REFLECTIONS ON MEMORY AND DEMOCRACY

Edited by
Merilee S. Grindle and Erin E. Goodman

Published by Harvard University David Rockefeller Center for
Latin American Studies

Distributed by Harvard University Press
Cambridge, Massachusetts
London, England
2016

Publisher's Cataloging-In-Publication Data

Reflections on memory and democracy / edited by Merilee S. Grindle and
    Erin E. Goodman.

        pages ; cm. — (The David Rockefeller Center series on Latin American
studies, Harvard University)

    Includes bibliographical references.
    ISBN: 978-0-674-08829-0

    1. Democracy—Latin America. 2. Memory—Political aspects—Latin America.
3. Violence—Latin America—Psychological aspects. 4. Latin America—Politics
and government. 5. Latin America—Social conditions. I. Grindle, Merilee
Serrill. II. Goodman, Erin E. III. Series: David Rockefeller Center series on Latin
American studies, Harvard University.

JL966 .R44 2016
321.8/098

To all those who suffered under authoritarian regimes and who are presente *in our memories.*

And to William, Eliot, Sofia, and Mateo, in the hope that they will come of age in a more democratic and just world.

Contents

III. Citizenship and Democratic Futures

Acknowledgments

In the fall of 2013, the David Rockefeller Center for Latin American Studies (DRCLAS) at Harvard University organized a "collaborative" on Democracy and Memory in Latin America. Its intent was to engage scholars from the social sciences, arts and humanities, and the physical sciences in exploring the relationship between democracy and the collective memory of violence, injustice, repression, and resistance in Latin America. The collaborative featured a distinguished lecture series, an art exhibition, a film series, an issue of the DRCLAS *ReVista*, and artistic performances.

As with all such undertakings, this collaborative would not have been possible without valuable support from many organizations and individuals. Funding was provided by the David Rockefeller Center for Latin American Studies and the following co-sponsors from Harvard University: the Ash Center for Democratic Governance, the Carr Center for Human Rights Policy, the Faculty of Arts and Sciences, the Harvard Film Archive, the Harvard Humanitarian Initiative, the Harvard Law School Human Rights Program, the Nieman Foundation for Journalism, the Office of the Provost, and the Weatherhead Center for International Affairs. Additionally, the Ford Foundation was an important sponsor of the two-day conference. We are deeply grateful to these organizations for their support and interest in this collaborative venture. In addition, many people were critical to turning ideas into real events. We thank the faculty members who formed part of the DRCLAS Executive Committee, and Resident Scholar Marysa Navarro for her intellectual contributions as well as all these organizations and individuals for their hard work and commitment to the project.

The collaborative culminated in a major international conference on November 1 and 2, 2013. This volume gathers many of the presentations at the conference (the conference program is included at the end of this volume). We feel enormously privileged that so many distinguished intellectuals and practitioners agreed to make presentations and were so engaged in the lively debates that ensued.

Many members of the DRCLAS staff helped coordinate these efforts, with particular thanks to Sophie Jampel. Thanks also to Marcela Ramos, Manager of the Arts@DRCLAS program, who put together the corresponding arts exhibition, "Memory and Democracy in Latin American Poetry," curated by Assistant Professor of Romance Languages and Literatures Sergio Delgado. In addition, interns Malusa de Nova and Silvia Percovich were essential at different stages of conference planning and throughout the semester; Kirin Gupta served as conference rapporteur.

This volume benefited from the advice and skills of several people, including DRCLAS Publications Director June Erlick, copy editor Anita Safran, translators Will Morningstar, Andy Klatt and Arielle Concilio, and anonymous readers of the manuscript. Our thanks to all of you.

Merilee S. Grindle
Erin E. Goodman
Cambridge, January 2016

Arpillera and photo courtesy of Marjorie Agosín

Prologue

Arpilleras

Marjorie Agosín
Translated by Arielle Concilio

In my dream I see them traveling through the windows of my sleep, walking through the naked trees damp with the autumn rains. They appear like glimmers of light in the shadows. The disappeared, constantly crossing the frontier between life and death, are caught like ghosts in the minds of those who knew them, or who want to know them, those obsessed with remembering them.

There is no burial place I can visit. They inhabit a space spun from frail threads, a vanishing place like the forests in winter. As a poet, I try to name them with carefully chosen words. In my writing, I search the empty rooms where they were once tortured. I sense them like sudden gusts of wind: they sweep across the vast arid deserts where we still comb the earth for their bones. I imagine them in the sea, in waters not sonorous but silent, tombs into which they were thrown by military helicopters.

Testimony involves a giver and a receiver. One person tells her story and another hears or reads it. As I write these words, and as you read them, we are bearing witness. Testimony is an act that occurs in courtrooms, in the most public places, but it also happens in literature, in the privacy of a bedroom where reader and writer unite in the space between the eye and the page. The word and the voice create a memorial to the absence, and to the silence that is the shadow side of any official history.

But there is a distinct type of testimony to which I would like to bring attention: the Chilean *arpilleras*. Onto burlap, a rough cloth known for its resilience, women sewed scraps cut from used clothes, blankets, and other everyday items in the style of patchwork. Often they used pieces of material that had belonged to their disappeared loved ones. And from these imperfect pieces they told their stories. These *arpilleristas* gave visual testimony to the forced disappearances that occurred during the military dictatorship from 1973 until 1990. Theirs are powerful memorials, for they bear witness to those seventeen brutal years and their aftermath, and create a tangible and tactile way to remember the dead.

In a country almost at the end of the world, at the foot of the *cordillera*, wise and courageous women stitched their family stories onto cloth, and somehow reconstructed the silenced memory of a nation. Everyday women, especially mothers of children disappeared by the dictatorship, created *arpilleras* to both remember their loved ones and to denounce a society dominated by authoritarianism and fear.

The *arpilleristas* tenaciously filled the absences in their lives with the presence of their hands full of materials, sometimes even including corporal objects such as pieces of hair. After the materials were chosen the process of constructing an *arpillera* began, rendering to these women a living memorial marked by a marvelous union of the senses of touch and memory. For their hands created not only works of visual beauty, but also of remembrance both personal and political. The Chilean *arpilleristas*, individual women telling their stories, sewing side by side into the night, were recording the collective history of the nation.

The Chilean *Arpilleras*

Since time immemorial, cloth has provided protection and served as adornment. And it has most often been associated with the feminine. Weaving and embroidering are tasks usually performed by women. It is generally a communal act performed in private, inconspicuous spaces.

I can still close my eyes and return to our timeworn home in Santiago de Chile, to the room where women sat in silence, their gazes fixed out the window at the Andean range with their hands always moving amidst needle, thread, and cloth. As a young girl with a small hand called in to card the wool, I understood that I was entering a place of intimate work, where intimate stories and mysterious secrets would be revealed. As I grew up I saw how stitching and mending was a way of repairing the world, a gesture deeply linked to a feminist worldview.

I was reminded of this when I began working with the *arpilleristas* 35 years ago. When I first met these women and observed their work, I knew I was witnessing something singular and marvelous. There was something about what was occurring in that room that could only be called magical. In their work, the art of memory united with the art of reason, as the search for the disappeared had a clear goal. All their emotions, including their resolve, could be observed in the magical act of sewing the patchwork.

I also was struck by the fact that these women were working with the torn pieces of the clothes of the missing, bringing life back to the literal shreds of their histories. For example, a blue shirt from the uniform a missing son once wore to school was used to create the sky that is always featured on each *arpillera*. That azure sky might still hold the stains, the scent of his sweat. The process of creating an *arpillera* with the real clothing of a loved one represents a sensual longing to touch and perceive, to remake and recreate. Moreover, the sensory experience of working with the fabric lends this art a sense of presence. The act of unweaving the cloth, of un-sewing and re-sewing to create a work of art beautifully integrated into a single fabric renders these acts of reassembling into an art of remembering.

The *arpillera* is stained also with longing. Born of an act of remembrance, the burlap becomes a sacred space, a sort of prayer site, when a woman records her loss in patchwork upon it. I remember how the women always kissed the little scraps of fabric they had found among the household items before sewing them to the burlap background. The process of layering the pieces by hand is a labor of memory, and it is also, more importantly, an act of resistance. Such tenacity reminded me of the figure of Penelope, who weaves by day and unweaves by night, recalling the presence of her husband Odysseus who has not yet returned to Ithaca. Another woman from Greek mythology, Philomena, embroiders her story into a tapestry after her brother-in-law Tereus rapes her and cuts out her tongue, rendering her unable to speak.

The Chilean *arpilleristas* have a story similar to Philomena's. During the military dictatorship, these brave women gave testimony to their private and collective lives through cloth and patchwork. Their testimony was not presented in a courtroom, nor through narrative literature, but through a visual medium. *Arpilleras* often tell the stories of disappeared children, of lives cut short often symbolized by a table with a missing chair, or a tree with broken branches. Or perhaps it is a window with the face of a woman, watching and weeping. Such domestic images represent broken families and also bridge the larger historical narrative of the disappeared, weaving the personal with the public.

The Chilean *arpilleras* were born in a period when the entire country seemed to be covered by a thick fog of silence. Fear kept people from speaking, from acknowledging how their families, and their country, had been torn apart. The witness borne by the *arpillera* is not a voice in the courtroom nor a word on the page. The art of the *arpilleristas* is distinctly domestic. In the early days, women pieced scraps together in their homes. Later, they came together to work in the rooms of the Vicars of Solidarity, where they were protected by the Catholic Church. In the stillness of the Santiago night, the women worked on the fabric, testifying to the private spaces of the home where a loved one had vanished.

From the recovery of the cloth that the disappeared once wore, to the incorporation of different materials like photographs and bits of hair into their handiwork, the *arpilleristas* participated in a constant dialogue with each other and against oblivion. Their dialogue relied upon the body, the hands, and even the voice, as one of the most central experiences was the chance to speak with the other women in the group, creating a conversation that became like a sacred ritual for its participants. Someone would break the heavy silence, and then the room would be full of voices and presences of those they so desperately missed—a son, a daughter, a husband torn away in the night. The women told their stories with their hands and voices as they worked to keep their memories, and indeed their own hopes, alive.

The Traveling *Arpillera*

I have come to think that the *arpilleras* represent a kind of portable memory. In the early years of the military dictatorship, when censorship was brutally enforced, the *arpilleras* were sent abroad by airmail and identified as mere artisanal creations. Later, many human rights workers began to carry the *arpilleras* in their suitcases and distribute them abroad. Clandestine travelers, like so many Chilean citizens who emigrated during those times, *arpilleras* began to appear in art galleries, schools, churches, in Amnesty International calendars, and, little by little, they began to inhabit the private spaces of the home. Simultaneously, these apparently ingenuous works of popular art came to occupy a place of great importance in the history of Chile. The *arpilleras* embody the feelings of the families of the disappeared, and they carry their testimonies.

Nomadic, like the disappeared loved ones visiting between waking and sleep, the *arpilleras* were always traveling. One of the *arpilleristas*, Doris Maniconi, told me that they were like letters sent in the wind, waiting for someone, somewhere, to receive them. We do not well know to whom each of them belongs, but we know that somewhere, someone will hold them in their hands, will talk about them; some people will place them on the wall and others will simply put them away until, one day, they look at the hidden box as if for the first time, understanding that this *arpillera* was created by, indeed is part of, another human being.

It is difficult to live with representations of grief and loss. The *arpillera* is an object brimming with beautiful colors and shapes, yet it contains a record of pain and violence. Looking at the *arpillera*, at the care put into the stitches, the uniqueness of each scrap of cloth, one is intimately drawn into its narrative. We think of the mother who made it. We wonder about her life and want to know her story. The family of the disappeared becomes our family, and we long to find our lost brother or sister, our spouse or our child, we want to encounter that life cut short, to reconstruct that future which was so cruelly dismembered.

Can one extract the *arpillera*'s secrets? Can one imagine in which moment of repose and on which night the *arpillera* was born? Where the *arpillerista* searched for the scraps of cloth? How she pieced them together? Where did she first begin her stitches? In the spaces of daily life, perhaps seated at her kitchen table? Or in the secret spaces of a society under dictatorship, in the concentration camps or the torture chambers?

Truly, something extraordinary is achieved through the sending and receiving of these *arpilleras*, for a bond of empathy is forged between the one who gives testimony through her handiwork and the one in the foreign land who holds it for the very first time. In seeing and touching an *arpillera*, one begins a dialogue with the woman who created it. One not only receives and responds to her memories, but also bears witness to her testimony. For the *arpilleras* are indeed testimony: painstakingly detailed accounts of the atrocities that were committed during the military dictatorship, as well as records of the resilient spirits of those Chilean citizens who refused to lose hope in the power of beauty and justice. Not only a piece of art or handiwork, an *arpillera* is in itself a call for justice and accountability, an aesthetic rendering of memory that serves as political testimony.

The *arpilleras* made visual representations of memory in a society that for 17 years made a pact with oblivion, where every expression of remembrance was a cause for suspicion, destruction, and ultimately silence. The *arpilleras* participated in a new form of verbalizing the past and present of Chile. Thread by thread, the *arpilleras* have created a collective memory and a common history out of very personal and singular stories. The *arpillera* is distinct from, for example, the AIDS Quilt, where each piece of cloth is prepared to become part of one immense quilt. The intimate nature of the *arpillera*, onto which life is narrated by a single being, means that the one who receives the cloth becomes the guardian of its story.

In the many years I worked with the *arpilleristas*, I attended their workshops and participated in their conversations, but the only thing I clearly remember are the *arpilleras* on the table. They are looking up at me, the observer, always asking with insistent voices: "Where are they? What happened when they were taken away?" And the insistence of the *arpillera* became my own. The questions, the memories belong to all Chileans. The work of ordinary women's hands forms part of a tactile imaginary of extraordinary historic importance in which each thread represents a life and renders forgetting impossible. Such are the calls of the Chilean *arpilleristas*, like Philomena reclaiming her voice.

1

Democracies in the Shadow of Memory

Merilee S. Grindle

Like a collection of *arpilleras*, this book is the work of many hands. It has been stitched together by journalists, writers, and poets; literary critics, political scientists, and historians; philosophers, economists, and linguists. Encompassing experiences of those who lived the recent past, *Reflections on Memory and Democracy* seeks to capture a variety of contemporary views of how history, and understanding of that history, are woven into the ways in which diverse societies engage in conflict and its resolution. It reflects on how communities create their present and future in the shadow of history.

We focus on countries of Latin America that have lived through periods of violence, repression, disappearances, injustice, and resistance and that have sought to build democratic institutions despite divisions and conflicts rooted in that past. We are intentionally eclectic, in that the book draws reflections from a variety of disciplines about how such societies stitch experiences of trauma and violence into lessons for democracy. As with the hands that produce an *arpillera,* we suggest that societies must tell stories about how those experiences are understood and remembered in contemporary life; at times, the stories can be discordant, just as an *arpillera* can be made up of pieces of cloth that do not always lie harmoniously next to each other.

Despite the variety of perspectives, contributors to *Reflections* converge to affirm three points. First, to be legitimate and durable over time, democratic institutions and societies must come to terms with pasts marked by violence, repression, and injustice. Second, coming to terms with history is a difficult task, fraught with ambiguity, uncertainty, misunderstanding, and the potential for failure. And third, visiting the sins of the past must contribute to the construction of new political institutions as well as create conditions to encourage the engagement of democratic citizens. While these lessons are not consistently echoed in the contributions, and while the volume does not seek to provide a uniform interpretation of the connection between memory and democracy—indeed, most of the following chapters provide insights into why the connection is problematic—it suggests the importance of exploring these themes and finding common ground for understanding the multiplicity of ways that the past influences the present, for good and for ill.

In a series of essays—some profoundly personal, others more traditionally academic—this volume encourages reflection on the recent history of Latin American countries from the 1960s to the present day. We are mindful, of course, that experiences of authoritarian repression and democratic beginnings, revivals, and reversals are not exclusive to this period, but transcend centuries. And indeed, conflicts over how Latin American societies are to be governed are emblematic of the entire 19th and 20th centuries. Yet we believe that by focusing on recent experiences we can provide insights that are relevant for other efforts to engage memory and democracy, both contemporary and historical.

The countries and the events we are concerned about are diverse. Beginning in the 1960s and 1970s, democratic governments in Chile, Argentina, Uruguay, and Brazil were replaced by repressive military governments. During the same period, and extending into the 1990s, authoritarian regimes held power in numerous other countries. In Mexico, for example, although the military was largely marginalized from direct engagement in national decision-making, the machinery of the dominant party state was effective in curtailing claims for democracy, including the use of systematic co-optation and repression of dissent. In Peru, an authoritarian regime re-established state authority in the midst of an ongoing and violent confrontation, and did so through a significant narrowing of space for dissent. Military, paramilitary and guerilla forces in Colombia vied as alternatives to state power and claimed lives across the country for almost 60 years. Paraguay suffered 35 years of authoritarian rule and the suppression of rights.

The list goes on. Seventy-five thousand people were killed in El Salvador's civil war in the 1980s, and untold numbers were disappeared. In Guatemala's 36-year civil war, military and civilian governments, paramilitary, and rebel organizations routinely engaged in violent and repressive acts against the population, and particularly against indigenous and rural groups, leaving behind as many as 200,000 dead or disappeared. Nicaraguans lived through the long-term repression of the Somoza regime and then saw the country militarized as it descended into civil war in the 1980s. Ecuador's *dictablanda* and military interventions in Honduras and Panama left their own scars of violence and instability. Cuba's revolutionary government has a long history of repressing dissidence, and democratic

Venezuela and unstable Bolivia have tested "third wave of democracy" trends in more recent turns to authoritarianism and repression.

Many of these authoritarian experiences were distinct from previous dictatorships. Rather than revisiting historical patterns of personalism and uncoordinated violence, these new regimes were more efficient and effective in using institutions of the state for political control. They made systematic use of violence, repression, disappearances, and fear to suppress resistance, protest, and human rights. They targeted enemies of the state broadly and used exile, torture, and executions as instruments of state power. At times, their actions were publicly justified as a response to the systematic use of violence and fear by those fighting in anti-state movements. Resistance to state repression and courageous acts of dissent were also notable in many countries. During periods of authoritarian rule, then, tens of thousands of individuals were imprisoned, killed, or disappeared, and millions lived with restricted freedoms and heightened vulnerability. All too frequently, the United States and other external actors were culpable in the commission of violence and repression, presenting an important international dimension of the connection between memory and democracy.

Collective memories of these events form a backdrop for the re-emergence of democratic processes that characterized most Latin American countries in the 1980s, 1990s, and 2000s. They spawned numerous efforts to avoid the repetition of history, such as constitutional conventions to create stronger institutions for sharing power and conflict resolution, peace accords to mend the fissures that led to confrontation, violence, injustice, and repression; and political pacts that eased the introduction of democratic elections. They encouraged efforts to engage citizens at local and national levels in participatory decision-making around democratic norms. They led to literatures, monuments, and public spaces that interpreted past experiences in contemporary life. Films and museums brought the meaning of violent pasts to younger generations. Archival, journalistic, and forensic initiatives sought to pin down what happened and when it happened; discovery of documents and new tools of analysis helped with the recording and rewriting of history.

Yet memory remains an elusive and contested terrain in contemporary assessments of what went wrong in the past and how democratic institutions can put it right. Divisions about how past crimes are to be understood and judged, how those accused of the abuse of human rights are to be held responsible for their actions, and how victims are to be compensated continue to generate debate and dissonance in many Latin American polities. In some cases, plans for memory museums and public monuments have brought out strong divisions about the meaning of historical events and how they should be represented. For many, understanding the past engages memories of loss, exile, and injustice and raises concerns about impunity and accountability. For others, the lessons have to do with the importance of order and stability in societies racked by violence and division. In some countries, the past is still silent.

Indeed, the connection between the lived experience of authoritarianism, the memories it has left behind, and the institutions of democracy that characterize many Latin American countries raise a number of questions, the answers to which are difficult to untangle. Sergio Bitar is correct when he writes that "There is not one history, there are many memories, many histories." These histories and memories can be appropriated and even manipulated for a variety of ends, as Katherine Hite has argued; it is important to note who is writing history. Over time, memory and its interpretation take on added significance as those who experienced injustice and violence die and new generations emerge who do not have first-hand knowledge of the impact of authoritarianism and know of repression only through the memory and interpretation of others.

Thus, what is learned from our memories may be ambiguous; moral boundaries can be called into question when divergent perspectives are compared and assessed. Even more troubling, memory can be as divisive as it is healing; an "overabundance" of memory can even make reconciliation as elusive as the memory itself, as generations of conflict in the Balkans and the passions of winners and losers of communal violence in many settings are kept alive by interpretations of past events. Concrete evidence may or may not authenticate what is recalled.

These are among the issues that are considered in this volume. Does the past, shaped by collective memories that are themselves constructed of narratives, shared experiences, and interpretations of everyday life as well as of violence, repression, and resistance, contribute significantly to collective commitment to new institutions for making decisions, resolving conflict, and creating consensus about broad lines of public policy? What are the enduring tensions and conflicts that result from collective memories of political pasts? How do collective memories survive and how are they transmitted across generations? What is the obligation of current and future generations to honor past struggles and to engage in conflicts and discussions about differing interpretations of the past?

These and similar questions were posed for a conference at Harvard University in early November of 2013. The conference, organized by Harvard's David Rockefeller Center for Latin American Studies, served as a reminder of the fortieth anniversary of the violent coup that toppled a long existing democratic regime in Chile—"the *other* September 11." On the Day of the Dead, when many societies in Latin America honor and remember those who have gone before, conference participants raised glasses to the memory of those who were victims of violence and impunity. They then set about discussing how such losses are translated into contemporary efforts to create stable democratic societies. A central organizing principle of the event was that historical events such as those in Latin America had to be approached from a multidisciplinary perspective, given the elusiveness of collective memory and its implications for contemporary life. Many of the papers delivered at this conference, including Marjorie Agosín's poetic prologue on the Chilean *arpilleras*, are represented in this volume.

In a now published version of her keynote conference address, Elizabeth Jelin considered a number of the uncertainties that surround the connection between memory and democracy in contemporary Latin America, uncertainties visited in the conference and in the contributions to this volume (Jelin 2013). She questioned the "duty to remember so as not to repeat," in terms of what lessons are learned in remembering. This is an issue addressed in chapters by Sergio Bitar and Salomón Lerner. She wondered when memory should begin—with repression or with the conditions that gave rise to it, a theme that is raised by Peter Winn and Bitar. Jelin also wondered why the violence of the past has been largely understood through a human rights lens rather than any alternative—a lens of social equity, for example—an issue of concern in this volume's contribution by Susana Draper. And she cautioned that memory can lead to a culture of "victimization" that ignores the potential for individual and collective agency, certainly a theme that is apparent in contributions by June Erlick, Michèle Montas, Marjorie Feitlowitz, and Ava Berinstein. Jelin also raised the issue of the connection between memory and active citizenship, a question that plays an important role in chapters by Frances Hagopian, Paolo Vignolo, Winn, and Lerner.

"The past is an object of dispute," Jelin concludes, and readers will find many unresolved questions in *Reflections*. Nevertheless, the following chapters are bound together by a common concern about learning from the past, how the past is known and remembered, and how societies build upon but also seek to move beyond memory in order to construct viable democracies. Thus, leaving many questions unanswered and available for future debate and discussion, the following chapters affirm that the connection between memory and democracy must be unraveled and considered as part of a democratic experience of citizenship in each country as it comes to terms with its own difficult and divisive past.

Three Themes, Many Perspectives

Societies that wish to sustain strong democratic institutions must come to terms with historical experiences of violence, repression, and injustice. Coming to terms with history, however, is extraordinarily difficult because memories diverge and conflict, are difficult to understand, and are not always respected in constructive ways. Democratic institutions based on an effective understanding of memory and history can help prevent the return of authoritarianism and political violence, but not unless large numbers of citizens become engaged in building and participating in them.

These three statements emerge in a variety of ways and although, as themes, they often overlap in the following chapters, we have adopted them as the organizing principle for the volume. More generally, we begin with a clear statement—memory is essential to democratic governance—and then show how problematic this straightforward statement is because of the nature of memory itself and its understanding in particular historical contexts. We seek, then, to find the difficulties embedded in a cliché, not to destroy the cliché, but to demonstrate the hard work over time that is implied in making it true. Societies stitch their own *arpilleras*, we find, some more effectively than others.

Remembering and Democracy: Memory and Its Place in
Democratic Institutions

Part I of the volume asks readers to consider the importance of dealing with memory if democratic institutions are to be effectively created, institutionalized, and strengthened. Four chapters explore the relationship between memory and democracy in terms of commitment to justice and accountability for past wrongs and of addressing the consequences of impunity. Thus, in these chapters, addressing the injustices of the past is taken as a fundamental building block for democratic legitimacy.

Yet this connection is not free of difficulties. Memory is essential—but it is important that what is remembered and how it is remembered be constructive of democratic rules and institutions. Each of the writers is concerned with the importance of not forgetting the past, but at the same time not letting it be an opportunity for the perpetuation of violence. These chapters ring with authentic and personal meaning, as each of the contributors was a participant in efforts to bring memory to bear on democratic institution-building. Sergio Bitar, June Erlick, Michèle Montas, and Salomón Lerner Febres provide testimony about the value of acknowledging the past in the present "from the trenches." The transformation of memory into effective institutions, they indicate, is a process, one that can become truncated, misdirected, and counterproductive if memory is distorted by amnesia or the desire for revenge.

Sergio Bitar has impressive credentials in terms of both living the past and discussing the importance of memory for leading off a discussion of the importance of memory in the construction of democratic institutions. After participating briefly in the government of Salvador Allende in 1973, he spent a year as a prisoner of the Pinochet regime in the notorious Dawson Island concentration camp and other such prisons. Then, after 10 years in exile, he returned to Chile, where he was active in the "No" plebiscite in 1988. Under the reconstituted democracy, he was one of the founders and, on three occasions, president of the Partido por la Democracia (PPD), a partner in the coalition that governed Chile between 1990 and 2010. He also served as senator, minister of public works, and minister of education. These experiences led him to affirm "achieving reconciliation in societies that have experienced a major crisis requires memory to understand what went wrong and to draw lessons from it. We must resist the temptation to simply put the past behind us."

Yet he also acknowledges the difficulty of putting this affirmation into practice. Memories have to be unraveled and understood in context, often a difficult task for those who have been directly affected by violence and repression. To quote from his chapter:

> It was difficult to explain how the apparently civilized colonel from the FACH (Chilean Air Force), who had visited my house when I assumed my position as Minister of Mining under President Allende, could just a short time later order his institution to resort to torture. Or, how people with whom we had interacted every day could become the first informers or creators of the rhetoric that would hide or try to justify what was happening.

The search for understanding, begun in internal exile, helped those on the left grapple with what went wrong while they held the reins of power. They questioned their previous ideological commitments and affirmed the importance of peaceful construction of democracy. This helped them achieve coexistence with the perpetrators of violence and terror, but left reconciliation as a more difficult challenge.

Since the military coup [in Chile in 1973], I have been committed to the construction of a civilized coexistence based on democracy and respect for human rights. My conviction was, and is, that reconciliation as a social process requires underlying political conditions that are not yet present, and that reconciliation will only progress if we are able to improve, day by day, the democratic underpinning of coexistence.

Reconciliation cannot be achieved, he writes, until the causes of the Pinochet coup and its repressive activities are agreed upon; those who justify the coup implicitly or explicitly endorse the violence, and those who seek to ignore it repress its meaning for the future. Until there is closure on this debate, there is the threat that the sins of the past can be repeated.

Mine was a privileged generation that fought for dreams, suffered through the dictatorship and actively participated in the creation of a new democratic society. But that legacy is still inconclusive if we don't preserve the memory of what it cost, the lessons for preventing a repeat in Chile and elsewhere, and enshrine the importance of protecting our essential values for the future.

This will happen, he argues, when the "culture of human rights" becomes common sense for citizens and embedded practice for institutions.

June Erlick, a journalist, writer, and activist in efforts to bring light to cases of abuse and violence against journalists in Latin America and around the world, relates her engagement in efforts to uncover the truth about a disappeared journalist in Guatemala and affirms Bitar's observations about a culture of human rights. Stories of what happens to journalists are important, she writes, because journalists are at the forefront of what democracies need if they are to work effectively—information, insight, the right to know. Just as peace accords were being signed to bring an end to almost four decades of civil war, she began to appreciate the extent to which a particular journalist's story needed to be told and retold if Guatemala and other countries were to be able to move beyond violence and repression. "After all, to forcibly disappear a person is to obliterate them" and the values they embodied. She set out on a quest to find the story of what happened to Irma Flaquer. In this quest, Erlick found universal meaning and implications in a personal history of courage and commitment.

The journalism that Flaquer practiced is one of the links Erlick finds between the personal and the general. Flaquer took on cases of blatant official violence—such as that of three teenagers who were shot to death in a restaurant simply because they had annoyed an important member of the elite—and stayed with them, demanding that justice be done, that impunity be challenged. "Facing the impact of disappearances on a society clearly sets out the principles of truth and accountability that drive the practice of transitional justice; one must reckon with the past to move forward," Erlick writes, echoing the affirmations of Bitar and Lerner. In Guatemala, however, the fate of Flaquer is still unknown, as are the fates of thousands more. Thus, the personal history underscores the more universal message.

Eventually, the Guatemalan government began to respond to pressures from families, the church, and other organizations to recognize the past—Irma Flaquer, symbolic of "all the Guatemalan journalists who had suffered repression during the dark days of Guatemala," now has a statue in her honor and a street named after her in the capital city. Erlick continues to hope that the truth about her will be known.

> There must be someone, I think, someone who gave an order, someone who took an order, someone who tortured her, someone who gave her water, someone who buried her, someone who feels guilty now as he gets older, someone who wants to speak before the memory becomes too old and painful, someone who wants to tell the truth, or the part of the truth that he or she knows.

This hasn't happened yet, and until it does, justice and coming to terms with the past will continue to haunt efforts to establish democracy in Guatemala.

In Haiti, Michèle Montas was also a witness to incomplete justice. In her moving testimony, she relates that she "lived in fear and silence when I was 12 to 14 years old, never fully understanding why there were so many taboo subjects at the dinner table or at school, or why there were, at times, dead bodies in the streets." After family members disappeared, she and her family went into hiding, part of a story of childhood under "Papa Doc" Duvalier. Her story became even more harrowing as she started to work at Radio Haiti when "Baby Doc" Jean-Claude Duvalier had come to power. Married to the owner of the radio station, she and others began, cautiously, bringing information to ordinary citizens, even those who lived in remote rural areas.

> We only covered politics by proxy, reporting not on Haiti but, for instance, on the fall of Somoza in Nicaragua in 1979 or in elections in the U.S., the neighboring Dominican Republic or Jamaica. We

slowly forced open the window left ajar by the demands of the Carter administration that aid be tied to the respect for human rights.... [It was] a very dangerous game, of cat and mouse, of evaluating, on any given day, how far we could go in being journalists.

When repression escalated in the aftermath of the U.S. election of Ronald Regan as president, Michèle and her husband, Jean Dominique, were forced to flee, returning only in 1986, after Jean-Claude Duvalier had been forced out of the country. In the following years, another period of exile was followed by a return to Radio Haiti and an effort to report on past and ongoing injustices. Then, her husband was assassinated on April 3, 2000, and gunmen came for her in 2002, killing one of her bodyguards. A third exile followed.

Montas weaves this story into a narrative about the importance of memory and the righting of past wrongs in creating the foundations of democratic governance. With the murder of her husband still pending resolution, and continuing impunity for Jean-Claude Duvalier, she questions the ability of the judicial system in Haiti to bring the past to bear witness against those who committed torture, murder, and disappearances. Although she finds sources for optimism about the future in evidence that some brutal acts have come to the courts and to the attention of the domestic and international media, "very little remains of concrete anchors of memory around a painful past that has left such deep scars on Haiti's present and future." Montas joins Erlick in asserting the responsibility of the media to revive memories of the past and expose violations of human rights. Journalists, then, have a clear responsibility to help develop the rule of law and construct democratic states, she concludes.

Salomón Lerner Febres, philosopher and university president, was also a participant in bringing memory to bear on the construction of viable and stable democratic institutions when, between 2001 and 2003, he headed the Peruvian Commission on Truth and Reconciliation. The commission assembled over 17,000 testimonies from victims of violence perpetrated by Sendero Luminoso, the military, and paramilitary groups, and authenticated 70,000 deaths and disappearances. In his role as president of the commission, he confronted the dilemma of memory and how it could contribute to democratic legitimacy, and also how it could undermine it. This chapter provides reflections that are deeply relevant to the stories told by Bitar, Erlick, and Montas.

The Commission for Truth and Reconciliation, writes Lerner, presented a clear case that "Peru could not aspire to become a durable and stable democracy if it could not ensure the transformation and eradication of certain habits and values, of certain institutional conditions, of certain ways of exercising power" that limited the ability to ensure the rule of law in the country. Thus, the commission sought to give voice to the victims, to provide a public accounting of violence, terror, and injustice, and to emphasize the importance of human dignity and rights to society and political activity. The commission's task was made difficult by the fact that acts of abuse and violence were committed by terrorists as well as the state, adding credence to those who argued that the state's violent actions were justified as a means of dealing with the threat to security posed by anti-government forces. As in Chile, then, reconciliation would be hindered by divergent lessons drawn from the past. Moreover, a legacy of racism haunted Peru and threatened the depth of its democratic commitment.

In recounting the story of the past, there was also tension between hearing the voices of victims and the desire for revenge and settling of scores. Lerner is clear, "We do not remember an episode of violence in order to become slaves of the past, but to humanize this terrible past . . . to clarify its meaning." There is also a danger of a "hegemonic" memory, when the past is used by those in power to stifle debate and the search for understanding. This was the great challenge for the commission—to ensure that the past was acknowledged, that its work would contribute to a common understanding of what occurred, that accountability would help build the citizens' trust so essential to democratic institutions, and that the country could move ahead in developing values based on the equality and dignity of citizenship and an enduring commitment to peaceful rules for resolving conflict.

The Challenges of "Capturing" Memory

Judicial procedures, commissions of truth and justice, the media, the school curriculum, language, public places of memory—they all seek to bring the past to light. But how do we know what really happened in the past? How are the pieces of the puzzle put together when some of the pieces are missing and when different actors may be working on distinct puzzles? These questions are central to three chapters exploring memory as a subjective reality and the possibility that what happened in the past may never be clear or may be lost to memory. Thus, through language and literary works, those who experienced violence, repression, and resistance are shown to have incomplete memories of the past through language and literary works; they are uncertain about what happened to them and their loved ones; they revise what they understood as truth. Those who lived through repressive eras wonder about the authenticity of their own pasts and their real identities. Activists who paid a price for resisting injustices discover the limitations of their understanding, and perpetrators of violence try to understand why they did what they did. They are tempted by forgetting and denial as a way to deal with uncertainty and pain.

Marguerite Feitlowitz assesses the work of three Argentine writers, Luis Gusmán, Alicia Plante, and Patricio Pron, whose characters struggle to understand what happened in the past. Those who are older are forced to question their courage under fire, their complicity with violence, and the guilt of their survival while others perished. Younger ones are uncertain about who their parents were and the extent to which they have been living in enforced amnesia and contrived history. There is mystery in unraveling the past, and, as time passes, new generations become "the detectives of their parents," attempting to understand what happened and the very personal histories of those who were actively engaged in conflict.[1] At times, they envy the danger, the struggles, and the almost blind commitments of their parents, hunters and hunted alike. Their own lives seem lost, as the memory of the past is lost.

Thus, for one of Gusmán's protagonists, the mind is "a file of murky things," and, for another, the past is so traumatic that those who experienced it cannot or will not speak of it. Documents of the past come to light, but raise questions about when they were written and under what conditions, and a tale is told of "an extensive web of repressed fact, disguised reality, disappeared persons, and identities that will be forever unknown." In a novel by Plante, a vague memory of a stolen baby, the chance encounter with the privileged son of the neighbor, a neighborhood that acknowledged but then "forgot" a kidnapping raise a disturbing question: "Was it really natural for everyone to let the facts fade?" The protagonist of Pron's novel, whose memory is defaced by drugs, argues, "You don't ever want to know certain things, because what you know belongs to you, and there are certain things you never want to own."

If personal memory is so fragile and unreliable, how can collective memory be trusted? Feitlowitz writes that ambiguity is part of memory.

> The ways in which we think about what happens is also part of history: our anxieties, dreads, and dreams; the precepts, categories, and genres that help us organize our thoughts and feelings; the ways in which we both resist and seek to recover individual and collective memories.

Novels, then, deepen the difficulty of linking lessons of the past to the present, the memory to the construction of democratic institutions. As

Feitlowitz asks, "How do you recount collective experience in a way that is personal, if those who lived through the dictatorship have been unable to do so?"

Susana Draper provides one response to this question. Rather than focus on the memories that are linked to trauma, she asks readers to consider the lessons of more ordinary memories, ones that involve communal and collective interactions, of living together and learning from each other. In an assessment of a memoir of activism and incarceration surrounding the 1968 student rebellion and massacre at Tlatelolco in Mexico, she asks what ideas are essential to democracy. Those who participated in historic events, such as the student activists in Mexico, believed deeply in the importance of freedom; their definition of democracy was about the freedom it would bring to citizens—freedom to participate, to make decisions, to have control of one's destiny. Ironically, it is the loss of freedom the students experienced when they were jailed for participating in the protest movement that causes one of them, Roberta Avendaño, to question the definition she had so fiercely espoused.

In prison for two years, she and fellow "special prisoners" set themselves apart from the "common prisoners," making a distinction between those who were educated and privileged and those who were expected to do manual labor, such as cleaning their quarters. Draper writes that "The women who live in jail open up a universe that had no place in the democratic demands of '68, as if they were an underworld in which the 'common' had nothing to do with the 'political.'" Gradually, however, prisoners like Avendaño were forced to interact with the common prisoners and, as she learned their stories—how did they end up in the women's prison?—she began to understand that the revolutionary vision she shared with other students would have little impact on these "other" women—for them, freedom only came with death. The democracy envisioned by common prisoners—poor, uneducated, and victimized repeatedly by life—had to do with equality and opportunities to live a decent life, free from poverty, powerlessness, and uncertainty.

Prison taught political prisoners new things about class, gender, and inequality; they had spoken and written of egalitarianism, they had acted on its behalf, but until prison, they had not lived it. "The question about democracy that was the basis for the movement arose out of a problem of inequality that is still unresolved and which makes it increasingly difficult to create links or bridges among people, languages and struggles." The crime of the government the students were protesting against, then, was not simply the denial of freedom, but its failure to address the inequality and poverty that defined so much of Mexico. Thus, "memory . . . helps to bring (once again) the problem of democracy within the context of social injustice."

Social injustice is equally apparent in Ava Berinstein's discussion of efforts to revitalize a sacred oral tradition of those who have long been victims of discrimination and poverty. The historical significance of Mayan oral literature, tracing back to pre-Columbian times, provides a lens into Mayan life and thought, both ancient and modern. When a language disappears, she writes, culture is imperiled, as "memories, shared histories, religious and ritual practices, folklore, and legends passed down from generation to generation are lost." Shared language helps preserve the past, but can be deeply threatened by conflict and dislocation. No better example of this can be found than in the fate of indigenous languages and peoples in Guatemala, a country that experienced years of official violence and in which terror and forced relocation were mechanisms of military repression. Now the Indigenous people of Guatemala face another battle that is the effect of cultural genocide: the battle to have a voice; the battle for freedom of expression.

Without a voice, how can collective memory be restored and cultural identity preserved? Berinstein shows that the work of linguists, anthropologists, and Indigenous Maya collection of stories and poetry can help to preserve knowledge of the past. The distant past—a pre-conquest history for Indigenous groups in Guatemala—is particularly fragile and needs the attention of scholars. In addition to this work of remembering and recording additional oral narratives, community radio is critically important in preserving a recent past and maintaining cultural identity. Community radio, Berinstein argues, provides an opportunity to "reflect and promote local identity, character, and culture," as well as a platform for sharing opinions, information, and diverse perspectives, and enabling a broad range of people to participate.

She demonstrates how open, community-based radio promotes participation, building and maintaining memory, and collective action. Language, and its preservation, thus go beyond memory to build citizenship among those who have historically been marginalized. As stated by a Maya educator in Belize, "Democracy is really a word that means that everyone should be a part of it; having a right to say anything; to have a voice." Sharing oral literature through community-based radio contributes to the revitalization of Mayan language and culture, hopefully inhibiting the progression of cultural and language ethnocide.

Citizenship and Democratic Futures

In previous sections, contributors have affirmed the importance of memory to democracy but then made the connection between them complicated by first examining the vulnerability of memory and then raising issues about what is democratic in democracies. In this section, a political scientist and two historians revisit the question of what memory should teach us. These chapters—one focusing on Brazil, one on Chile, and one on Colombia—demonstrate that democratic institutions must be fortified and maintained by active citizen engagement in collective decision-making, representation, and demand-making. Memory must be understood in context, the authors assert, because efforts to bring the past to bear on democratic institution-building create new contexts for political interactions and participation.

When societies are able to address the difficult process of coming to terms with the past, lessons are learned and alter behavior, new political actors emerge, and new rules shape responses to issues of collective life. Frances Hagopian, in considering "the weight of memory" in the past, present, and future of Brazil, demonstrates how a transition to democracy created the possibility for new politics in that country. Thus, in the historical experience of authoritarianism, elites learned "the value of tolerance, moderation, and democracy itself" from the authoritarian past. The past also encouraged citizens to express themselves politically in new, more autonomous arenas, and to "develop non-hierarchical, participatory norms, and recognize the potential of a broad gamut of representative, accountability, and justice institutions." In this regard, the development of a culture of participation and democratic norms fundamentally altered the old political frameworks.

In linking memory and democracy, then, Hagopian urges scholars and activists to take a longer-term approach to how institutions emerge and become institutionalized over time. She agrees with Erlick, Montas, and Lerner, who argue strongly that past wrongs must be put right in order to create the bases for democratic societies, but she indicates how this is but a step in the direction of creating societies with new norms and institutions. In Brazil and elsewhere, parties of the left, economic elites, labor unions, and the Catholic Church "'learned' not merely to respect democracy and not to mobilize for revolution or knock on the barracks door, but also not to cling to policy preferences that their opponents could not abide"—they learned the importance of negotiation, tolerance, moderation, and consultation, as well as concern for the reach of state power. Moreover, social movements unleashed by the experience of authoritarianism and the space provided by new democratic institutions "set in motion a political transformation that led to more representative, participatory, and accountable democracies." Older and new forms of association allowed "ordinary" people to voice their concerns and make demands for public goods and services.

Thus, one response to the concern raised in other contributions about how to move from restoring memory to strengthening democratic government is to focus attention on the engagement of civil society in ways that reinforce the importance of participation, voice, and representation of interests. This latter factor, which Hagopian implies can be fostered and supported under democratic institutions, provides insurance that these same institutions will perform appropriately, that equity will be respected, accountability sustained, and rights observed. Pressure for fair representation must come from a variety of sources, and focus on political participation and the ongoing reform of local and national political institutions. Learning from the past is not enough if part of that learning does not incorporate the importance of citizenship and political engagement in building and sustaining democratic governments.

Peter Winn agrees with Hagopian about the importance of vibrant participation of citizens in democratic environments, but shows how the lessons learned in Chile by the political elites who crafted democratic institutions in the wake of the Pinochet regime did not learn enough from the past. He questions the "dominant negative assessments of the democracy of the Allende era," indicating that during this period, ordinary people learned to use political processes to take control of their own destinies, a practice not encouraged by the "pacted" democracy that replaced the dictatorship. The re-creation of democracy in Chile was based on an agreement not to return to the divisiveness of politics in the early 1970s; nevertheless, Winn suggests the importance of revisiting the meaning of this period in the wake of widespread student protests in the 2010s. For many, the Allende years were a time of authentic participation in political decision-making.

Winn shows how the experience of organized labor in the Allende period engaged many in ways that were certainly repressed under Pinochet, and that have been discouraged under the current regime. Using a case study from the 1960s and 1970s, he explores an "extraordinary exercise in direct democracy," when "the rank and file workers took control." At a critical meeting, "many took to the floor to vent decades of resentment at company repression, exploitation and denial of union democracy." Equally meaningful for the labor movement, the national confederation of labor unions began direct elections for its leadership, and workers began to organize across industries in particular locales. Self-managed industries became commonplace. Democracy was widened by lowering the age for voting and allowing illiterates to vote, by the governance of universities, and by elections for community leadership. In reaction to the politics and policies of the Allende years, middle-class and elite women became activists for change, also a positive (if ironic) contribution of that time.

Eventually, demands for participation and conflicting agendas and an escalation of violence fed into the military takeover of 1973. But Winn's point is often forgotten—in the years before the coup, many of the least powerful people in Chile found political voice for their demands and participation. Moreover, organized workers who had experienced direct participation began to emerge again in the late 1970s as important actors in the struggle to bring down the Pinochet government. Winn indicates that the workers, remembering those early years, were disappointed when the *Concertación* government's approach to "never again" was to limit the extent to which democratic institutions would permit direct response to their demands. Leaders of the student protest movement of the 2010s, however, "remembered" (none of them were born at the time) the pre-coup era as one of democratic politics that engaged the entire population in citizenship.

Paolo Vignolo views public spaces as essential to democracy because they provide numerous and distinct opportunities for participation and for recognizing the importance of history and memory in contemporary life. He takes us to the "city of the dead" in Bogota, the central cemetery, and how it is being reclaimed as a city of the living. For Vignolo, in this place "different population groups have developed funerary practices, ancestor cults, and different ways to evoke memory, making the cemetery a privileged space to communicate with the beyond, but privileged also for the exercise of active citizenship and to reassert ethnic, political, and cultural meanings." In part, it is the intermingling of ethnicities, political perspectives, and social classes among the dead that draw the living closer together because citizens are forced, in this site, to acknowledge history and to reflect on the causes and consequences of conflicts of the past. Moreover, activities such as pilgrimages and rites at the sites of popular saints provide opportunities to elude the rules of dominant institutions such as the Catholic Church or governments that want to control the space.

Like other contributors, Vignolo points to debates about what is remembered and how it is remembered; but he also points to issues such as how space is used, how it looks, and who has access to it. Each of these issues can be a means for encouraging citizen engagement. In the space of the cemetery, still under construction as a place of memory, performance arts are solidifying the link between the past and the present and the possibility for peace. As a large public demonstration for "peace, democracy, and the defense of the public good" showed in April 2013, spaces for participation are important for building democracy.

> Among the people fed up with the militarization of daily life and brought together by a coalition of the government, labor unions, and parts of the left could be found the invisible and marginalized face of the country: settlers from far-flung rural areas, Indians defending their traditional form of property, representatives of black communities on the Pacific coast with their own collective property rights, and campesinos from every part of the country. . . . the *Marcha Patriótica* put all its impressive political and electoral potential on display in the streets of the capital. Long-deceased victims of unpunished atrocities were vicariously endowed with legal standing and embodied by the demonstrators, raising their voices to demand an end to hostilities. This event represented a new vision of the country's national memory.

The city of the dead thus became a site for reconciliation and bringing together those with diverse agendas to appreciate the possibilities of an end to violence and the promise of peaceful resolution of conflicts within a framework of democratic institutions open to all citizens. Vignolo sees "memory building as a bottom-up participatory process" that, in Colombia, finally has the support of public institutions and thus can be incorporated into the rules of the game that support democratic resolution of conflicts.

Many Voices, Many Perspectives

Harvard's conference on Democracy and Memory included perspectives from a broad range of disciplines on the connection between these concepts in the recent past and present of Latin America. Indeed, the conference was organized around the contributions of various disciplines and, although the organization of this volume is distinct from the 2013 event, the scholars who participated addressed important questions about how different disciplines shed light on a complex relationship. Not all of the participants in the conference chose to prepare papers for *Reflections*. In the final chapter of this volume, Erin Goodman provides an opportunity to hear from conference voices not included in the preceding chapters. She reviews the presentations these participants made and suggests how their contributions broaden perspectives about how memory and democracy intersect and interact.

Thus, Goodman indicates the important questions raised in sociology by Elizabeth Jelin, considers how Katherine Hite explains the utility of the perspectives of political scientists in illuminating the links between democracy and memory, and echoes the thoughts of Juan Mendez on why international law is important in the domestic politics of nations. She discusses Stephen Kinzer's perspectives on the international dimensions of political events in Guatemala and Maria Teresa Ronderos' work in encouraging debate about Colombia's past and present through the provision of information and voice; both participants share Erlick and Montas' commitment to the role of the media in discussions of justice, human rights, and impunity.

Other disciplines add to the voices that Goodman reflects. In many countries, architects have been active in planning, interpreting, and commemorating the relationship between democracy and memory. In exploring presentations by Julian Bonder and Gustavo Buntinx, Goodman recalls Vignolo's chapter on the role of public spaces in recovering, interpreting, and passing on memory in the present and future. She presents Marysa Navarro's thoughts about Spain's coming to terms with the long years of the Franco dictatorship, and indicates how John Dinges and Kirsten Weld explore the role of archives and archivists in the documentation of the past and its importance in the reconstruction of democratic societies. She brings yet additional perspectives to the complex of questions raised in the volume and at the conference.

Reflections on Memory and Democracy in Latin America does not resolve the issue of the connection between these two concepts. As with many other works that consider the relationship between memory and democracy in the wake of violence and repression, we conclude that the cliché, "the past must be reconciled with the present and future if democracies are to be vibrant and durable," encourages too simplistic an understanding of the connection. Memory and democracy may be linked, but before they are, dilemmas of what is remembered, what lessons are drawn from it, how those lessons are used to construct new democratic institutions, and whether a link reaches beyond institutions to citizenship—all these must be addressed in the particular context of individual societies. There are, we found, indeed "many histories and many memories." In most Latin American societies, additional *arpilleras* remain to be stitched.

PART

I

Remembering and Democracy: Memory and Its Place in Democratic Institutions

2

Memory as a Pillar for Democracy and Reconciliation in Chile

Sergio Bitar

Achieving reconciliation in societies that have experienced a major crisis requires a national effort to bring out what happened, to understand what went wrong, and to draw lessons from it. We must resist the temptation simply to put the past behind us.

Real reconciliation can only be achieved if we create institutions that respect and guarantee the rights of all sectors of society and enable disagreements to be resolved in a democratic fashion. Reconciliation cannot, therefore, occur while ignoring the past. Learning from our collective experience is a fundamental step in building a common future and lasting reconciliation. In the case of Chile, it is important to remember the human rights violations committed by the civic-military dictatorship from 1973 to 1989, and also to understand and acknowledge the political and economic conditions that led to the coup.

A Personal Experience

I have to confess that reconciliation has not been the political goal that has inspired my public actions. Since the military coup, I have been committed to the construction of a civilized coexistence based on democracy and respect for human rights. My conviction was, and is, that reconciliation as a social process requires underlying political conditions that are not yet present, and that reconciliation will only progress if we are able to improve, day by day, the democratic underpinnings of coexistence (*"convivencia"*).

I have not had to reconcile myself with persons who violated human rights. Even today I don't seek reconciliation with those who still justify violence. I can coexist with those people, but I cannot be reconciled with them.

For me and for thousands of my compatriots, the essential task right after the coup was to survive. The shock was monumental. The bombing of the presidential palace, La Moneda, with President Salvador Allende inside, the assassination of friends, the disappearances, the torture, the prison, and the exile—it was difficult to endure all of these without breaking.

As time went on my feelings and reasoning started evolving. From those first days in 1973, I observed that, as peaceful as Chilean society had seemed, it had enormous potential for violence, which could erupt when the norms were broken or worse, when they were broken through state terrorism. It was difficult to explain how the apparently civilized colonel from the FACH (Chilean Air Force), who had visited my house when I held the post of Minister of Mining under President Allende, could just a short time later order his subordinates to resort to torture. Or, how people with whom we had interacted every day could become the first informers or spokesmen of the rhetoric that would hide or try to justify what was happening.

I never felt hatred nor the desire for vengeance. But indignation became for me a motivating force to combat injustice. At that moment, no one was aiming for reconciliation or even trying to organize people to fight; we simply lived to overcome our circumstances.

I found it healing to tell the story of my life on Dawson Island in 1975, as a political prisoner, and to leave it a testimony for my children, and for all children. However, I put the text away for more than eight years and returned to it only in 1983. Upon rereading it, I realized that there were bits that I no longer remembered. I felt the fragility of memory, and the strength of the mind to block out bad memories in order to allow us to move forward. But if we forget tragic events, they could be repeated. I learned through my own experience that we must keep our memories because they can both heal us and keep us alert. In 1987, when Pope John Paul II visited Chile, publishers dared to launch the first edition of my book *Isla 10*. It became a bestseller as Chileans wanted to understand what had happened.

This opening of past experience led to an important evolution in Chilean political thinking, especially in the left. On the one hand, the abrupt end of the Chilean road to socialism and, on the other hand and later, the crisis of "real" socialism in Eastern Europe, along with the attractiveness of European Social Democrats' experiences, all contributed to a review of ideological positions. It opened the way for reassessing democracy and its institutions, and the idea of broad coalitions became important to the moderate left in Chile and Latin America. The examples of governance in democratic countries also opened up new perspectives and showed us new national paths forward.

In exile we had begun to organize ourselves, help others who arrived, and launch international campaigns to protect human rights and condemn the dictatorship. To seek a political way forward we had to ask ourselves seriously why the democratic process had failed and the coup happened—what did we do wrong? Unlike many others, I had a self-critical vision that I expressed in the book *Chile: Experiments in Democracy*, which was published in the United States, Mexico, Brazil, and Chile (where it was titled *El Gobierno de Allende, Chile 1970–73*). The main aspiration and goal of the book was to unite democrats in Chile and abroad who shared a respect for human rights, to fight the dictatorship and rebuild democracy through peaceful means.

At that time the fight was for what today appears to be a modest goal: that the justice system would offer, at the very least, legal recourse (*habeas corpus*) when someone disappeared. It was an almost futile battle. Only a very few judges acted with dignity and offered some consolation. We tried to stop the violence, combat fear and, through those efforts, protect social mobilization.

The process of political and social convergence began early. A first meeting of leaders connected to democratic socialism and the Christian Democrats was held in 1975 in Colonia Tovar, Venezuela, with the support of the Ebert Foundation. They would later be joined by liberals from the right.

One name that must not be forgotten is that of Cardinal Silva Henríquez. Along with other denominations and church leaders, he defended life and offered hope in the midst of despair. That may have been the moment when the Catholic Church was closest to the heart of the majority of Chileans. No one, not even the church, talked about reconciliation then.

Rediscovering My Country and Moving On

Chile's transition was a slow process, as are many transitions worldwide. In fighting the dictatorship, the progressive convergence of political forces and their coordination with workers' organizations, professionals, women, students, and the Catholic Church grew into a political power capable of defeating Pinochet. The Group for the new Constitution or the Group of 24 in 1980, the Democratic Alliance in 1983, the National Agreement in 1985, the Assembly for Civility in 1986, the Free Elections Committee in 1987, and the *Concertación por el No* in 1988 were successive steps that allowed the plebiscite to triumph in 1988. All these steps were not aimed at forging reconciliation, but at dislodging the dictatorship from power.

In 1984, when I was allowed to reenter Chile and the L stamped on my passport was removed, my exile ended and my "un-exile" began. I found a very different country. Only little by little could I see that the familiar parts were still there, albeit buried. I felt the oppression of the dictatorship and sensed the contempt for those civilians who supported it. I understood that although all of us Chileans lived in the same country, we thought very differently, and that it was essential to reorganize a country based on democratic rules and tolerance for diversity. It was unacceptable for one to crush the other through force.

Parties, social organizations, and civil society continued to fight for lessening the ideological strife with persistence and patience. As time went by, some factions of the dictatorship began to incline in favor of a return to democracy. Cardinal Francisco Fresno's call for a National Agreement attracted people who were open to seeking the truth. My book *Isla 10* was read by people in the Navy. I began to feel hope that this could bloom into a spirit of coming together.

The 1988 plebiscite to decide on whether Pinochet would be given an additional term, and the triumph of the NO vote, marked a historic change. We took on the enormous task of reconstructing the institutional democratic foundations, neutralizing hatred, and seeking unity among Chileans. The *Concertación* (a coalition based mainly on Christian Democrats and Social Democrats) acted with conviction to re-establish the authority of the civilian government over the military, ensure respect for human rights, seek justice, and focus on reducing poverty.

The National Commission for Truth and Reconciliation was an audacious step that President Aylwin took in 1991. Its precepts of truth and justice, also hailed by the church, were rejected by many supporters of the dictatorship. Pinochet, still Commander in Chief of the Army, protested and threatened: his argument was that, far from contributing to reconciliation, the truth would open wounds and provoke hatred. On the contrary, the Commission's work brought peace, dissipated fear, and led to a demand for justice in the tribunals. It became an international example, observed later by South Africa.

To identify lessons that might be useful for Arab nations and some countries in Asia and Africa, my colleague Abraham Lowenthal and I recently interviewed former presidents of countries that had managed transitions to democracy. With all its lights and shadows, Chile achieved something unlike any other country in looking for truth and justice, and keeping memory alive. These results are also due to the moral force of women and the families of those who were detained and disappeared, of the *Vicaría de la Solidaridad,* and of many human rights organizations.

From the beginning of democratic governments, it was clear to me that reconciliation could only emerge from each person's spirit to the extent that truth and justice moved forward. It was also apparent that there would never be only one version of history, but many; not one memory, but many; and though we will always disagree on some issues, we can coexist if we cling to democratic norms and respect for human rights.

After President Aylwin's National Commission for Truth and Reconciliation, the Frei government followed up with the "Roundtable Dialogue," engaging in conversations with the military, human rights organizations, and lawyers; the Lagos administration organized the "Valech Commission" to identify those who suffered political imprisonment, torture, and abuse; and President Bachelet opened the Museum of Memory. Then came the trials and the reparations. After many attempts, Congress succeeded in approving Chile's entry as a member of the International Criminal Court and the Committee against Torture (CAT).

Is Reconciliation Possible with Those Who Justify the Coup?

The debate about the causes of the coup is still unresolved, perhaps because such a resolution logically comes with a risk: to find justification for the coup may once again provide justification for human rights violations.

No one is free from responsibility for what happened. Each person has to draw his or her own lessons from the past. Mine are that the Allende administration, of which I was a part, created tension and polarization that served as an excuse for others to reject the government's legitimacy and unleash a military coup. Whatever the reasons for the coup, however, nothing, under any circumstances, can justify human rights violations. There is a moral boundary that must not be crossed. Those who seek refuge in political justifications for the coup are ultimately justifying violence against their fellow citizens. Those who, in turn, ignore the causes of the coup and don't honestly examine the lessons of that period, also contribute to its repetition.

From that experience we drew political lessons that have guided our later decisions. We pushed for change by fostering a majority capable of confronting the enormous economic and political power of the dominant non-democratic forces. We have continuously educated the public, being aware that in Chile more than 40 percent of the population voted for Pinochet's regime to continue in power. I also learned to mistrust the voices of the extreme left that loudly proclaimed intransigence, providing fodder for the fascist-inspired groups. Constructive and democratic changes must be forged through successive reforms, profoundly linked to the assent of the citizenry.

It was very difficult to reconstruct coexistence with a living dictator who had headed the Army for more than eight years and then became a Senator for life. In 1998, Pinochet entered the Senate without an election, installed through a constitutional rule that he himself inserted in his 1980

Constitution. I was sitting within ten meters of him in the Senate for a number of months. He was responsible for so many crimes, and there he was, voting, with the same right as the senators chosen by the people, surrounded and protected by some senators who served as his bodyguards. Maintaining my composure was difficult. Reconcile? Impossible. The goal was to change the rules and get him out.

The extended presence of Pinochet delayed the whole process, particularly changes in the judicial branch. Barring a few notable and honorable exceptions, the Chilean judiciary had been subordinated to the dictatorship. The Chilean transition to democracy was strengthened by the European decision to try Pinochet for the assassination and disappearance of European citizens. The actions of Judge Baltasar Garzón (of Spain) and the British justice system were invaluable, and reflected the recognition that human rights are a universal value, guaranteed in international agreements. Without this decision, Pinochet would never have been held accountable and the story of our transition would have been a different one. Impunity would have weakened our democracy and strengthened the anti-democratic sectors that had justified the dictatorship's actions. An important segment of the Chilean right has still not drawn the line between justifying the coup and justifying the violation of human rights.

The Future: From Personal Memory to Social Memory

Notwithstanding the explosion of memory that occurred in Chile on September 11, 2013, on the 40th anniversary of the coup, there is still an essential step we must take to leave a legacy that endures and sustains a common future. We must move from the personal memory of those who lived their own experience to a collective memory for those who come after us. Forgetting is an illness of our time. Many wish to forget, thinking that we will then be more at ease. But memory is a source of healing and hope. Memory has its own dynamics; it is not a way of clinging to the past but of gaining knowledge to help build a new world.

Mine was a privileged generation that fought for its dreams, suffered through the dictatorship, and actively participated in the creation of a new democratic society. But that legacy is still inconclusive if we don't preserve the memory of what it cost, learn the lessons for preventing a repeat in Chile and elsewhere, and enshrine the importance of protecting our essential values for the future. Have we built the foundations to coexist in a democracy? Certainly. Has memory helped to build those foundations? Absolutely. Has Chile achieved reconciliation? Not yet. The culture of human rights is still not yet deeply rooted. The mission for all of us is to turn it into common sense.

If memory helps democracy and democracy is a precondition for reconciliation, we Chileans should work together to forge common futures based on deepening democracy and respecting the rights of everyone. A priority task is to elaborate a new constitution, together, with widespread participation. The existing constitution, despite having been amended during this democratic period, drags the illegitimacy of being imposed in 1980 by Pinochet, in the midst of a dictatorship, without respect for any democratic rule. Chileans now demand a future agenda that represents a common project. A constitutional process developed in a working democracy may help us to agree on norms and institutions that revere the values of liberty, solidarity, participation, and a collective will. This step, among others, will favor reconciliation.

3

Searching for Irma: A Public and Private Quest for Memory

June Erlick

Irma Flaquer is still missing.

The courageous 42-year-old reporter was swept from the streets of downtown Guatemala in 1980. Her car was ambushed by two vehicles, her son shot to death by her side, while she was dragged out by her hair, never to be seen again.

I was assigned to investigate the case of Irma Flaquer in 1996 as a part of the Inter American Press Association's Unpunished Crimes Against Journalists project. To tell the truth, I was disappointed in the choice of assignment. Irma's was the oldest of the eight cases to be investigated in Guatemala, Colombia, Mexico, and Panama. It was the only case involving a woman. My first reaction was that this was a cold case of some obscure reporter (I had never heard of Irma) that was being chosen only because she was a woman. Besides, I had lived in Colombia for a decade and had known Luis Guillermo Cano, the editor of *El Espectador*, who had been assassinated in 1986, in broad daylight, as a result of his newspaper's courageous reporting on the burgeoning drug trafficking. He had helped me with my visa when I won an Inter American Press Association (IAPA) scholarship to study and report from Colombia in 1977. I can't say I knew him well, but he had treated me as a cub reporter with infinite kindness and respect. I had assumed I would be assigned that case and didn't lobby for it. Someone else did.

I felt selfish, putting my personal interests first in my desire for that particular case. After all, through my work with the IAPA, I knew that journalists like Luis Guillermo Cano were being silenced throughout the hemisphere. Years later, as I worked on this chapter, as I read through my colleagues' contributions, I was particularly struck by Haitian journalist Michèle Montas' description of her childhood. Like Irma in Guatemala, Montas grew up in a culture of fear and silence "never fully understanding why there were so many taboo subjects at the dinner table or at school, or why there were, at times, dead bodies in the streets." When she was 17, her family had to go into hiding when an aunt and four cousins were forcibly disappeared during the dictatorship of François Duvalier. Montas, as she tells us in her chapter in this book, decided to become a broadcast journalist because she "could no longer accept the deafening silence of my childhood and because [she] refused to hide ever again."

Irma Flaquer in Guatemala, I learned, also got her start in broadcast journalism, at a Catholic radio station—for the prosaic reason that she needed to earn a living to support her two sons and had had voice training in her father's traveling theatre. She started with necessity, but was soon broadcasting "what others don't dare say." She soon migrated to print journalism with a column seeking to do just that. It didn't take much investigation to figure out that her story was an emblematic case, even if an old one. I began to investigate what had happened to Irma Flaquer just about the time the Guatemalan Peace Accords were being signed in 1996. The country, which had just endured 36 years of bloody civil war, was immersed in a deep silence and a culture of fear at that time. Irma's career had spanned nearly the entire period of the war, and she was not about to be silent. Her newspaper column was simply entitled "What Others Don't Dare Write."

I soon found out that my good friend Stephen Kinzer, author of the classic *Bitter Fruit*, had known Irma. In the foreword to the book I eventually wrote about the Guatemalan reporter, he observed,

> During the holocaust that descended on Guatemala during the 1970s and 1980s, government-sponsored death squads roamed the country with impunity. Anyone who protested, anyone who organized, anyone who challenged the established order was liable to be killed. The lucky victims met sudden death in street-corner assassinations. Others were made to "disappear," often suffering through long periods of unspeakable torture before being murdered. All this was done with the collusion of the country's leaders and at least the tacit approval of their supporters in Washington and other foreign capitals.

In such a climate, a person of conscience faces a stark choice between safe submission and dangerous activism. Irma Flaquer chose the latter. Certainly, she understood the risks of this course. Her passion for justice and her deep sense of patriotism, however, led her to use her talents to confront the brutal system under which Guatemala was suffering. Ultimately, she became another of its victims.

Irma wrote constantly about the human rights abuses in her country, about corruption, about the failure of the legal system. She wrote until she was told that she could no longer write her column because workers at the newspaper's printing plant had been threatened by bomb attacks in retaliation for her writing.

While I was investigating the case, while I tried to reconstruct what had happened the day she was taken, I began to ask why she had stayed, why she had kept on. When she was a 22-year-old reporter, she was beaten up by a group of market women at the service of the presidential palace. Government authorities at that time often used mobs to do their dirty work, in this case beating up a young female reporter to keep her silent. The plan backfired; instead of being silenced, she received international publicity and support. Her photo with a blackened eye appeared in *Time* magazine. Less than a decade later, in even darker times, a car bomb tore through her automobile as she opened its door, injuring her hearing and her writing hand and sending her to the hospital, followed by a year of recuperation in which she began to write short stories and swore off journalism. She couldn't stay away though and soon accepted another newspaper job. She kept reporting and writing until a couple of months before her disappearance.

My investigation became an intensely personal quest to recover her memory, to find out why she stayed, even why she had holed up in her apartment faced with a blatant death sentence. Why had she not left for revolutionary Managua, where she could have found a supportive haven, or for Miami, where she had a loving sister?

Her story was intensely Guatemalan. She loved the hand-embroidered blouses of the local indigenous women; she enjoyed eating Guatemalan typical dishes. She wrote about specific Guatemalan corruption and specific human rights abuses; her columns were never abstract or universal. Even when she wrote about foreign affairs, as she did with the U.S. elections or the Sandinista Revolution, she was always writing in terms of the impact on her beloved Guatemala.

Realizing that about her, I perhaps overreacted when Argentine and Chilean colleagues, seeing the photo of the attractive blonde and hearing that she had disappeared, would inevitably ask, "Is she Argentine?" "Is she Chilean?" I'd immediately correct them. But one day a Chilean friend, having looked at the photo and having asked the same question and having received the same explanation, sighed wistfully and declared, "She's one of us."

Peter Winn's chapter in this book about the memory of politics reminds me that Irma shares with Chileans the memory of a democratically elected leftist government. In Guatemala, it was the government of Jacobo Arbenz, which Kinzer describes so powerfully in his book; in Chile, it was that of Salvador Allende. Winn points out,

> It might be a dissident collective memory, but many Chileans recalled the Popular Unity era as one of deepened democracy, when government policies favored the majority and they felt empowered for the first time—and in 1990 expected the restored democracy that they had fought for to restore as well some of that empowerment and some of those policies.

This dissident collective memory, as Winn aptly puts it, also existed and exists in Guatemala with a deeply polarized vision of the past. That memory of democracy shaped Irma's writings and her quest for justice.

But just as memory may be collective, I began to understand from my investigation that memory could be so very specific—down to the tortillas Irma liked and the cuss words she used—and at the same time universal. Soon after this encounter, something would happen that would show me powerfully how memory in Latin America—and perhaps everywhere—operates on those two very powerful levels, the intensely personal and the intensely universal.

Of course, the first intensely universal meaning of her disappearance—and indeed of the whole Unpunished Crimes Against Journalists project—is the very fact that Irma was a journalist. It's not that journalists are more important than the doctors, lawyers, poets, workers, housewives, or scholars who are murdered or disappeared in an attempt to silence their voices. Journalists, however, represent the public's right to know. Journalism makes democracy work. It seeks the truth about the most complicated stories. It denounces abuses of all types. It is the way the world gets to learn what is happening in countries that may be distant from the main international scene.

From 1995, the year before I began my investigation of Irma's case and 2004, the year my book about her was published, 341 Guatemalan journalists were assassinated while performing their journalistic duties. During this period, only 35 people had been arrested in connection with these cases. That is, 85 percent of the cases went unpunished, according to the Committee to Protect Journalists. And these figures do not reflect the darkest days in which Irma herself practiced journalism nor the current situation in Guatemala, complicated by drug trafficking and escalating violence.

Irma herself explained the role of the journalist as she saw it:

A completely impartial attitude just isn't understood in this environment, where political and personal interests play such a very important role. Nevertheless, I believe—and I will always believe—that the
obligation of the honorable journalist is to tell the truth to his or her
readers. It doesn't matter if the truth affects the right or the left, or
if the truth makes the government look good or favors the opposition . . . I believe my obligation is to tell the truth, no matter whom it
hurts. (*La Hora*, March 3, 1961, translated in Erlick: *Disappeared, A
Journalist Silenced*, p. 60)

Irma's story took place before the days of the Internet and even easy
international calls. As I learned more about her and her journalistic work,
I realized that it was not only her incisive columns that were important in
Guatemala's time of darkness. Irma served as a source for foreign reporters
to get information about human rights abuses reported about internationally, hoping that other governments and civil society organizations might
be able to act to stop the bloodletting.

I found out that another friend, Pulitzer-Prize winning journalist Shirley Christian, had also used Irma as a source and had written about her by
name. Not only did Shirley have the original article she wrote about Irma
and the Guatemalan situation, but she had her notes, which she photo-
copied from her yellowed reporter's notebook to share with me.

Christian's interaction with Irma illustrated what I had discovered about
the collective and the particular nature of memory. The United States had
no clear-cut policy at the time of the interview, wavering between pressure from human rights activists and geopolitical concerns about a Central
American region that could become a pawn for the Soviet Union. Christian
was reporting at the time for *The Miami Herald*, then the most influential
voice in the coverage of Latin America. Most of the U.S. foreign press paid
little attention to Guatemala, instead focusing on revolutionary Nicaragua
or war-torn El Salvador.

An exiled Guatemalan labor activist had suggested Christian talk to
Irma. She would talk freely, he told the reporter. Not many people would.
Christian flew to Guatemala City and the interview took place at *La Nación*
newspaper. She quoted Irma in her article.

If you want to cry out for the dignity of the human being in this
country they say you are a Communist. I am as Communist as Jimmy

Carter, but here, liking Carter instead of Reagan means you are on the left. What is certain is that Guatemala is going to explode sooner or later, whoever is president of the United States.

Christian then went on to describe Irma, "Irma Flaquer, establishment woman, is speaking. Private secretary to former President Julio César Mendez Montenegro in the 1960s, she now is assistant editor of a newspaper that plays by the rules. She knows the right people. Establishment, but outspoken." The headline on the August 10, 1980, story was "U.S. Has No Real Policy While Guatemala Boils."

Christian asked Irma repeatedly whether she could use her name. And the Guatemalan reporter insisted that her name be used. To be effective, Irma knew, she could not be anonymous. Yet to have her name published might be a risk, because not only was she denouncing human rights abuses but condemning the United States for its failure to take a stance.

In the corner of the lined spiral reporter's notebook, the notes read, "blonde hair, green eyeshadow." What Christian remembered after so many years were Irma's long, well-manicured fingernails. She remembered the reporter as a special, concrete individual, as well as a courageous reporter who dared speak out when most of society was silent.

One of Flaquer's best-known investigations, one cited even by taxi-drivers in Guatemala City today, involved a case of impunity, and she kept writing about it and insisting on justice for years.

The story started in a very ordinary fashion. Three teenage boys from the Paiz Maselli family were having a good time after a soccer victory by dining out at a popular fish restaurant in a tree-lined neighborhood of Guatemala City. They were joking around and teasing each other in the somewhat raucous way teenage boys are prone to do.

The bodyguards of a rich and politically connected entrepreneur went over to the boys' table and asked them to be quiet because the businessman wanted to enjoy his lunch in peace.

One of the boys retorted, "Why should we? It's a free country."

A few minutes later, the bodyguards returned and, without warning, opened fire. They killed two of the boys, injuring the third. Businessman Jorge Köng Vielman, a military commissioner for the local zone where the restaurant was located, hadn't done the actual shooting; he ordered his de facto bodyguards—members of the ambulatory military police—to do something about the ruckus.

The boys' father fought for justice, seeking Irma Flaquer's help in writing about the case. The businessman was eventually sentenced to jail for eight years and eight months. In a brief democratic opening in the Guatemalan justice system, the Paiz Maselli became a symbol, a test for democracy and peaceful solutions. However, the case was overturned on a technicality in 1978, and Köng went free.

Irma had written about the case for months, keeping it alive in the press. The 1978 reversal appeared to be an important factor in Flaquer's slowly understanding that the rule of law might not work, despite her best efforts. She tied the impunity in this case to the growing impunity of terror in the country, the terror to which she herself eventually succumbed.

If ESA (the death squad known as the Secret Anti-Communist Army) doesn't exist, then those sentenced to death shouldn't exist, not should those who have already been executed. It's like the case of the Paiz Maselli brothers. They were killed, and then the court declared that no one killed them. The assassin's bullets were fired by somebody called nobody. Such an absurd thing could only happen in Guatemala.

My parents, the university and life itself have taught me that if a rock breaks a window, someone threw it. If two boys are murdered in front of witnesses, someone pulled the trigger. If several people appear on a death list and are later murdered, not only logic, but the most basic common sense says that someone didn't want to take the responsibility.

Even though Irma observed that an absurd and tragic killing and an equally absurd and tragic court ruling could only occur in Guatemala, one can now see that her struggle for justice in the courts in Guatemala was part of the ongoing Latin American—perhaps universal—struggle against impunity. She felt that her journalist's voice could always point out to justice, but she was realizing that the power of the press was not always enough to obtain justice from a legal system that did not work. She studied law at the university to understand it better; she studied psychology to give more effective and direct help to citizens than journalism could accomplish. But as frustrated as she could feel at times with journalism, she always returned to her profession. No other profession provided so many opportunities to try to tell the truth. No other profession gave so much leeway to the effort to make the rule of law work. No other profession allowed one to write the first draft of history, to construct memory, as painful as that could be.

After the official investigation for the Inter American Press Association was over, I continued to work on the case, using my own money and time to return to Guatemala to look into Irma's life and disappearance.

And even though I no longer had an official relationship to the IAPA, I continued to call Ricardo Trotti to share details of the case with him. The energetic, committed Argentine headed up the organization's impunity project, as the Unpunished Crimes Against Journalists had become informally known. I think my enthusiasm and passion were contagious. The case of Irma Flaquer became the first ever that the organization took to the Inter-American Commission on Human Rights.

The IAPA charged before the Commission that the Guatemalan state had violated several articles of the Inter-American Convention on Human Rights: the right to life (Article 4), to a fair trial (Article 8), to freedom of expression (Article 13) and to judicial protection (Article 25), "all in relation to the general obligation to respect the rights (Article 1) recognized in the Inter-American Convention on Human Rights." The Washington D.C.-based Commission is an autonomous dependency of the Organization of American States (OAS). Both its mandate and creation stem from the Inter-American Convention on Human Rights.

On March 2, 2001, the Guatemalan government signed a friendly agreement with the IAPA under the auspices of the Commission. Then-President Alfonso Portillo acknowledged the institutional responsibility of the Guatemalan state. Guatemala was beginning its long and unfinished road towards democracy, which involves an accounting for the past to pave the way for a more just future—a process of transitional justice. Irma's case became an integral part of this process.

In Frances Hagopian's chapter in this book, she points out that equal access to the judicial system and equal protection under the law are more "aspirational" than "real," observing,

> What has enabled judiciaries to take bold jurisprudential steps against impunity has been a sea change in the guiding norms of the judiciary itself—from the formalist, positivist legal cultures that historically protected conservative interests in Latin America to one guided by a juridical vision committed to the defense of human rights that applies doctrines derived from international human rights law.

International organizations such as the IAPA and the Inter-American Human Rights Commission can encourage the fight against impunity in both an aspirational and, we hope, "real" fashion.

The second point of the agreement with IAPA asserts: "The State deplores and acknowledges that the forced disappearance of the journalist, Irma Marina Flaquer Azurdia, on October 16, 1980, was despicable and endorses the view that it is urgently necessary to continue with and vigorously reinforce administrative and legal measures aimed at identifying those responsible, determining the whereabouts of the victim and applying the appropriate criminal and civil punishment."

In other words, the Guatemalan government was reopening the investigation into Irma Flaquer's disappearance. But along with the opening of the case—which I hoped would turn into the legal quest to seek the truth of memory, the memory of truth, of what happened to Irma—the agreement was a textbook blueprint for memory-making. Like much of what has happened in Guatemala since the peace accords were signed, and like much of what has happened throughout Latin America, the blueprint has been carried out unevenly and sometimes with unintended consequences.

For me as an investigator, as an author, as someone who was trying to discover the truth about Irma, the agreement put the memories I had been retrieving into the context of an official collective memory. The text struggled with the issues of transitional justice and how to best implement it and paid heavy tribute to memorialization in a mostly constructive way.

In looking at the agreement between the Guatemalan state and the IAPA, I seek to look at the many layers of memory-making as they pertain to her particular case, the disappeared in Guatemala, and the struggle to find the ways of connecting memory to building democracy in Latin America.

Transitional Justice

In Guatemala, as in Chile, Argentina, Brazil and Uruguay, as in the rest of Latin America, as in the rest of the world that has signed the International Convention for the Protection of All Persons from Forced Disappearance, disappearance is still a crime. Even in countries that have granted amnesty to the perpetrators of human rights abuses, disappearance is an exception. It is a crime that is continuing, a present crime, not a past one. Thinking about disappearance that way makes it possible to try perpetrators in spite of amnesty laws, which cover crimes of the past.

Before beginning to investigate Irma's case, I understood that concept as an abstraction, perhaps as a way to achieve at least a quota of transitional justice. As I came to know Irma's relatives, friends, colleagues and readers, I began to understand that with forced disappearance, there is no closure. There are no bones, no burial, no knowledge of what happened, of the person's last words and whereabouts. There are only questions. And pain. It is indeed an ongoing crime against humanity.

Marjorie Agosín says it so well in the prologue to this book: "The disappeared, constantly crossing the frontier between life and death, caught like ghosts in the minds of those who knew them, or who want to know them, those obsessed with remembering them."

Anabella Flaquer explained the impact of her sister's disappearance at a mock inquest—a symbolic courtroom—at the 1996 IAPA General Assembly in Los Angeles, California. The audience included two Nobel Prize winners, three former Latin American presidents, newspaper executives, editors, and human rights activists. It was at that meeting that Colombian writer Gabriel García Márquez gave his now-iconic speech about "The Best Job in the World," meaning journalism. Irma's dedication to journalism could not lessen her sister's pain, although Anabella recognized her sister's commitment.

> My sister told me, "Anabella, if I die, don't cry. Just know that I will be very happy, because I have died fighting for what I most love." But ladies and gentlemen, how can I stop crying if I have lost not only my sister, Irma Flaquer, the journalist, but my moral support, my counselor, my confidant? I am left an orphan again, robbed of my human right to bury a loved one.

The crowd gave Anabella a standing ovation. She knew that even as she was talking from the bottom of her heart about Irma, there were many in the audience who also had lost family members in forced disappearances. Many came to tell her their own stories and to empathize with her plight.

In Argentina and Chile, even before Guatemala, governments employed forced disappearance to try to silence and control political opposition. Like Irma, individuals were yanked from the streets, dragged from their beds, or picked up from protests. Most never appeared again.

Many of the countries established Truth Commissions; Guatemala had two, one sponsored by the Catholic Church and the other by the UN-sponsored Commission for Historical Clarification. Both sought to create an extensive documentation of the 36-year internal conflict dating from 1960 to the United Nations' brokered peace agreement of 1996. The Commission for Historical Clarification describes its mission "to foster tolerance and preserve memory of the victims."

Both commissions had great visibility. They differed not so much in their conclusions as in their perspectives. The Guatemalan bishops believed that the path to healing and reconciliation in their country needed to reveal and document the truth about the overwhelming prior abuses and atrocities. The Recovery of Historical Memory project (REMHI) was published as a four-volume report, *Guatemala: Nunca Más: Informe proyecto interdiocesano de recuperación de la memoria histórica* (in English, published in 1998 as *Guatemala: Never Again*).

The first volume discusses the impact of the violence, from both an individual and collective perspective—again, the thread of how the individual illuminates the collective, and the collective provides context and power to the individual experience. The second volume focuses on the methodology of horror, documenting the organizational methods and strategies employed by the army, intelligence divisions, police units, and death squads. The third section provides a very detailed historical overview. REHMI found the total number of people killed was over 200,000; 83 percent of the victims were Mayan and 17 percent were Ladino, mixed-race or of Spanish descent like Irma. REHMI also concluded that state forces and related paramilitary groups were responsible for 93 percent of the violations documented, and that the guerrillas were responsible for 3 percent of the human rights violations and acts of violence.

The last volume spells out REHMI recommendations, including a call for reparations, a statement of government responsibility, public commemoration of the victims, legislative and judicial reforms, demilitarization, and a greater concern for human rights. With the exception of the call for legislative and judicial reforms and the call for demilitarization, the bishops' report seemed to be setting out guidelines similar to those of the friendly agreement reached between the Guatemalan government and the Inter American Press Association on the Flaquer case.

Soon after the REHMI report was released, the bishop who had spearheaded the project was killed. With the brutal murder of Bishop Juan Gerardi, impunity and the operation of the justice system became a focus of international and Guatemalan attention.

The friendly agreement between the IAPA and the Guatemalan government took place in the context of critical history in the making. Transitional justice, seen in previous examples such as South Africa and Chile, now came to the reality of Guatemala, an amazingly beautiful country with an equally sad and contorted history that sometimes seemed to evoke Colombian author Gabriel García Márquez's magical realism— with a coup against an elected president staged by the United States, a bishop murdered in his own home, and infants strangled to death for being Communists. Irma's story in a way made this overdose of injustice manageable; her reporting and writing during her newspaper career took on many of the abuses and corruption of power eventually discussed in the REHMI and the UN report. The agreement to reopen the case was a step toward justice.

To face the impact of disappearances on a society it is necessary to set out the principles of truth and accountability that drive the practice of transitional justice: one must reckon with the past to move forward. "Transitional justice helps societies comprehensively address legacies of disappearances by establishing the records of the disappeared, seeking criminal accountability for those responsible, restoring public trusts in institutions, and issuing reparations to the families of the disappeared," states the International Center for Transitional Justice.

One of the figures who loom large in the disappearance of Irma Flaquer is that of Interior Minister Donaldo Alvarez Ruiz, a civilian who had long-standing ties to the Flaquer family. As a matter of fact, when I began to investigate the case, I was told by an activist, "Everyone knows who did it; it was Donaldo Alvarez, and he lives in Miami."

The real story proved to be much more complicated. Alvarez may have tried to save Irma's life, knowing she was on a death list. He summoned her into his office, told her to leave the country immediately and wrote her a check for her fare, which she did not accept, retorting, "It's not enough for a return ticket." He may have washed his hands of the case afterwards; he may even have ordered her death to prove his loyalty to the government. The more I investigated, the more complex the story became. Transitional justice is not a picture drawn in black and white; perpetrators are sometimes also victims; people act in unexpected ways because of ties of blood and friendship.

What is clear, however, is that Alvarez has never been found for questioning—on this or any other case, let alone being held accountable for his own acts. At the initiative of Guatemalan Nobel Prize winner Rigoberta Menchú, an arrest warrant was issued against Alvarez for torture and political assassination. In a close call he was almost captured in Mexico, but the Mexican authorities showed up too late and Alvarez slipped away. His whereabouts are still unknown.

When I began investigating Irma's case and discovered that things were not as simple as they had seemed at first, that the black and whites devolved into greys, I considered writing a novel. I had recently taken Marguerite Feitlowitz's course in literary translation at Harvard and knew the power of fiction in describing the uncertainties of the past, in rendering memory into the forms one wanted to take. I am struck now by her essay in this book, which takes a look at how Argentine novelists wrestle with history.

The ways in which we think about what happens is also part of history: our anxieties, dreads, and dreams; the precepts, categories, and genres that help us organize our thoughts and feelings; the ways in which we both resist and seek to recover individual and collective memories. "History" is the play of rupture and continuity: we struggle to articulate happenings whose depth, complexity, and horror strain effability.

In the end, I chose the path of explaining history through biography, rather than in the form of a novel. After all, Irma was a journalist: she lived for the facts and she died for the facts. And as history has evolved, more facts have emerged. Four years after the friendly agreement was signed, investigators from Guatemala's human rights office accidentally discovered the secret Guatemalan National Police Archives, the existence of which had been firmly denied for years. The estimated 75 million pages of materials are providing new evidence for justice in Guatemala. In addition to the written documents, hundreds of rolls of still photography, lists of police informants with names and photos, vehicle license plates, video tapes and computer disks are both the raw materials for memory-making, but also for pursuing justice.

"Despite [its] terrible legacy, Guatemala represents today an extraordinary example of how information can advance the cause of justice over the barriers of impunity," writes Kate Doyle of the National Security Archive in a 2005 article posted on the organization's website.

Guatemalan investigators have drawn on victims' accounts, forensic records, published human rights reports, perpetrators' testimonies and thousands of declassified U.S. documents obtained by the National Security Archive under the Freedom of Information Act in an attempt to provide some historical and judicial accountability for what happened during the war. Openness advocates have used the government's silence about the war to press their case for the passage of a national freedom of information law. Prosecutors have incorporated U.S. declassified documents into legal battles targeting military and police abusers in key human rights cases. And now Guatemalans are discovering their own buried, hidden, and abandoned records from the files of the repressive Guatemalan security services.

The newly discovered police archives, which cover a century of police operations, promise to be one of the most revealing collections of military or police records ever discovered in Latin America. The appearance of these documents has created an extraordinary opportunity for preserving history and advancing justice that the Archive is mobilizing to meet.

Only a few scattered references to Irma have been found in the National Police Archives, none of which directly deal with her disappearance. Every time a document is found, Irma's sister Anabella is contacted in Miami. Anabella has given her DNA, and every time a body is discovered that might possibly be that of Irma (and it has happened more than once), she is contacted for dental records or more information.

The investigation is still technically open, but other priorities, new violence, and a limited budget stymie attempts for justice. On a trip to Guatemala, Anabella and I had the opportunity to visit the National Security Archive together. Hundreds of workers—many of them international volunteers—were digitalizing documents. We walked through the cavernous site that had once been a munitions depot. Anabella looked at the stacks of papers and said wistfully, "I feel as if my sister is here in this place. I feel as if we can find the truth and justice can be done."

Reparations

As part of the agreement between the Guatemalan state and the Inter-American Press Association, the state agreed to pay reparations to Irma's family.

Throughout Latin America, reparations are an integral part of the process of searching for both memory and justice. Many times, the reparations are made to indigenous families whose entire source of income has been lost because of the murder or disappearance of a loved one.

In Colombia, Guatemala, Peru, and other countries in Latin America and beyond, reparations make up an important part of the reconciliation process. Peru, for example, is moving forward at a rapid rate. As Peruvian expert David Scott Palmer writes in the Fall 2014 issue of *ReVista, the Harvard Review of Latin America,*

> The Ollanta Humala administration (2011–2016) has moved forward on the exhumations of mass graves, almost completely thwarted during the previous government. These include several in Ayacucho, such as the communities of Chungui and Huancapi and the military bases in Huanta and Los Cabitos. This government has also reopened individual and collective victims' registries, and significantly increased budget allocations for the Reparations Council. According to official reports, its budget increased from US$16 million in 2011 to US$46 million in 2012 and US$57 million in 2013. An additional 475 communities have received collective reparations, averaging US$36,000 each, about twice that paid per community at the end of the [Alan] García government. Individual reparations began in late 2011; by the

end of 2013, fully 69 percent of registrants (54,840 of 79,564) had received compensation averaging US$12,700 per victim. Other types of reparations, including education, health and symbolic, have also gone forward at significant levels over the past two years.

In Irma's case, reparations of thousands of dollars were made to Irma's family members. One of the initial questions that came up was defining who were the people to receive reparations—her surviving son and her sister were obvious choices. So was her grandson, whose father was killed when Irma was kidnapped. But one might say that her cousin—who was like a little sister—and other family members might have received reparations. So might have all the journalists of Guatemala and Guatemalan readers, who had lost a journalist who was willing to struggle with the truth, who was a role model for generations of journalists to come.

Sergio, the surviving son, used the money to temporarily get his life together with rehabilitation and therapy for his alcoholism and emotional trauma. Anabella made a down payment on an apartment in Miami. Alejandro, the grandson, used the money to finance his engineering studies.

Over and over again, the family brought up the issue of "blood money." Reparations were not a payoff for keeping silent nor a way of saying that the case was closed because compensation had been paid. Anabella told me that she had considered not taking the money. She mused continually, thinking what her sister would have done in her shoes.

Irma's disappearance changed the family's life both emotionally and financially. Sergio, who had been on a kibbutz in Israel when his mother was killed, sank into depression and substance abuse. Alejandro, four years old at the time of his father's murder, was brought up by a single mom, and eventually a distant stepfather. Anabella, a single mother in Miami, could no longer count on her sister to connect her with her homeland or to provide her with countless hours of advice.

Despite a bit of initial conflict about who was to receive reparations and who was to be excluded, the entire family united around truth-seeking. In part, this attitude was helped along by the agreement itself, which not only included monetary reparations but also symbolic ones.

A scholarship was established for a Guatemalan to study journalism. Mimi de Maza, the cousin who had a sisterly relationship with Irma, has attended many of the ceremonies. A university chair in journalism with Irma's name was also established as part of the reparations. Since Irma had written extensively about women prisoners, a program was set up for women prisoner education.

In watching the process of making reparations, I again discovered the fine line between the individual and collective. The reparations helped the Flaquer family, but they did not change their lifestyle or their commitment to justice. Yet the fact that money was involved made the state's admission of guilt more tangible. And through the additional reparations, the state was acknowledging that Irma's life of service to journalism and human rights was to be perpetuated through scholarships and education.

Memory-Making

The emphasis on memory-making in the friendly agreement reached with the Guatemalan state should not have surprised me. It did. For years since then, ever since I had been reluctantly assigned the case for the IAPA's impunity project, I had begun to see how the process of the reconstruction of the memory of Irma—both as a journalist and as an individual—was at least as important as finding the details of her disappearance or even the quest for justice.

After all, to forcibly disappear a person is to obliterate them. It is to make them into less than a human being. In a culture of silence, that obliteration is doubled because of the fear of guilt by association. If one is a friend, colleague or relative of a disappeared person, one risks the same fate.

Of course, as is widely discussed in this book, many throughout Latin America did not accept this imposed obliteration. The mothers and the grandmothers became eloquent spokeswomen for their relatives; today, the children and grandchildren of the disappeared and murdered have joined with them throughout Latin America in a quest for justice and memory.

Guatemala seemed so silent—it was indeed silent—when I began to investigate the story of Irma. It was not the friendly agreement that broke the silence in the case of Irma; my reporting and the resulting book may have started the process, but the state's recognition of its own responsibility made memory into a public affair.

To me, the most meaningful of the measures was, once again, a highly personal and a collective one. The friendly agreement called for the erection of a monument to journalists who sacrifice their lives for the right to freedom of expression, symbolized in the person of Irma Flaquer. Irma was meant to represent all the Guatemalan journalists who had suffered repression during the dark days of Guatemala. Thus it was made clear that the monument was not to Irma herself, but to her memory as a part of a collective memory of courage.

A second place of memory became the public library, again as mandated by the friendly agreement. All material related to Irma's life was gathered in this wing of the library, and the room was dedicated to peace.

The street where Irma lived was named after her. I was present—with Anabella and members of the Inter American Press Association—at the unveiling of the plaque in downtown Guatemala. The street is a non-descript one in a busy section of town near the Central Park. At best, it might be called a working-class street, a transient, car-logged street. When I began my reporting, I had difficulty finding anyone who had known her or even who knew that she had lived there. Now the street had a name, a place where memory could be recovered.

I had spent hours and hours in Guatemala's public library newspaper archives, copying Irma's columns into notebooks. I felt I heard her sing-song soothing voice and her cackling laugh as I read her columns and news stories. Many of these newspapers had been untouched for years, as far as I could gather from their physical appearance. Therefore, it was personally pleasing to me when the friendly agreement mandated the compilation and publication of a book containing a selection of the best columns and articles by the disappeared journalist. My book had not yet been published in Spanish; indeed, it would take almost a decade before it appeared under the title *Desaparecida* in a joint Guatemalan-Venezuelan publishing venture. The publication of the book would make her writings widely available in Guatemala.

A documentary about her life, journalistic career, and disappearance was also produced as a result of the friendly agreement. A rather standard compilation of photos and interviews, the documentary nevertheless was another way of extending Irma's memory into the public sphere. I must confess that I have a dream that a Latin American film director someday will read my book or the book of her writings or see the original documentary and decide to put Irma onto the big screen. She deserves it.

Over and over again, I found myself saying that to myself: "she deserves it." Not that Irma deserves it any more than any other journalist or any other human being that was a victim of repression, but that she is one individual who makes us pay attention to the collectivity of the individuals who have suffered.

The process of implementation of the friendly agreement taught me a lot about the evolving situation in Guatemala and the meaning of transitional justice in memory-making and beyond. With the admission of responsibility for the disappearance of Irma Flaquer, the government was going beyond Flaquer's political position. Unlike in the United States during the

Cold War, when a person was either "good" or "bad," "friend" or "enemy" depending on political affiliations and could be punished accordingly, the Guatemalan government acknowledged that the state had a duty to protect a citizen who was a public figure. Whether the government of the time had actually executed her disappearance or not, the state had to protect her under international conventions as a well-known journalist and founder of a human rights commission. The former state had failed to do so, and the current state now had to admit that responsibility.

Guatemala accepted the responsibility as a state, not as a government. It was not the government of Alfonso Portillo, the president in 1996 when the Peace Accords were signed, who disappeared Irma Flaquer or neglected to protect her when she was disappeared. That happened during the government of General Romeo Lucas García. By accepting responsibility as a state in signing the friendly agreement, Guatemala was accepting the responsibility of history. Guilt and responsibility do not go away at the end of every four-year term.

The friendly agreement also illustrated the important role of international organizations in helping to achieve justice through memory, memory through justice. All through the Guatemalan struggle for transitional justice, international organizations ranging from the Inter-American Press Association to the Committee to Protect Journalists to the National Security Archive to the Roman Catholic Church to the United Nations have been present as companions, not dictating what Guatemalans should do but helping them develop their own blueprints.

I've spent a lot of time analyzing the contents of the friendly agreement because its stipulations seem like an effective way to explain the process of restorative justice in one particular case. But the story neither begins nor ends there.

The family began to talk about a funeral mass after a member of the human rights commission mentioned that a priest friend had recently performed the rite for a disappeared person. A Jesuit priest friend, Father Ricardo Bendaña, offered to perform a funeral mass for Irma after consulting with his superiors to see if this was ecclesiastically possible. The mass is actually known, in the absence of a body, as a "paraliturgical celebration," but the rite was an important acknowledgment of what everyone knew already. It was a chance for closure, an opportunity to mourn in community.

Anabella arrived early from Miami to Guatemala and drove around the city with other family members, hand-delivering invitations. Ana Victoria, Irma's niece and Anabella's daughter, now 21 years old, stayed behind in Miami. She was afraid.

The mass was performed in Guatemala City's spacious colonial cathedral on September 5, 2001, barely a week before the destruction of the twin towers in New York would once again change the world's geopolitical makeup, a scant week before thousands of Americans and those world over would once more learn the meaning of the word "disappeared."

The cathedral was filled with young people who had heard of Irma's story and had been inspired by it; it was attended by older people who knew Irma or knew of her. She would have been 63 years old that day.

Rolando Paiz, the brother of the two murdered youth in the fish restaurant, talked about Irma's crusade against impunity. A niece, Isabel Ruano Azurdia, sang a song that she composed in Irma's honor. Writer Enrique Wyld reminisced about her life and work. In a certain sense, it was like every other funeral mass, a site of remembrance, a collective creation of memory.

Then Viana Maza Chavarria, Irma's young cousin, spoke, saying that she was speaking in the name of all the youth of Guatemala.

I was only two years old when Irma was kidnapped. I don't remember the moment when everything happened, but I think it [the experience of having a relative disappear] is more powerful than that. It is something that I have inherited, a learned fear, a tremendous absence that won't leave one in peace. It is something that is transmitted from generation to generation.

Some lived the experience directly, but we grew up with it; it has always been part of our lives. Irma, even if she wasn't there, was always part of my life. I heard about her. I always heard her mentioned within the family, but it wasn't until a few years ago that I had the opportunity to read what she had written. One day I came home and my mother had on the dining room table a few photocopies that attracted my attention. I began to read and I couldn't stop. It was a book that Irma had written, and it gave me goose bumps. I also read some of her columns.

It was then I realized who my aunt had been: her intelligence, her capacity, her talent and, above all, her bravery. My admiration for her increased, and I felt myself identifying with her. The truth is, I don't know if these qualities are inherited, but they reached me somehow. It is very important that a woman can achieve everything like she achieved; to see her photos and see how beautiful she was; and at the same time know that her blood is in our veins.

I think we are the children of war. We are the sons and daughters of this quantity of evil that drowned our country for such a long time. It is not easy. I imagine that it was not easy to live during the war, but now we have a double task. We have a bitterness that is very difficult to manage. It is something we have learned, but at the same time, we do not feel it directly.

I have a group of friends. The group is made up of the son of a military man, the son of a guerrilla commander, the daughter of an exiled couple, the son of some hippies, the daughter of someone who didn't have the least idea that there had been a war in Guatemala— that is, a bunch of children of people who couldn't even stare each other in the face. I think this is a beautiful thing . . . I think that things are changing and if they have not changed, they are about to change and we want them to change. We are getting there, and I think it will be easier with your help.

Why? Because I have fallen in love with my country and I want the best for its people. Because we are trying to do a lot with our poor resources and I think that this country's youth is one of the principle components of the present in this country. Because I have a cousin whom I love a lot who lives abroad and whom I cannot see because Guatemala frightens her. Because I am not afraid to speak out and I believe this is the greatest gift that Irma left me.

Her words rang out in the large cathedral. The mass continued. Outside, it was raining steadily and the sound mingled with the sounds of the mass. For the first time in 21 years, there was an acknowledgment of Irma's death and also of her life and work.

Viana's words are optimistic; she sees a future for Guatemala that has not yet quite materialized. Yet things that Irma could not have possibly predicted have taken place. Trials took place involving soldiers, police, and paramilitaries prosecuted for international crimes;for example, Felipe Cusanero, an ex-paramilitary leader, was convicted and sentenced in 2009 to 150 years for the forced disappearance of 6 indigenous people between 1982 and 1984. Others are convicted for forced disappearances and crimes against humanity in connection with the massacres at Dos Erres and Plan de Sánchez. Pedro García Arredondo, a former police chief, was convicted in August 22, 2012, in connection with the disappearance of Edgar Saenz, a student. General Efraín Rios Montt was brought to trial and convicted for his role in the "scorched earth" campaign in the 1980s. Even though the verdict was overturned on a technicality, just as the Paiz Maselli case had been years earlier, dozens of Ixil men and women had a chance to make their voices heard, to testify about the abuses they and their families had suffered. The silence was broken; the memory was recognized and digni-fied, and justice (almost) served.

When I look back on the long process of the investigation of Irma's case and the subsequent friendly agreement with the Guatemala government, I feel a mix of satisfaction and frustration. Where there was silence before, there is now pride. Passersby walk down Irma Flaquer Street in downtown Guatemala; students read beneath her image in the public library; women prisoners have taken countless workshops in her name, and aspiring reporters have attended journalism school with a scholarship named after her. At a recent International Women's Day parade, a young woman with bright red hair strutted down the avenue with a poster of Irma Flaquer. There were no words. There didn't have to be any.

The family has received reparations. The Guatemalan state has issued an apology and has taken responsibility for her disappearance. The case has been reopened.

No one has been brought to trial. A thorough investigation has never been carried out. Donaldo Alvarez, who played a key role in the case, has not been captured. Irma's bones have never been found. There has been a funeral mass, but no burial. Time goes on, and both witnesses and per-petrators are getting older. Every time I read a story about a former Nazi perpetrator being arrested in some corner of the world, I think about the Guatemalan perpetrators hiding in many cases in plain sight in the United States and Latin America.

Every time a book is sold, every time I write an article, every time I give a talk, especially in Spanish, I hope that someone will come forward. There must be someone, I think, someone who gave an order, someone who took an order, someone who tortured her, someone who gave her water, someone who buried her, someone who feels guilty now as he gets older, someone who wants to speak before the memory becomes too old and painful, someone who wants to tell the truth, or the part of the truth that he or she knows.

I know that Anabella feels the same way. Every time she has received a call about possible remains, the hope is revived. Every time, thus far, the hope is dashed. But memory is still being made and justice still remains to be done.

Irma Flaquer is still missing.

4
Unearthing Haiti's Buried Memories

Michèle Montas

> *Bay kou bliye, pote mak sonje.*
> *Those who inflict pain forget, those who carry the scars remember.*
> —Haitian proverb

I lived in fear and in silence when I was 12 to 14 years old, never fully understanding why there were so many taboo subjects at the dinner table or at school, or why there were, at times, dead bodies in the streets. In the summer of 1964—I was 17—my family had to go into hiding, as an aunt and four cousins were summarily "disappeared." It was under the dictatorship of François Duvalier.

I became a broadcast journalist because I could no longer accept the deafening silence of my childhood and because I refused to hide ever again. I reported on the news in the early seventies, under the younger Duvalier, and I inadvertently became the news, with prison, three exiles, my journalist-husband's assassination during a theoretically democratic season, and an attempt on my own life in 2003. Through all of it, I came to focus increasingly on one essential building block of any sustainable democracy, its judicial system. Haiti's judiciary has been anchored for the last two centuries on a class system excluding the majority of Haitians, and on a traditional culture of impunity and of memories denied. The institution of justice was further perverted and "vassalized" during the 29-year dictatorship of the Duvaliers from 1957 to 1986.

Almost three decades later, the links between memory, justice, impunity, popular participation and a sustainable democracy, discussed from our individual perspectives in this collection of essays, have been brought to the forefront in Haiti by two ongoing judicial cases.

As a journalist and as a survivor, I am a plaintiff in bothcases currently before the same appellate court in Port-au-Prince, testing an anemic judicial system and the prevailing culture of impunity. One case is that of my late husband, Jean Dominique, a Haitian broadcast journalist assassinated in April 2000. He had known jail and exile and had his radio station destroyed, under the two Duvalier regimes. However, he was not killed under the dictatorial regimes he had fought against, but during a democratic season in Haiti's recent history. The second case is that of Jean-Claude Duvalier himself, named President-for-Life in 1971 by his father, François Duvalier, overthrown in 1986 by a popular uprising, and who returned in 2011 after 25 years in exile. I have joined 28 other victims of his regime, demanding that the former dictator be tried for massive violations of human rights and crimes against humanity.

Not unlike the *arpilleras* described by Marjorie Agosín, both cases reflect the ongoing struggle to weave the painful memories of the past into the present and into the difficult construction of the rule of law in Haiti more than 25 years after the fall of the Duvalier dictatorship. These two judicial cases are stitched into the fabric of a recent past marked by violence, repression, injustice, and resistance.

Reporting under Fire

Returning from graduate studies at the Columbia School of Journalism, I started working at Radio Haiti, a privately owned independent radio station that had opened in 1972. It was under the regime of 19-year old President-for-Life Jean-Claude Duvalier, who had "inherited" our country from his father. Since 1957, the media had become the echo chamber of the regime, publishing full speeches, never analyzing, questioning, or even simply reporting. Radio was mostly entertainment. Jean Dominique, the agronomist turned journalist who owned Radio Haiti and later became my husband, had introduced news in Creole, the language of the majority of Haitians, at a time when the information that the radio was able to provide about international events came from wire services and official speeches from the regime, all in French, the language of the traditional elite.

As the regime of Jean-Claude Duvalier tried to project a better image to international aid providers, particularly the United States, official censorship (editing newspapers before they were published, cutting out articles in foreign publications with any mention of Haiti) was no longer enforced, but the repressive apparatus was fully in place—and we knew it. The government repeatedly closed independent publications and radio stations. Journalists were beaten, jailed, and forced to leave the country. The self-imposed censorship under the young Duvalier insured that these occurrences were seldom if ever reported. The existence of hundreds of political prisoners, many arrested under François Duvalier, could only be noted when a few, under international pressure, were released. The situation in the "Triangle of Death," the three notorious prisons in Port-au-Prince, and the corruption that siphoned millions of state revenues into private family accounts were never reported. The murder in 1976 of investigative journalist Gasner Raymond of the weekly *Petit Samedi Soir* by "unknown assailants," and the physical assault and arrest in December 1977 of Bob Nerée, editor of the opposition weekly *Jeune Presse*, made it clear that, under the thin varnish of "liberalization," the repressive system set under François Duvalier was alive and well.

In the meantime, beginning in the early seventies, a silent revolution was underway. Cheap portable transistor radios, distributed at first by churches across the country for evangelical purposes, gave access to information through AM frequencies to a majority of Haitians, the uneducated peasants as well as the slum dwellers in the cities. They had lived isolated for two centuries by language (French was that of the elite who controlled governments or the administration of justice) and by geography (the peasant majority lived for the most part in remote mountain villages, without electricity or phones). When we started broadcasting news in Creole, the language of all Haitians, in the early seventies and when, for the first time, radio started echoing voices that had never been heard before—of coffee growers, of Madan Sarah, the peasant women carrying produce to the cities, or of fishermen along the coast of the island—a profound transformation took place in a society where exclusion had always been the norm and where the brutal repression of the dictatorship had further atomized the population.

In the early seventies, when François Duvalier, on his deathbed, named his son as his successor and President-for-Life, we, at Radio Haiti, started to rebuild memory on cultural matters, interviewing historians, sociologists, writers, artists, covering voodoo ceremonies (a taboo subject at the time for the elites), or enacting radio plays about historical figures of resistance. We then increasingly touched on social and economic issues. We interviewed coffee growers on the prices they were paid by speculators for their beans. We investigated the flow of boat people out of Haiti or reported on the contracts governing the hiring of Haitian sugar cane workers for the *zafra* (harvest) in the Dominican Republic.

At first, we only covered politics by proxy, reporting not on Haiti but, for instance, on the fall of Somoza in Nicaragua in 1979 or on elections in the United States, the neighboring Dominican Republic, or Jamaica. We slowly forced open the window of truth-telling left barely ajar by the demands of the Carter administration that aid be tied to the respect for human rights. And we started reporting on peasant uprisings in the Artibonite Valley and the rebirth of associations and labor unions that had been banned under François Duvalier.

Building memory after so many years of silence was difficult and limited in scope. The lives and disappearances of family members or times of jail or torture under both Duvaliers remained shrouded under a thick black veil. We could not mention political prisoners except in passing when a few were released under international pressure.

In August 1977, the American Ambassador to the United Nations, Andrew Young, brought President Carter's human rights demands to Jean-Claude Duvalier with a list of 104 political prisoners to be released. We could cover Young's press conference. We could not interview the released prisoners on the conditions of life in Fort Dimanche, the notorious political prison of the Duvalier regime. We could not mention those who were on that list and were never released, and the "disappeared" remained a taboo subject until the fall of the regime in 1986.

It was a very dangerous game, of cat and mouse, of evaluating, on any given day, how far we could go as journalists. And we knew we were walking a very tight rope. The rope was brutally severed on November 28, 1980, after the U.S. presidential election when the Carter administration was voted out of office. That day in Port-au-Prince and across the country, all newly created political parties, labor unions, student associations, and independent media were crushed in one single blow, with hundreds of people arrested. We were singled out, and our studios at Radio Haiti were physically destroyed by the political police. All our journalists, including myself, were handcuffed and taken to the notorious Caserne Dessalines barracks for questioning. Some were tortured, jailed, and later sent into exile. Two days later, Colonel Jean Valmé, chief of the S.D., the political police, announced the dismantling of a "vast communist plot." Valmé had been looking for Jean Dominique who was not at the station at the time. I learned later that there was an order to kill my husband on sight. Jean and I were to reunite again a few months later in New York, where he had joined me from his own exile in Venezuela.

Silencing and Recovering Memory

Over the following six years, with Radio Haiti destroyed, with a number of small publications closed, and with Haitian journalists in exile in the United States, Venezuela, or Canada, local media retreated into the guarded silence of the early seventies. Foreign news had once more replaced national coverage on radio broadcasts, with brief news bulletins on cultural and social events. But all investigative journalism, about boat people leaving the country in droves or land conflicts in the Artibonite Valley, had become a thing of the past. Except for rare articles, the fate of the hundreds arrested and exiled on November 28, 1980, was shrouded in silence.

Three years later, emboldened by a papal visit to Port-au-Prince in 1983, and by John Paul II's statement that "things must change in Haiti," the Catholic Radio station, Radio Soleil, started airing programs denouncing the lack of justice or health care, not in a traditional news format but often in the shape of radio skits. In 1985, when the station started to denounce the terms of a constitutional referendum that would restore multi-party politics on condition that all parties swore allegiance to President-for-Life Jean-Claude Duvalier, its people were forbidden to broadcast news. Radio Soleil's transmitters were sabotaged and on January 31, 1986, it was forcibly closed.

Very little news was aired or printed in the larger media during that six-year period, but memory of repression, of resistance, of democratic gains and dreams, remained alive in many alternative ways. The recorded sermons of a few Catholic priests, proponents of liberation theology, were clandestinely circulating in 1984–1985, as were songs of resistance from the Haitian diasporas, honoring the fallen heroes of the dictatorship. At the time, another alternative "media," the traditional "telediol," the vital word-of-mouth grapevine that predated media in that very oral society, also played a key role in transmitting information and keeping memory alive within communities, and from neighborhood to neighborhood.

The fact that memory had been kept alive was evident on November 28, 1985, the anniversary of the crackdown of 1980. That day, demonstrators in the town of Gonaives were remembering the victims of the repression five years earlier, while protesting high unemployment and poor living conditions. The army opened fire on the crowd, killing three schoolboys. The event triggered the fall of Duvalier, as protests spread like wildfire. Jean-Claude Duvalier was forced to leave the country on February 7, 1986.

Upon our return to Port-au-Prince a month later, we journalists had unwittingly become the news. There were close to 60,000 people at the airport welcoming Jean Dominique and Radio Haiti back. More than five years after its destruction, the station was rebuilt with contributions from hundreds of people. Joining intellectuals, technicians, and local industrialists were hundreds of small shopowners, market vendors, and peasants, who contributed 50 centimes or 10 gourdes (a dime or two U.S. dollars at the time) so they could get "their" voice back.

During our 63 months in exile, then, we had not been forgotten. It meant that we had earned trust, and it came with added responsibilities.

Journalists were to be the truth-tellers but were also expected to be the protective shields against any return to the repressive methods of the past. And for the first time in 200 years, peasants, artisans, workers demanded to be the ones writing history. They wanted to be heard.

From 1986 to 1990, rebuilding memory after 29 years of dictatorship became about justice, about unveiling buried truths, about analyzing the obstacles in reviving institutions that had been systematically dismantled. It was about building a democratic society. The role expected of the media, particularly the radio in a country where a 52 percent illiteracy rate curtails access to print, was clearly articulated in a survey Radio Haiti did in 1986 in Cité Soleil, the largest slum in Port-au-Prince. The majority at the time ranked justice and freedom of speech as their highest priority above food and shelter, and they expected the media to press on justice issues, justice for past repression and violence, and a larger social justice agenda.

The Conseil National de Gouvernement (the National Council of Government), a joint military and civilian provisional government with General Henri Namphy at its head, was then ruling the country. It was an exhilarating but dangerous season, one of direct threats and indirect repression, one of resistance and defiance, one of military coup after military coup. Political and civic leaders were killed. Radio stations were sabotaged. The façade of our station was riddled with bullet holes, our journalists constantly harassed. During that tumultuous transition period, we were reporting on ongoing events: the short-lived, informal people's tribunals in Côte de Fer in 1986 set up to try local "macoutes," the armed militia of the previous regime; street demonstrations against the army to insure the successful vote of a new constitution; killings of human rights defenders or political leaders; a voting day drowned in blood in 1987, by Duvalierists with the complicity of the government; peasant massacres in Jean Rabel or Piatre.

While we continued to give a voice to victims of the past, it became obvious that covering ongoing news was in itself building memory, since what we had inherited, with the army in power, was a veiled form of Duvalierism without Duvalier. The 1987 Constitution kept the former officials of the dictatorship from holding power for the following 10 years, but the "macoutes" and the army officers close to the fallen regime remained active in blocking any elections.

On the day of the first scheduled elections, on November 29, 1987, voters at the Ruelle Vaillant polling place, or those standing in line to vote, were mowed down by armed commandos. The offices and homes of members of the electoral commission and several radio stations were firebombed or attacked with grenades. Military leaders, who had either orchestrated or condoned the murders, canceled the election and retained control of the government.

At the time, we bore witness to the resistance from all sectors of Haitian society to any return of a dictatorial regime and reported on the hundreds of new grass-root organizations burgeoning throughout the country. We investigated the failings and inadequacies of a judicial system, weakened by the dictatorship. This was particularly vital at the local level, where for 30 years villages knew only the rule of the Section Chief, deputized by the army, who had the combined role of arresting officer, jailer, judge, jury, and executioner, exercising complete control over rural areas.

In 1990 a popular parish priest, Jean Bertrand Aristide, became the first democratically elected President of Haiti with 67 percent of the popular vote. He was chosen as the flag bearer by a strong democratic movement, which had paid a heavy price for the respect of basic freedoms of speech and association.

In 1991 a bloody military coup overthrew President Aristide, after less than eight months in office, and he was forced into exile. The media was once more targeted. In the first few months after the coup, two broadcasters were killed, one after being arrested and tortured, another one abducted and "disappeared." Unidentified armed men came one night and started firing on our home. Radio Haiti as well as other radio stations had to close and, once more, we had to go into exile.

The media fell into silence or tight self-censorship, with one exception, an alternative network of local community radios which would broadcast recorded news, on and off, on a small scale. Part of that guerilla journalism was waged across the border, in the Dominican Republic, where Radio Enriquillo, a Catholic radio station, was broadcasting news programs in Creole about the situation after the military coup. When the Catholic hierarchy in the DR ordered the broadcasts stopped, the news was imaginatively sung in Creole and became one of the few reliable sources of information for Haitians within the country, one that could not be readily silenced.

From the beginning, the coup against Aristide had been rejected by the Organization of American States as well as the United Nations Security Council, and heavy sanctions forced the military to finally relinquish power three years later, after a brokered agreement. On October 15, 1994, with the help of the U.S. military, the constitutional government of Jean Bertrand Aristide returned to power.

We came back to Haiti that same year, 1994, to repair our damaged equipment, gather, once more, our team of journalists, and train new ones. From 1994 to 2003, we were gathering data of the abuses of the military coup, filling the gap on the three years of brutal military rule (September 1991–October 1994), focusing once more on justice issues and the work of the Truth and Justice Commission (Commission Nationale de Verité et de Justice) tasked, in 1994, with investigating human rights abuses during the military regime. Its scope did not cover the "sins of the past," the violations of human rights under the dictatorship of the Duvaliers, which were never officially investigated. The Commission presented its final report to President Aristide and the judiciary on February 5, 1996. It contained crucial facts and names of alleged perpetrators, but was not widely picked up by the majority of the media.

The report covered in particular the Raboteau massacre. On April 22, 1994, at dawn, soldiers and paramilitary forces raided the seaside slum of Raboteau, in Gonaives, where residents had rallied in support of the deposed president. They indiscriminately fired on unarmed dwellers, going house to house, beating and arresting people of all ages. Many who had retreated to the harbor were killed or wounded on the beach or in the fishing boats. Many more were arrested and tortured. Families could not collect the bodies of the dead, so no exact count exists of the number of dead and disappeared.

At Radio Haiti, we amplified the report of the Truth and Justice Commission, particularly on the massacre, an emblematic case. In Raboteau, with the enthusiastic support of the local communities, we uncovered additional truths. We spoke to survivors, lawyers, and witnesses, and reported on the preparations and holding of the unique trial that followed in 2000.

Jean Dominique, who had covered so many of the atrocities of the massacre, was not there for the trial itself. He had been assassinated six months before.

The Jean Dominique Case

On April 3, 2000, Jean Dominique was gunned down in the courtyard of our radio station, Radio Haiti Inter. This outspoken journalist had survived past dictatorships. He had exposed human rights abuses, political corruption, and state-sponsored violence under military regimes as well as elected governments. Jean's assassination in a democratic season stunned Haiti and had massive ramifications. So did our daily struggle to find justice, not only for Jean, but also for the many victims of the dictatorship and for the political killings that had gone unpunished since 1986.

Unlike other high profile political killings, Jean Dominique's case did not fade away. Week after week, month after month, hundreds of people demonstrated in the streets, demanding justice for the man they called their "voice," the advocate of the "peyi an deyo," the "outside country," as the majority of peasants, excluded from citizenship for 200 years, are often called. To many, the assassination of Jean Dominique under a democratically elected government (that of Aristide's successor, René Préval) meant that democracy itself was at stake.

For three years, while we continued our work as journalists, we scrutinized every public aspect of an investigation beset by violence and threats. It is a case where suspects have died in custody, where witnesses and corpses have vanished, where the Senate refused to lift the parliamentary immunity of a suspect, where a judge, frightened for his life, had to seek political asylum abroad, where the police have been unable or unwilling to carry out arrest warrants against former army officers.

We would systematically expose not only the roadblocks on the path to justice, but also the lack of independence and the structural inadequacies of a judicial system left largely moribund by 29 years of dictatorship. During this period, in which I anchored alone the daily news broadcast that Jean and I had anchored for many years together, I counted on the air the days since we had started demanding justice on Jean's assassination, 3,232 days. On Christmas Day 2002, two hired gunmen came for me, at my home. One of my bodyguards was killed. As constant threats were directed at our reporters, the newsroom took a collective decision. Radio Haiti had to be closed to prevent further loss of lives. We turned off our transmitters and I left Haiti that same day, on February 22, 2003, to go into my third exile. It was again during a democratic season, under the second mandate of Aristide, who had succeeded Préval in February 2001.

Every year after Jean Dominique was killed, journalists' associations and the media have kept on covering the slow-moving judicial case and mark the anniversary of the assassination with special programs, airing his editorials. In 2004, American movie director Jonathan Demme produced an award-winning documentary, *The Agronomist*, about Jean's life as a journalist and the recent troubled history of Haiti, from the Duvalier years to 2003. The Creole version of the documentary continues to be aired over and over again on Haitian television, keeping memory alive.

A month after Radio Haiti was forced into silence, in 2003, the investigative judge assigned to the case formally indicted six people as the alleged perpetrators and accomplices of Jean Dominique's assassination. On April 3, 2003, from my New York exile, I filed an appeal, demanding that, along with the gunmen, the sponsors of the crime, those who had engineered it and paid the hired killers, also be brought to justice. I continued to work from abroad, through the courts and through Haitian media that relayed the popular demand for justice from large segments of Haitian society and from journalists.

From 2003 to 2010, the Jean Dominique case remained under media scrutiny. The three alleged perpetrators and accomplices broke out of jail in 2004, as Aristide was forced to leave power. Most of the documents pertaining to the case disappeared mysteriously from the investigation file. A succession of judges was assigned to the case. In 2006, as Préval began his second term, he created a commission of journalists to assist the judiciary in pursuing crimes against reporters and media personnel. That commission also contributed to keep memory alive.

For six years, the case went from the appellate court to the Supreme Court and was finally reopened in 2009, when an appellate court judge was assigned to find "the intellectual authors" of the crime. I was able to testify again in person in 2011. I was then working in Haiti, under continuous U.N. protection, no longer a journalist but a Senior Adviser to the Special Representative of the Secretary General who headed the United Nations Mission in Haiti. I had been asked to serve as liaison between the Haitian institutions, gravely impacted by the January 2010 earthquake that had destroyed all public buildings in Port-au-Prince, and the United Nations Mission whose upper echelon had been decimated by the catastrophe. More than 250,000 people had been killed, a million and a half were without shelter, and our last places of memory had been incidentally erased.

At that time the "sins of the past," the crimes committed during the dictatorship, were still shrouded in silence. There were no memorials anywhere reminding the young of the families massacred in Jeremie in 1964 simply because a son or a nephew had joined the fight against Duvalier, or of the hundreds who were executed or died in Fort Dimanche, the political prison of the dictatorship. There were no memorials anywhere for those who were killed under successive military coups. Other anchors of memory had also been leveled by the earthquake. The torture chambers, once used personally by the elder Duvalier in the basement of the white gleaming National Palace, and the Caserne Dessalines, the former army barracks where many were detained and tortured in the '80s, were reduced to rubble by the earthquake. All the Catholic churches in Port-au-Prince collapsed. In one, people attending a mass celebrated by then-Father Aristide had been massacred during military rule. In another, a well-known human rights defender had been abducted and executed during a ceremony in remembrance of other victims of the military, during the '91–'94 coup. *It was as if the earthquake had leveled memory itself.*

What remained of the Jean Dominique file had to be retrieved from the rubble of the Palais de Justice, the headquarters for the courts. Two former Haitian presidents, René Préval and Jean-Bertrand Aristide, several senators, and former military officers had to testify *in 2013* before the investigative judge assigned to the case by the appellate court. The judge recommended on January 17, 2014, that nine people be charged, including a former senator of Aristide's Fanmi Lavalas party and four close associates. The former senator, who is also a former executive officer at the Aristide Foundation, is accused of having ordered the killing. Three others are also accused of planning the crime and five, previously indicted, of executing it or covering it up.

Fourteen years after the crime, for the truth to be known the appellate court has yet to formally bring charges, which would result in formal arrests and a trial. But getting to that preliminary report would have been impossible without the supportive role played by the media in constructing memory and the even larger popular mobilization in street demonstrations, talk shows, or social media around this specific crime, as was the case around the 1994 massacre in Raboteau.

The Jean-Claude Duvalier Case

A few months earlier, on February 28, 2013, another head of state was also forced to testify, this time as the accused, a unique occurrence in Haiti's history. The case against former dictator, Jean-Claude Duvalier, is presently before the same appellate court, at the same preliminary stage of investigation as the 14-year-old case against Jean Dominique's assassins.

In a move that stunned the country, the former dictator returned unexpectedly from exile on January 16, 2011, 25 years after he was forced to leave power. I am also a plaintiff in the case against the former "President-for-Life," specifically for the massive crackdown of November 28,1980, the day so many of our journalists at Radio Haiti were arrested, some tortured, unlawfully jailed for several months, and forcibly exiled. Today we are only 29 plaintiffs, intellectuals, agronomists, teachers, and peasants, against a regime that has made thousands of victims.

The experience was sobering, as somehow there seemed to be a complete breakdown in memory about what the dictatorship had represented and the price paid in the last 25 years to regain basic rights of free speech and free association. I remember systematically calling former political prisoners or members of families whose sons or daughters disappeared under the 15-year rule of Jean-Claude Duvalier, to convince them to go to court with us and bear witness. Many refused.

I suddenly sensed that, in spite of the existence of a democratic government, fear—insidious, senseless—had returned. So did the pain of wounds that never healed. This was further reinforced as Duvalier was allowed to freely move around as he still does. What was most disheartening was the apparent amnesia of the larger society, which has seen so much violence, so many killings left unpunished, that met the return of Duvalier with indifference, until he was forced last year to testify before an appellate court.

Twenty-five years after the end of the dictatorship, most Haitians are too young to remember. As Merilee Grindle underlines in the introduction to these *Reflections*, "memory and its interpretation take on added significance as those who experienced injustice and violence die and new generations emerge who do not have first-hand knowledge of the impact of authoritarianism." From 1986 to 1988, the media, particularly our radio station, had extensively covered the violent demonstrations in the streets against the "*macoutes*." At the time, we had given voice to the testimony of dozens of survivors. All seemed to have been washed away by the tumultuous transition to democratic rule, by the many military coups, and by a series of political murders left unpunished, or disappearances left unsolved.

Today the courts have to decide on whether Duvalier should be tried for massive violations of human rights, murders, torture, and forced exile, or simply for financial crimes, as a lower-court judge had ruled earlier. Twenty-two of the 29 plaintiffs against Duvalier, from all walks of life, as well as four Haitian human rights organizations, are now regrouped under an association, the Collective Against Impunity, demanding that Jean-Claude Duvalier be held accountable for the massive violations of human rights under his 15-year regime and for crimes against humanity.

In April 1971 he had "inherited" our country from his father, along with a ruthless repressive machine. Considering the difficulty faced by the country in 2011, one year after the earthquake, and considering the prevailing climate of impunity in Haiti, Duvalier could have imagined that he would never be prosecuted. And that, without prosecution, he could quietly reclaim his assets frozen in Swiss banks and be reinserted in Haiti's political future.

Instead he was summoned by the public prosecutor on January 17, 2011, then formally accused the next day by the state and by a handful of victims of his regime of massive human rights violations and embezzlement, as the Haitian government reopened a previous lawsuit brought against Duvalier and associates in France, the United States, Switzerland, and Haiti among other countries, for stealing public funds, as well as for human rights violations.

Beyond getting justice, our individual pleas meant, symbolically, speaking out on behalf of those who could not, or would not speak out. We felt strongly that our personal grievances suffered under Jean-Claude Duvalier—executions, disappearances of a parent or a husband, illegal arrests and detention, torture or exile—represented, beyond the judicial case, those thousands of victims of both Duvaliers, from all social classes and walks of life, who had been denied the right to justice.

Pursuing the case against the former dictator, before the same courts that had been so corrupted, intimidated, and weakened by years of dictatorships, was also an attempt to jump-start a judicial system that has been, so far, unable to respond to the demands for justice, and to force that system to function. As in the emblematic case of Jean Dominique, we hope, in the long run, to make a substantial dent in the culture of impunity that has prevailed in Haiti, particularly since 1957.

We also felt an added responsibility since our generation, as Sergio Bitar notes in these *Reflections*, was a privileged one, having "fought for dreams, suffered through the dictatorship and actively participated in the creation of a new democratic society," no matter how imperfect. We wanted that uphill battle to also be inscribed in a larger historical legacy, that of the struggle of the Haitian people for human rights. Haiti was the first nation that ended slavery in this hemisphere, and one that supported liberation movements throughout the Americas in the nineteenth century. Let's remember that one condition for the support given by Haiti's President Alexandre Petion to Simon Bolivar, who, in 1816 received shelter and weapons from our new Haitian Republic, was that freedom be given to all slaves in the territories liberated from the Spanish crown. Haiti was also one of the 19 signatories of the Nuremberg Charter and a founding member of the United Nations.

From February to May 2011, the plaintiffs and Jean-Claude Duvalier testified before the first instructing judge, Carves Jean in the judge's chambers. Only one of Duvalier's former ministers was heard, with no follow-up investigations being carried out as required by law. A new prosecutor in the case ruled that the Haitian Penal Code carries a statute of limitations that prevents any prosecution for the murders, disappearances, torture, and other grave violations of human rights committed by the Duvalier government from 1971 to 1986. In January 2012, the instructing judge himself ruled that Haitian law did not permit claims of crimes against humanity and he dismissed those charges, while upholding the accusations of embezzlement, to be treated by a criminal court as a simple misdemeanor punishable by a maximum jail term of three years.

But an appeal was filed, and public hearings were scheduled before the Appellate Court, from December 13, 2012 to May 16, 2013. For the first time in Haiti's recent history, on February 28, 2013, the former dictator was forced to appear publicly at court and answer the questions from a panel of judges. He was formally charged with corruption, theft, and misappropriation of funds. That was a turning point. Even though the courts have yet to issue a decision on whether Duvalier should be tried for massive violations of human rights, his appearance in court galvanized those who had chosen not to speak out until then.

Roadblocks to Justice

Can a former dictator be tried in Haiti? The question is important in exploring the links between memory, impunity, and the democratic mechanisms that can prevent the return of another repressive regime.

The obstacles to a fair trial in the Duvalier case are embedded in the judicial system itself. Its antiquated penal code, dating back to 1825, does not incorporate new offenses such as terrorism (in this case state terrorism), crimes against humanity, money laundering, or most of the financial and economic crimes that would be relevant in this case. The system functions in complete disregard for the international conventions Haiti has ratified and that should preside over the national legal framework. Haiti has ratified the Universal Declaration of Human Rights and the International Covenant on Civil and Political Rights. In the American system, Haiti is a party to the American Convention on Human Rights or Pact of San Jose (1979). Haiti has also accepted the jurisdiction of the Inter-American Court of Human Rights (1998). Although the Haitian Constitution stipulates (section 276.2) that "international treaties or agreements once approved and ratified in the manner prescribed by the Constitution, are part of the country's legislation and repeal all laws that are opposite," this principle, and international standards, are not applied in the courts. Such rules are not even part of the curriculum of law schools in the country.

The judicial system is still largely dysfunctional, even though some individual judges have shown courage and honesty in handling sensitive cases. The system's independence from the executive is tenuous at best. Bureaucratic procedures have long been a substitute for justice. Few criminal investigations ever reach any conclusions, with a negative impact on the plaintiffs as well as on the rights of the accused. The catch phrase "l'enquête se poursuit" (the investigation continues) is used derisively to mock judges and prosecutors alike, as investigations by judges as provided for in the Napoleonic Code never seem to end. Judicial reforms, started 28 years ago, have still not reached their goal. The structures that were to be put in place to reinforce the system have yet to become functional. Scarce resources and the lack of training for court personnel are still plaguing the system, in spite of the creation of l'Ecole de la Magistrature, the Magistrate School.

The challenge today in taking Jean-Claude Duvalier to court is to reform, in the process, the judicial system itself to get it finally to respect and defend the basic rights of Haitians. Merilee Grindle asks the question, "Does the past, shaped by collective memories . . . contribute significantly to collective commitment to new institutions for making decisions, resolving conflicts and creating consensus about broad lines of public policy?" We are talking here about using the "sins of the past" in building consensus for the need to reform an old discredited institution and changing that institution into a viable pillar of a democratic future. It's about "the transformation of memory into effective institutions."

To the difficulties in modernizing and reforming the judicial structures, we should add the political context of Duvalierism without Duvalier. As noted earlier, this phenomenon has continued, on and off, for many years since February 1986 and the formal departure of the dictator himself. The system remained in place through the military regimes that followed. The atmosphere surrounding the court procedures against the former President-for-Life has been a difficult one for the victims. The Collective Against Impunity has consistently denounced the noxious atmosphere of the appellate court hearings inside and outside the courtroom; the lack of the most elementary respect towards the victims, treated as if they were the accused; and the ambivalent attitude of the prosecutor, supposedly the "defender of society," but who systematically sided with Duvalier's lawyers.

By May 2013, when the hearings were closed, most of the 29 plaintiffs had not been asked by the appellate court to testify. Nor were the military commanders of the regime accused by the plaintiffs of murder and torture ever called, whether by the First Instructing Judge or by the court. The state has taken no measures to use the technical assistance offered by the Inter-American Commission on the well-documented violations of human rights under Jean-Claude Duvalier's regime. There was no request for information nor any search for evidence addressed to other countries or international instances.

Outside the courtroom, a revisionist discourse and attempts at rewriting history have targeted the young Haitians who have little if any knowledge of the dictatorship. As we noted earlier, many young people under 35 are unaware today of what it means to live in fear and be deprived of basic liberties, even though they experienced periods of military rule. So many have never learned from parents, from schools, or from places of memory the sacrifices made for press freedom and the right of association they now enjoy. The aggressive campaign led by the former officials of the dictatorship has at times used threats and intimidations, as when a group of Duvalier's partisans tried to disrupt a press conference by Amnesty International on September 22, 2011, focusing on crimes committed by the dictatorship.

Today, the government, the international community, and the political parties, many of which were decimated under the two Duvalier regimes, seem to consider elections as the only yardstick to assess the state of Haitian democracy, and there is a tendency to see the quest for justice as a thing of the past, irrelevant to the future of Haiti. The head of state, President Joseph Michel Martelly, declared that he was ready to amnesty Duvalier, at a time when the former dictator had not even been charged. He visited the former dictator and other former leaders and officially invited him in 2012 to the commemoration of the two-year anniversary of the January 2010 earthquake. The government, in the name of "reconciliation," has also seen fit to invite Duvalier to the official Independence Day celebration, on January 1, 2014, ignoring his status as a defendant. When this invitation created an uproar from several human rights organization in Haiti and abroad that denounced the government's apparent support of impunity and its trivialization of the dictatorship, the head of state paid lip service to the victims, declaring in a speech on January 13 to the National Assembly, that forgiveness and reconciliation do not mean "forgetting and rehabilitating."

In spite of the charges of embezzlement brought by previous governments against Duvalier, with hundreds of documents establishing the siphoning of more than $600 million into private accounts, the former dictator has been given a presidential pension. His properties, seized in 1986, have been returned to him. He has a diplomatic passport and police protection. Well-known Duvalierists are members of the present government, with the minister of the interior being the head of the Duvalierist party, the PUN. The sight of the former President-for-Life circulating freely in the chic restaurants or jazz concerts, while technically under house arrest, sent a clear message of ongoing impunity, at least until he was forced to appear in court as a defendant and to answer the questions of a three-judge panel.

In the aftermath of Duvalier's return in 2011, the traditional Haitian media were echoing the arguments used by his lawyers that the Haitian Penal Code's statute of limitations prevents any prosecution for the murders, disappearances, torture, and other grave violations of human rights committed by the dictatorship. Little space was given to the opposite argument, the existence of conventions signed by Haiti and of numerous international rulings establishing that there can be no statute of limitations for crimes against humanity or disappearances defined as ongoing crimes.

Abroad, there were some positive signs towards rebuilding lost memory and supporting the victims' efforts. The call for the trial of Jean-Claude Duvalier came early on from international institutions, civil society associations, and human rights organizations worldwide. In February 2011, a month after Duvalier's return, the UN High Commissioner reminded the Haitian government of its obligation "to investigate the well-documented serious human rights violations that occurred during the rule of Mr. Duvalier, and to prosecute those responsible for them." "Such systematic violations of rights cannot remain unaddressed. The thousands of Haitians who suffered under this regime deserve justice," said High Commissioner Navi Pillay. She called on the Haitian authorities to send a message to the world "that their national courts can ensure accountability for serious violations of human rights, even in difficult humanitarian and political contexts."

A month later, UN Secretary General Ban Ki-moon declared, "It is of capital importance that the Haitian authorities take all legal and judiciary measures in the case of Jean-Claude Duvalier. Trying those who commit crimes against their own people is a clear message to the Haitians that impunity will no longer rule in their land." Following a deposition by the Collective Against Impunity, on March 28, 2011, in Washington, the Inter-American Human Rights Commission ruled that

> The government of Jean-Claude Duvalier was characterized by systematic violations of human rights such as extrajudicial executions, forced disappearances and torture. Under international law, such acts constitute crimes against humanity . . . Haiti now has a unique opportunity. The investigation and punishment of these crimes could become a fundamental step in strengthening the rule of law and restoring confidence in the Haitian justice system.

At the March 28 hearings in Washington, the former ministry of justice of the Préval government represented Haiti and pledged to prosecute the violations of human rights under the Duvalier dictatorship.

In addition, organizations such as Amnesty International and Human Rights Watch have documented these violations with evidence of arbitrary detentions, torture, deaths in custody, killings, and disappearances. Their reports from the time of the dictatorship were reissued, as were their remarks on the present case against Duvalier. This has been an invaluable asset in the uphill battle to revive memory and boost public support for a trial.

Invaluable also has been a recent ruling by the Swiss courts. In December 2013 they definitively ruled for the restitution to Haiti of the funds misappropriated by Duvalier and frozen in Swiss banks since 1986. The tribunal agreed on seizing the funds that would be used to improve the living conditions of the Haitian people and to reinforce the rule of law and the struggle against impunity. The government has had no official reaction and has not formally notified the Haitian courts of the results of the long and painstaking legal work done in Switzerland that established the illicit origin of Duvalier's funds, even though previous Haitian governments initiated the court actions.

Lawyers Without Borders in Canada, the International Center for Transitional Justice, The Institute for Justice and Democracy in Haiti, and Human Rights Watch have supported the Inter-American Commission and have urged the government of President Michel Martelly to assign enough human resources to the investigations and the prosecution. They have called upon the international community to support the fight against impunity and the search for justice in Haiti. The Collective Against Impunity has also received legal support from the Open Society Justice Initiative with an advisory *amicus curiae* filed with the courts in December 2011. It has received steady technical support from Lawyers Without Borders, who have worked with the plaintiffs throughout the process, and legal advice from Human Rights Watch, from the Haiti office of the High Commissioner for Human Rights, and other international organizations.

However, international support from foreign governments, quite strong after the unexpected return of Jean-Claude Duvalier, has since trickled down to periodic declarations of principles, as other priorities like elections, governance, or economic recovery seem to take precedence over justice and the rule of law. The international community has done little to pressure the Haitian government into meeting its human rights obligations. A 2013 letter addressed to that effect by the Collective Against Impunity to Latin American troop contributors to MINUSTAH, the United Nations Stabilization Mission in Haiti, received no answers. It was only after public appeals in February of that year that diplomatic missions in Haiti, the Organization of American States, the United States, Canada, France, and Switzerland assigned observers to the proceedings at the Appellate Court.

While the courts in the Duvalier case are still withholding a decision on whether Jean-Claude Duvalier should be tried for crimes against humanity and massive human rights violations, the Raboteau trial held in 2000 in the town of Gonaives could give some hope to the plaintiffs in the Duvalier case that justice and the truth, nourished by memory, can be achieved in Haiti. In October and November 2000, 50 people were put on trial for their role in the massacre. Thirty-seven, including the military coup leaders General Raoul Cedras, Colonel Michel François, the former chief of national police, and paramilitary leaders Emmanuel Constant and Louis Jodel Chamblain, were tried in absentia. Sixteen of the 22 defendants in custody were found guilty of having participated in the massacre. The trial lasted six weeks. Five years later, on May 3rd, 2005 the Haitian Supreme Court overturned the sentences on a technicality. By then, the 15 imprisoned defendants had escaped during a mass jailbreak.

Regardless of the end result, what the Raboteau trial meant and the way it was conducted are the important factors. Praised by Amnesty International as "one of the most significant human rights achievements in America" in a 2004 report, and considered by Human Rights Watch as a "scrupulously fair trial," it was a landmark unprecedented in recent Haitian history. For MICAH, the United Nations International Civilian Support Mission in Haiti, the Raboteau massacre trial "proves that the Haitian Justice system is capable of effectively prosecuting" human rights cases, "while respecting the guarantees of the 1987 Constitution and International Treaties to which Haiti is a party." Thus, for the first time, those who had used violent repression against their own people would be punished, and this meant that the highest-ranking officers from the disbanded Forces Armées d'Haiti (FADH), the Haitian armed forces, as well as the top leaders of the brutal paramilitary Front Révolutionnaire Armé pour le Progrès d'Haiti (FRAPH), the Revolutionary Armed Front for the Progress of Haiti, had at last to account for their crimes.

According to Brian Concannon, an American lawyer and president of the Institute for Justice and Democracy, a non-profit organization based in Boston, who has worked on the case and written about it, "Haiti's Raboteau Massacre trial was a major, though under-reported, development in international law in 2000. The case is a milestone in the international fight against impunity for large-scale human rights violations."

The fact that the trial took place in a poor neighborhood of fishermen and small merchants meant even more, as it signaled the end of a two-century-old elitist justice system. It also signaled that 14 years after the end of the Duvalier dictatorship and nine years after the bloody military coup of 1991, the rule of law and the respect for human rights could become a reality and that impunity might no longer rule the land. The case opened the possibility of justice. It also demonstrates what is needed for further trials.

One important element of the trial was the mobilization of the population of Raboteau and the determination of the survivors to demand justice. While the Duvalier case has recently received more public opinion support, the mobilization that existed against the regime in the eighties has faded, as memory of the repression has been superseded by the tumultuous transition to democracy. And this might be one of the basic differences between the Raboteau trial, a future trial of Dominique's assassins, and a possible Duvalier judgment.

A second element that made the Raboteau case a success, in spite of its final outcome, was the political climate at the time and the unique support it received from the state, which was also the case during part of the Dominique investigation. In Haiti, the state theoretically has the obligation to investigate violations and pursue the perpetrators, a responsibility it has seldom taken. And again this is one of the major differences with a possible Duvalier trial.

A third element is the patient five-year preparatory work leading to the Raboteau trial where, from the start, the local justice of the peace wrote down witness statements when people came back to the ravaged neighborhood, as did members of the local branch of Justice et Paix, a human rights group affiliated with the Catholic Church, that also gathered medical records substantiating the abuses. The Truth and Justice Commission in its 1994 report transcribed detailed testimonies on the massacre. Before the trial took place, the government at the time opened a Bureau de Doléances, a registry of complaints that helped bring additional information to the prosecutors and was a coordinating office to handle logistics and assist the victims and witnesses. In contrast, at this stage of the proceedings against Duvalier, most of the burden has fallen on the victims' shoulders.

The fourth element at the Raboteau trial that would need to be duplicated in any Duvalier trial is the unprecedented international technical assistance provided to the prosecutors in Gonaives from 1995 to 2000. An international team of forensic anthropologists studied the remains of presumed victims in 1995, noting for instance ropes around the neck of an exhumed skeleton. DNA samples were taken from the bodies and matched with relatives to identify the victims. Two Argentine military experts had investigated the Raboteau massacre at the court's request in 1999 and concluded, based on command responsibility, that the military leaders were guilty under both Haitian and international law.

One important lesson of the Raboteau trial, later demonstrated when Duvalier was summoned to answer questions from the Appellate Court publicly, or when former Presidents Preval and Aristide testified before the judge on the Jean Dominique case, is that the powerful are not above the law, whether as the accused or as witnesses, and that impunity cannot continue to rule the land.

Rebuilding Memory

Rebuilding memory from the period of the dictatorship, after the tumultuous transition to democratic rule, is a difficult undertaking. The mass deaths caused by the earthquake of January 2010 and the most immediate concerns of sheer survival pushed many further into voluntary amnesia about the bloody years of the dictatorship, and very few concrete anchors of memory remain of a painful past that has left such deep scars on Haiti's present and future.

A case in point is that of Fort Dimanche, called Fo lan Mo, the Fort of Death, where thousands of political prisoners were tortured, executed, or died of malnutrition under the regimes of the two Duvaliers. On April 26, 1986, three months after Duvalier was overthrown, several hundred demonstrators marched to the Fort, demanding that it be turned into a memorial for the disappeared of the dictatorship. The army opened fire on the peaceful march. Eleven were killed, their bodies thrown into a mass grave at Ti Tanyen, an area outside Port-au-Prince where the dictatorship had disposed of dissidents before. In 1987, the Fort, symbol of the bloody dictatorship of 1957–1986, was declared a national monument. In 1991, the new mayor of Port-au-Prince announced that it would become a museum where the instruments used in the torture chambers would be displayed, so no one would ever forget.

Today, 27 years later, a slum community of shacks and makeshift housing called Village Democracy has been built over the ruins of Fort Dimanche and is home to hundreds of people displaced by the earthquake. To the mass graves of Ti Tanyen, where many victims of the dictatorship and of the military regimes that followed were buried, the thousands of unknown dead of the 2010 earthquake have been added, blurring the lines between a man-made repression and a natural catastrophe.

Yet, carried largely at the beginning by a few victims of the regime, the buried truths of the dictatorship are increasingly being brought to the surface of collective consciousness. More of the survivors, intellectuals or peasants, who initially hesitated to come forward and reopen old wounds, have begun more recently to stand up to the aggressive Duvalierist propaganda and to testify on radio stations or public venues about the regime. While many express little faith in the judicial system, former political prisoners have testified on torture, mistreatments, and executions within the Triangle of Death, the three major detention centers of the dictatorship. Villagers have been testifying on mass arrests, and mothers have been speaking of sons kidnapped by soldiers and never seen again.

As the Raboteau trial and the recent judicial report on the Jean Dominique case illustrate, memory can be shared and kept alive by the media, by informal communication networks including social media, and by civil society as a whole. Such communications play a critical role in any search for justice, the truth, and a sustainable democratic system.

Once more, memory is being rebuilt around specific dates of remembrance. A systematic campaign was launched last year by a number of survivors of the dictatorship to mark the many anniversaries of the repression of the sixties. On April 26, 2013, a series of activities, rebuilding and nurturing memory, marked the fiftieth anniversary of April 26, 1963, one of the darkest days of the dictatorship, that day when, as a teenager, I saw slain bodies littering the street where I lived. Church ceremonies, films, photo exhibits, conferences linking the dictatorial rule of the two Duvaliers and analyzing the impact of the dictatorship on today's Haiti were held in Port-au-Prince, creating a space for the survivors to speak out.

On February 7, 2014, various events marked the date when Duvalier was driven from power in 1986. They brought together a record number of people, many of them young students, discovering for the first time the realities of dictatorship, the price paid for the rights they enjoy today, and the true meaning of the "never again" expressed by their parents. Discussions and debates on the impact of the dictatorship on today's Haiti were held at the university and other public venues, on radio and television, as well as social media. A documentary, *The Reign of Impunity*, by Haitian director Arnold Antonin, with testimonies from victims and executioners, was broadcast simultaneously that day on all the major television channels in the country.

Beyond a "*devoir de memoire,*" the duty to remember, these commemorations have engaged younger generations in a conversation about repression, the cost of freedom, justice, and democracy. That conversation, whether focused on past events or ongoing judicial cases, can further fuel the efforts "to bring memory to bear on democratic institution building."

5

Memory and the Search for a Democratic Society

Salomón Lerner Febres
Translated by Will Morningstar

The consolidation of democracy remains an urgent and unfinished task for many societies worldwide. Although the left- and right-wing totalitarian paradigms of the 20th century no longer retain the surprising degree of acceptance they once held, these authoritarian tendencies have not disappeared. Violence, corruption, the excessive concentration of political and economic power, and threats to citizens' liberties by their governments continue to be constant risks and challenges to democratic stability.

This is particularly apparent in societies that are going through political transition, whether in a move from violence toward peace or a step from authoritarianism toward a system based on freedom. In such countries, the task of the construction of democracy is far from limited to the achievement of peace and coexistence accords or the adoption of institutional or constitutional reforms. While these steps are indispensable, what remains in these societies is a need and obligation to respond to an intense and wide-ranging discomfort, the product of the memory of past abuses perpetrated against the population—on a large scale in some cases and selectively in others—by repressive governments or armed insurgents. Thus, the idea of facing this past through memory and the recognition of victims' rights have become additional indispensable elements of democratic consolidation.

Although the discussion in this chapter is conceptual rather than about specific cases, it will nonetheless be based on and linked to its origin in concrete experience. In fact, these reflections about memory, violence, and the development of democracy are tightly bound to the process of truth-seeking that Peru started well over 10 years ago and, in particular, to my personal experience as member of the Truth and Reconciliation Commission of Peru established in 1991, which I had the honor of chairing, as well as to the experience of the country's transition to democracy and peace.

The work of this commission, which aimed to investigate the grave crimes and human rights violations committed during the armed internal conflict in Peru, allowed us to clearly see the relevance, for a society entranced by political transformation, of looking back directly at its own past in order to examine it, learn from it, and do justice.

I understand that the process that played out in Peru beginning in 2001 is neither unique nor exclusive, but rather representative of an international trend. Thus, the efforts undertaken in Peru in order to confront the legacy of a violent past have reflected many of the dilemmas and lessons that have taken place in a number of countries in the region in recent years. I am referring, of course, to the events in Argentina, Chile, El Salvador, and Guatemala, nations whose truth commissions undertook investigations into the past and sought justice for victims before such a process occurred in Peru. Likewise, after Peru's experience, other Latin American societies have been faced with the challenge of responding to their own histories of violence as a premise for constructing peace. Today, the most outstanding case might be that of Colombia, where peace negotiations to put an end to an almost half-century of violence have the moral charge of responding not only to the interests of political figures and armed actors, but also, and most importantly, to the victims' rights to truth, justice, reparations, and guarantees that such atrocities will never happen again.

My reflections will be centered mainly on the importance of memory and the search for truth as ways of confronting the past in societies emerging from situations of repressive authoritarianism or from periods of armed conflict. From this perspective, these ideas are framed within the set of institutional practices that have come to fall under the term of "transitional justice." The underlying principle behind these practices goes back, in its contemporary history, to the horrific crimes committed during the Second World War. Once these acts came to light, the international community adopted the belief that some crimes are so heinous that they cannot simply be forgotten but demand justice and, certainly, recognition. In this way, the imperative of justice, and consequently, that of the memory of past acts, began to gradually gain legitimacy and indeed became a necessity that few could question today.

In time, although very slowly, the idea gained strength in the global consensus that the horrors of war and authoritarian repression cannot be left behind or overcome simply by turning the page and looking toward the future. In this context truth and memory acquired increasing importance for those who question how to consolidate peace. But—and this is fundamental—we have also come to understand that achieving peace is not the definitive endpoint of overcoming authoritarianism or armed conflict, but rather the most basic condition on which to form political systems where fundamental rights are respected and promoted. The social transformations of which we speak, which require the engagement of truth and memory as conditions for justice, lie beyond democratization. Therefore we need to uncover the likely connections between collective memory work and the consolidation of a democratic political institutionality.

The Practice of Memory

In recent decades, the promotion of collective memory has become an enormously important political issue, and has come to be considered to be an unavoidable element in the policies adopted by nation states in order to adequately confront the legacy of violent or authoritarian pasts. Many societies have turned, since the mid-1970s, to a variety of mechanisms oriented toward recovering the truth about widespread perpetration of criminal atrocities, and promoting the memory of what happened. In institutional terms, this has typically taken the form of truth commissions: official but independent bodies dedicated to investigating the crimes committed in order to expose them publicly and to correct the historical record of the past.

These commissions have generally served as platforms for supporting the demands of victims. Truth, justice, and reparations—beyond guarantees of "never again" (*Nunca más*)—are the basic rights that can make a difference for those affected by grave human rights violations. Nonetheless, truth commissions are not the only ones to recall the memory of violence. In a public process of confronting a violent past, memory takes up other spaces and has other sources. Courts and state archives also come to be providers of resources for recovering evidence and collective representations of what happened.

Parallel to institutional efforts and often contradicting them, the affected populations have discovered the importance of deliberately cultivating their own recollections of their suffering. Consequently, in many societies transitioning to the use of official commissions, there are widespread unofficial initiatives supported mainly by churches, NGOs, and universities. This chapter touches upon these two areas of the practice of memory—the official and the unofficial—and identifies some elements that should be included when analyzing them.

In its present phase, the political and moral assessment of memory has its origins in the period immediately following the Second World War. The attempted extermination of the Jews of Europe, which manifested as a true genocide, gave way to judicial proceedings against the leaders of the Nazi regime after the Allied victory. In subsequent decades, these proceedings have come to be the basis of the fundamental idea that some large-scale crimes are so atrocious that they cannot simply be forgotten. From then on, the global community has become convinced that, beyond court justice, such experiences must somehow be recognized, protected, promoted, and ultimately, studied and understood. This "symbolic residue" is made up of individual and collective memory of abuse and suffering, of the factors and circumstances that made them possible, of the ways in which the affected population has confronted such adversity, and of the ways in which this population and the wider national community, has recognized, silenced, or denied this tragic past.

Of course, loosely speaking, the memory of violence is a social practice that has always existed, although its current institutional presence and the political weight that it has taken on are associated with the development of transitional justice. This concept and its embodiment can be understood as the intersection of practices and mechanisms oriented toward constructing sustainable peace in societies that have emerged from times of conflict, violence, or massive systemic violations of human rights. The mechanisms include the prosecution of the perpetrators, the revelation of the truth about past abuses, the provision of reparations to victims, and implementation of reforms of institutions linked to the violations. At the same time, the mechanisms of transitional justice respond to and find their legitimacy in the legal progress and moral consensus reached in recent decades, establishing the rights of victims to truth, justice, and reparations within the context of political transition, whether from authoritarianism to democracy or from violent conflict to peace. Thus, the present value of memory as a collective practice of political-moral importance may be considered as an integral element of the contemporary conception of political transitions. To say it plainly, an understanding of the role of memory can lead to an understanding of a wider phenomenon: the weight of the cultural life of a country in political transition.

What Kind of Memory Is Needed?

Naturally, the notion of memory can be defined in different ways. Memory and its functions come in many forms, including the collective practice of contending with past acts of violence or repression. In this context, I propose an understanding of memory that provides effective support for the consolidation of a government based on democratic coexistence.

To do this, I wish to avail myself of my experience in the search for the truth in Peru, and to briefly describe how my country's Truth and

Reconciliation Commission came to understand memory of the violent past and its potential weight in the political future of a country at the beginning of a transition to democracy.

At this point it is worth offering some basic information about the process of seeking truth that developed through the assembly of the Truth and Reconciliation Commission. A consideration of the Peruvian case will help to indicate some of the fundamental links between the construction of democracy and the necessity of confronting a violent and unjust past through institutional and social efforts of remembering.

Peru's most recent political transition toward democracy took place between the years 2000 and 2001, moving away from an authoritarian and corrupt government to a civic life that would no longer accept moral degradation and political disrepute as its hallmarks. It was also a move toward peace after almost twenty years of armed conflict begun by a terrorist organization that left in its wake serious and massive human rights violations committed both by the organization itself and by the state that fought against it.

To say that this was the most recent political transition to democracy implies, obviously, that Peru has experienced more than one previous attempt at democratization, and also that it has experienced several failures. Several dictators and several of attempts towards democracy have alternated repeatedly for the better part of the almost 200 years of republican Peru. And while the causes of this unfortunate back-and-forth are various and complex, one of the most important explanations can be found in the deficient, precarious, and superficial conceptions of democracy that have been prevalent in a country living, ostensibly, under the rule of law. Suffice it to say—if we are only to speak of recent decades—that while we refer to the years 1990–2000 as those of the authoritarian regime, in reality the governments of 1980–1990 were democratic only in form, not in substance. During these administrations, under theoretically democratic presidents, the state's behavior in responding to the challenge of the Shining Path terrorist organization took an exceptionally bloody form against the unarmed civilian population.

I make this observation to determine what exactly was the role assigned to a truth commission in the context of the political transition in 2000–2001. At that time the country was emerging from ten years of authoritarianism and twenty years of armed conflict, during which tens of thousands of human rights violations had accumulated. Unequivocally the most responsible actor for this toll was the organization Shining Path, which began a war against the state and against Peruvian society in May 1980, just when the country was beginning to return to democracy after twelve years of military dictator-ship. But it is equally important to recognize that the security forces of the Peruvian state likewise engaged in a campaign of indiscriminate violence, operating under the premise—not only wrong but, above all, atrocious—that terror should be fought and destroyed with terror. Yet it was not only the armed institutions of the state that failed during these years. Neither the successive Congresses, nor the offices and magistrates of the justice adminis-tration, nor many others managed to propose and demand a humanitarian strategy of pacification for the protection of the population from arbitrary violence. There was, then, a generalized institutional fracture that—while it did not itself produce the violence—created an environment for the deploy-ment of Shining Path's criminal violence and its counterpart by the police and the armed forces.

Peru thus began a political transition contending with a legacy of years of indiscriminate violence; amidst institutions, customs, and values that ran counter to the interests of citizens and to the basic right to life for a huge number of citizens; and under the pressing demands for truth and justice by once systematically ignored relatives and friends of those who were murdered and disappeared.

The decision to create a truth commission, adopted by democratic forces during the transition, arose in the first place and in an immediate way from this last consideration. Just like many other societies that have confronted periods of prolonged and severe repression or general armed conflict, Peru had a need to offer satisfactory prompt responses and agile measures to a huge number of victims. These responses could not come through the ordinary institutions of the state, not only because of their material inability to act diligently in these cases, but also because the vic-tims were historically the most marginalized people in Peru.

Following the lead of other Latin American countries like Argentina, Chile, Guatemala, and El Salvador, as well as South Africa's experience of emerging from the apartheid regime, Peruvians decided to create an entity for the recovery and public exposure of violence. This entity was called "Truth and Reconciliation Commission," and it was given a wide legal mandate that included the following tasks: to clarify the crimes and human rights violations committed during the period of violence; to con-tribute to the execution of justice; to provide an explanation of the factors that made the violence possible; and to propose measures for reparations and institutional reform.

The Commission worked for twenty-six months, doing extensive legal, historical, and anthropological research, and it made a political-moral interpretation of the period based on its findings. By the end of its work, the Commission was able to gather 17,000 victim testimonies and compiled an extensive final report, which was presented to state officials and to the wider society in August 2003.

In the report, the Commission established beyond any doubt that there had been almost 70,000 disappeared or murdered victims in Peru, and that both the security forces and Shining Path had committed crimes against humanity. The final report documents the main patterns of human rights violations, including murders and massacres, extrajudicial executions, forced disappearances, torture and cruel, inhumane, or degrading treatment, sexual violence against women, violence against children, violations of collective rights, and violations of due process. It establishes the main economic, political, and psychosocial ramifications of the armed conflict on affected individuals and groups, and it explains the social and cultural contexts in which these crimes transpired.

The final report of the Truth Commission aimed beyond a meticulous reconstruction of the facts and an incontrovertible demonstration of the penal, political, and moral responsibilities they incurred. Its aims were not limited simply to give voice to the victims—although it would have been a big enough accomplishment if it had—and offer official respect to the most marginalized and excluded Peruvians—something unheard of in our country—and to recognize these individuals as full citizens, like the urban citizens who enjoy their rights and the protections of institutions. The report aimed for more: without hiding or diminishing the value of these serious responsibilities, it sought to offer an extensive analysis of how Peru could not hope to become a stable and durable democracy without seeking a transformation and eradication of certain habits and values, certain institutional conditions, and certain forms of the exercise of power that for centuries have weakened all efforts to make the rule of law take root in our country.

The activity conducted by the Truth Commission thus transcended the necessary establishment of the facts to become a broader social exercise of reflection, recognition, and self-recognition. It is this kind of exercise that we call "memory."

The unprecedented activity of the Commission was undertaken with the aim of restoring the civic dignity and health of a country that has been devastated by civil war. Although such devastation could be compared to a natural disaster by virtue of its destructive results, it is, in fact, completely different because it resulted from the action and will of human beings. In a civil war, it is not only the consequences of actions that challenge us as moral beings, but also the actions themselves: the capacity of certain groups and individuals to commit atrocities, to inflict unlimited suffering, to remove the human dignity of those considered their enemies or of those who are simply instruments of their plans. These manifestations of human cruelty affect our physical existence, but also, and more destructively, our psychological existence, our mental and moral reality. Thus, the memory of violence or political repression can never be the same as that of any calamity caused by nature.

From the perspective of the Truth and Reconciliation Commission of Peru, the work was about memory realized in its richest and fullest sense, which should not be understood as a simple evocation of events that have occurred nor as a mere intellectual experience. Rather, it is a communion of experiences infused with affect, which aims to bridge the gap between the past and present so as to expand the meaning of events that, as mere facts, have been closed off by the passage of time.

Yet the harms, the abuses committed in the past cannot be erased. They are part of an eternal chain and they will stay that way forever. There is only one thing to do, and that is to re-appropriate the facts by recognizing and accepting them, imbuing them with a new level of intelligibility.

This is the only meaningful way to situate, in a human frame, the acts of the past which, as such, are immovable and which we tend to push away in a civilized community simply because of their horrific cruelty.

To be sure, there will always be those who insist that in the face of such violence the most sensible attitude is to forget. But forgetting is never a true remedy; indeed it aggravates and exacerbates harm. Pretending that nothing happened is the spineless, self-interested position of people who can't be bothered. To advocate forgetting implies indifference to pain and thus betrays the principle of solidarity that is one of the foundations of civilized life. Such a comfortable attitude of easy resignation to the remembered pain is also a waste of the opportunity to deal with past damages and to fight against the perpetuation of their effects. Ultimately, it is to accept an empty view of the present because one does not have the courage to dig into its roots.

In contrast, the deliberate exercise of memory appears as a braver, more honest, more effective way to cope with what causes pain and is yet part of the chain of existence. Each of us knows how to recover, from our own pasts, the truths, painful or otherwise, that have become important for our own life histories. However, in the case of violence that is exercised against the political community, memory must also be collective. Just as the human community is founded on dialogue, it must also rest on a legacy of shared memories as a function of its necessary plurality.

That said, individual memory used insincerely can give us a disfigured version of the past and one can assume the cynical position of intentional forgetting. In addition, not every exercise of collective memory has the properties of neutralization and humanization that I have pointed to above. There are certain pathologies of communal remembrance: one example is manipulated recollection, which is occasionally imposed by the powerful onto the weak. A false version of historical truth may be used to betray the lived experience of various communities, a way for the victors to prolong their violence through official narratives presented as truth. When these pathologies of memory occur, they rob the victims of their material well being and destroy the subjective sense of humanity. The symbols and affect, and the interpretation of life and destiny reside in identity.

It should be clear, therefore, that the collective memory of which we speak is not memory fabricated as a political instrument but a communitarian remembering that is true to the facts and respectful of the experiences to which those facts pertain. Similarly, if memory for the purposes of domination needs to be repudiated, so too should memory for purposes of revenge. Episodes of violence are not to be remembered in order to enslave us to the past, but rather to humanize the terror they contain, to detoxify their meaning. Therefore, the detailed memory of wrongs that motivates revenge is, ultimately, a submission to the past. It imprisons rather than frees. It degrades the present rather than lifts up the past. The ancient Greeks taught that one way to attain freedom is to break the fatal circle of revenge. Memory must serve to break us free rather than entrap us in a never-ending cycle of wrongs and reprisals. Finally, together with memory used for domination and memory for revenge, there is perhaps the most insidious way of treating a violent past. I am referring, again, to the kind of memory that annuls itself, that renounces its own being, that abdicates its powers in order to espouse a constructed regime of forgetting, resulting in a cynical and final denial of our human condition.

Here is a question to ask in the cases of societies hoping to surmount their legacies of violence and repression: what type of memory could we use to lead a reconciliation with the past without its becoming a simple evocation and conformity with the violence? This question may have many answers depending on the different circumstances of each society, its own historical tradition, the level of development of the conditions of its citizenry, the robustness of its institutions, or where it stands on matters of equity and recognition of its inhabitants.

But it is reasonable to say that, even while considering the different circumstances and historical specifics, the work society must undertake will always be about (or it *should* always be about) formulating an ethical memory, a memory exercised from the standpoint of our essential and inalienable freedom. Thus, remembrance must be conscious of our conscience: we choose to remember, and our memories appear before us in a shape that suits the needs of our identity. No one can remember for us. No one can impose on us our own past.

Not only must this ethical memory be free. It must also reflect our condition as social beings. Merely a shred of the pastbelongs only to us as individuals, and this is all the more true when memory is of a history of violence. Such a past is necessarily communal and, therefore, in order for memory to have collective relevance, it must be born out of an intersubjective dialogue, a mutual understanding made up of our individual affects. The dialogue must not be directed to select facts, but rather to express the experience of these facts in a manner acceptable to all. It is within this confluence, and only within it, that commemoration and not only remembrance is possible. This shared remembering of violence opens doors for condolences, for the experience of shared suffering and a sincere repentance, which means, ultimately, the promise of reconciliation. Ethical memory will be, then, an act of encounter and not of isolation, of integration and not of exclusion, and it will be animated in the first place by the principle of recognition.

The exercise of collective memory contains an interesting paradox. Memory sends us into the past, to be sure, but in doing so it also has the ability to lead us toward the future. Communitarian memory is, above all, the first step in the project of the future for a society which, like that of Peru or Colombia, has suffered a deep and terrible cycle of violence. Nothing truly valuable and enduring can be built on the foundations of forgetting or of selective, partisan memory. A society that wishes to be peaceful and democratic, a nation of people reconciled among themselves and with their own history, can only develop out of a brave exercise of ethical memory.

Memory and Truth

Memory and truth must be conceived in ethical terms because that is how they can most effectively reach their public function of moral restoration and self-reflection, indispensable tasks for any attempt at the restoration or construction of democracy. This implies, certainly, the association of memory with a complex notion of truth. It must not be conceived solely as a recuperation of specific facts about the past, which is necessary but insufficient. Rather, it must also lead to a reliable interpretation within a context that includes such facts and efforts and that makes them possible in the first place. In reconstructing the truth and memory of a society when we confront the legacy of violence and authoritarian abuse, it is most important to recognize the institutional and cultural fabric in which human beings live. Abuse, atrocity, arbitrary exercise of power do not occur in a vacuum but rather within a framework of values and in association with certain conceptions of power and ideas about the value of human beings against those who exercise repression or violence.

It was for this reason that the sociohistorical interpretation completed by Peru's Truth and Reconciliation Commission (TRC) gave special consideration to the problem of racism. It is always important to stress that in the TRC's interpretation, the idea that the violence had any kind of ethnic motivation—the idea that Shining Path had been representative of indigenous demands against a Creole and occidental state that had ignored and devalued the diverse forms of ethnic and cultural experience that coexisted in our country—was ruled out from the start. Although the point about inequality is unfortunately true, it is profoundly false that Shining Path had been a defender of the rights and ways of life of indigenous Peruvians. This is so not only because there was nothing in Shining Path's Marxist/Maoist program that spoke in favor of these rights, but rather because the machinery of death that this organization embodied was just as violent or more violent and harmful to the rural population, Andean or Amazonian, than the forces of the Peruvian state.

Thus, the theme of racism emphasized by the TRC indicates a different direction. It was not ethnic differences that triggered the violence, but rather the old racist idea of the state and of the various urban social classes—namely, that the indigenous, brown population was substantially inferior and lacked property rights—that provided the cultural context in which that population became so vulnerable and in which the indifference of the authorities, the media, and various institutions could be so rigid and unwavering. This is crucial for understanding the most relevant historical link between the work of the Commission and the perspective of democratization in Peru and, by extension, in other societies emerging from periods of violence.

One primary link, of course, is the call that the Commission makes for the institutions to function in defense of the fundamental rights of the people. In the circumstances of the current transition, this demand is more important than it might seem at first glance. The functioning of the institutions for the protection and guarantee of the civil, political, economic, social, and cultural rights of people is precisely what had been absent in the various unsuccessful experiences of democratization that Peru had undergone over the last two centuries.

It would not be enough for a new transition to be understood only as a restoration of the transfer of power through free elections: it should aim toward the construction of a society of citizens. The message of the Truth Commission is that a democracy can only hope to be sustainable when it is meaningful for all those who live within it: when they feel they are truly citizens because they see that their fundamental rights are being protected and, when these are threatened, that the Peruvian state will enact its institutional mechanisms to punish those responsible, bring compensation to the aggrieved, or procure the means by which a fundamental right may be truly fulfilled.

Now, as I have mentioned above, if the Commission calls for the functioning of the institutions to guarantee human rights and provide truth, justice, and reparations to the victims, the resulting message demands even more for the future of democracy. Noting the central problem of racism speaks to facts that are deeply entrenched in our social organization, beyond the design and pragmatics of our institutions. It is a phenomenon of the cultural order—representations of the other—which brings us to deny human qualities to those who are different from us and to hold their dignity and their lives as less valuable than those of other members of the political community. Thus, the question of democracy is situated in the order of symbols, values, and the public imagination, and it demands actions and transformations that are beyond the reform of standards and organizations. It is an essential shift for the constitution of a citizens' republic and, above all, of people equal in value, who live together in a more humane society. This requires changes in education, a fundamental requirement in the constitution of our political community. But beyond education, it is about transformations in the public discourse, in the way we express ourselves so that contempt and abuse, so common in our daily interactions, are rejected and stigmatized, if not removed entirely.

Memory and a Demanding Conception of Democracy

The beginning of this link between memory, truth, and democratization rests on a complex notion of the processes of the construction of democracy. Although it is now an outdated idea, democracy in post-authoritarian or post-conflict contexts used to be conceived of as consisting fundamentally in the adoption of a strategic agreement among the warring factions. In such situations, these factions would be represented by members of the regime in power on one side and the leaders of the democratic political parties on the other. In a situation where the state attempts overcome an armed conflict, however, the subjects of the negotiation would be the armed organizations and the state represented by its leaders.

In either case, democracy would be the result of a conjunction of treaties or accords through which the warring parties agreed to make a peaceful transition to a new political situation. This would involve a transaction. Forging a democratic transition demands a certain clarity about the interests of multiple actors and a considerable amount of flexibility to negotiate around those interests. The goal, a new system of peace and democracy in which the multiple political armed actors would come to a compromise to respect the rules of the game and desist in the use of force to achieve their goals, is always a morally valuable aim in itself. Added to this is the inauguration of a new institutional architecture presided over by a constitution, but followed by various reforms and new legislation to assure the order of the liberties and the respect for pluralism and the fundamental rights of citizens.

Such a scheme of political change would imply paying a price. And, in general, that price is forgetting all the abuses and atrocities committed in the era left behind. In order for the negotiating parties to feel secure about the stability and durability of the new order of things, it would be necessary for them to receive guarantees that, given the new balance of power, they would not be prosecuted or called to respond to crimes and violations they had committed in the past.

This paradigm of transitions, despite being oriented to the achievement of a democratic order, has an obvious and severe limitation that, in the long run, could conspire against the aims to which it aspires. And, of course, those who are excluded from the benefits of the agreements, those who are never asked if they were satisfied with the price to be paid, were the victims of the massive atrocities committed by the dictatorship or by armed actors. These victims would be asked to bear the cost of the transition, to give up on justice, on seeking the whereabouts or the fates of their loved ones, on receiving some sort of reparations for the damages or losses they had suffered. Ultimately, they would have to accept that the new democratic order would be constructed without their being offered any recognition, without restoring their human dignity and citizenship.

The approach to transitions and to the construction of a democratic order has changed substantially in recent decades. This change, with philosophical roots as well legal and political ones, can be summed up in the newly accepted idea of the rights of the victims of massive and serious human rights violations. It is now about the right to truth, to justice, to reparations, and to guarantees that it will never happen again, principles that have become increasingly accepted and incorporated in many forms into the international legal consensus and, in some cases, have become a clear, unequivocal legal obligation for states.

When such a change happens, one of the first good things to come out of it has been memory. The place of memory in this context and its most concrete connection with the idea of democracy can be found in the phenomenon of recognition. Memory, as described in the previous sections, is, in a very particular and urgent sense, a process through which society performs an act of recognition in two senses of the word: the sense of acceptance of the things that occurred and the public tasks and obligations that subsequently emerge, such as institutional reforms and the pressing need for justice, as well as in the sense of the public affirmation of the dignity of those who were assaulted and violated. A society that recognizes the victims is repairing the enormous damage of exclusion with respect to their capacity as moral beings, incorporating them respectfully in the political community and recognizing them fully as political subjects: that is, as citizens. Memory and the recognition it brings are crucial building blocks of the foundation of every serious democratic effort: the citizenship of all members of society and, therefore, the effectiveness of their rights and the obligation to act publicly when those rights are endangered.

Democracy and Citizenship

To conclude, this reflection is pertinent to considering the intrinsic link between democracy and citizenship, a link that has mostly been broken—if it ever existed—in societies devastated by authoritarianism or violence.

Democracy is essential to citizenship. It is impossible to talk about well-being or peace without asking, at the same time, about the existence of an effective, democratic life. We know that depends on the satisfaction of our basic material needs, but also on the realization of our moral aspirations. These aspirations, certainly, have varied throughout history depending on the particularities of specific civilizations. In today's world, the fundamental goal of moral well-being is the respect of the inherent dignity of every one of us. This general principle was anticipated in many different ways by the wisest thinkers of the modern world. In speaking about the Enlightenment, Kant identified the obligation to think for oneself as the unavoidable mandate of our time, and thus he put in the center of our social world the idea of the autonomy of the rational subject. At the beginning of the 19th century, Hegel's intense political reflection centered on the demand for recognition as the nucleus of human sociality. And, later in the same century, Alexis de Tocqueville proclaimed that the world was advancing inevitably toward equality. Autonomy, recognition, and equality—ideas central to our social imagination—are also the criteria for our well-being as members of a social and political community.

The democratic system is, in our civilization, what guarantees the realization of these ideals. Saying this implicitly affirms that democracy is much more than a set of rules for the accession and exercise of power. Understood in its institutional dimension, democracy is actually this set of rules, and as such is seen as a social agreement about the distribution and practice of power. But at the same time, the democratic order is a way of life, an environment, the space in which each of our unique and irreplaceable ordinary lives unfold. And thus democracy, in its institutional dimension, takes on reality in this set of rules that institute and simultaneously control power, and in its dimension as the social environment—the social ecology, so to speak—it is embodied only in its actors, who are its citizens.

I have argued that there may be no peace rightly understood if there is no democracy. I suggest now that a democratic system is just an empty shell, an insincere formality, if the subjects who live within it do not have full citizenship. Political science—unimportant when compared to real national experiences—teaches us nonetheless that the quality of citizenship is not a monolithic phenomenon that exists in any complete way, without fissures; it does not exist in the abstract. Citizenship is, rather, a dynamic and multifaceted condition, subject to progressions and regressions, directed by the particular history of each society. This finding should not lead us to dilute the strength of our demands on present-day democracies. Rather, it invites us to call attention to the double responsibility of our societies: they must aim, with the same level of effort, to establish their democracies as institutional systems and to foster the flourishing and expansion of the condition of full citizenship for all. However, we do run the risk of reducing democracy to its electoral aspect, of only understanding citizenship in its political dimension. The classic theory of the phenomenon of the citizen tells us that this is the result of the gradual broadening of the rights of subjects.

These rights are not only political, but also civil and social, and all of them appear together in the great achievement of our time: the doctrine of human rights. It is important to note this natural multiplicity of citizenship, or else it would be difficult to understand in what sense a genuine citizenship could become a real source of moral well being for the people and therefore an expression of the integral development that has been longed for. Reduced to its political dimension, citizenship would be achieved each time a subject participated in his or her society, whether through the simple act of voting or in some more active way. Nevertheless, the phenomenon thus bounded, the questions always remain of what satisfaction, what level of self-realization can a subject effectively extract from such a specific activity. In asking ourselves whether citizenship is the only faculty we have to intervene in the institutional management of public affairs, we propose a question with far greater consequences: of what value, truthfully, is democracy as a space for human achievement?

One conviction shared by prominent thinkers about the theme of democracy is that it is, above all, a way of life. This argument situates the problem on a wide plane of reflection, which also contains the convergence of ethics, psychology, philosophical anthropology and others strains of thought about our human existence.

This space finds itself dominated by one central concept: sociality. This is the necessary—not contingent—character of our existence in society. Sociality is not always valued in the same way. Tzvetan Todorov, a sharp contemporary essayist, recalled that in the Western philosophical tradition, there are at least two ways of addressing the problem. On one side are those, like Montaigne, Hobbes, or Freud, who accept social existence as an inevitable and necessary evil with which we must learn to coexist. Others, like Aristotle or Rousseau, similarly admit the necessary character of this coexistence, which they see not as a source of discomfort, but rather as the condition of human fulfillment. We are incomplete beings, but in the process and the promise of the fulfillment of our nature, this possibility of becoming more complete comes to fruition through our existence among others, through our extension through them, through our openness to those who are at the same time both different and like ourselves.

In the tradition of democratic thought we find, though with certain shades of difference, a similar division. From the perspective of a strictly liberal understanding, democracy is called to guarantee that individuals can pursue their own rightful goals through peaceful and legal means with as little interference as possible from the state or from other members of society. Democracy is, then, a social contract, a system of precautions designed to allow individuals to realize their full selves, subjects known as *homo clausus*, following the apt label of sociologist Norbert Elias. Other thinkers figure it differently. They see in a democratic regime the possibility that people are linked in relationships of solidarity and civility and that they live out their coexistence—that is, their community in citizenship—as an opportunity for reciprocal complementarities.

Naturally, in order for this most ambitious understanding of democracy to become reality, it is essential to transcend the sphere of political rights and responsibilities and to think about the properties necessary for such a system of coexistence. What should remain excluded, in principle, is the possibility of a situation in which passive citizens are set against the rest, or against the state. This passive existence—possible only when all we hope for is not to be interfered with in our business, or when we pin all of our hopes on the stewardship of the state or the government—can only lead, in the majority of cases, to a sluggish civic life or, even worse, to bastardized forms of democracy such as civil serfdom or patronage, the secular evil of Latin American republics. The center of the construction of a democracy oriented toward instituting a space of human fulfillment—that is, of development—is the root, trunk, and branches of an active citizenship, a system of civic existence in which citizen participation is not the exception but the rule. If democracy can come to be a vital force in societies emerging from authoritarianism or violence, if it can instill in these societies a more human character, it will happen through the constitution of a civil society that is strong, full, and healthy, that serves as a real agora, a common place where citizens can come together for shared learning.

It is no accident that at this point I bring in the notion of learning. If we are thinking of democracy and citizenship as requests for fulfillment, we must see them, at the same time, as spaces of self-education and mutual education. What is learned in these spaces? It is not necessarily technical skills nor theories, but rather something more subtle and difficult to define, something that various thinkers have labeled as civic values, the first of which is without a doubt the cordial acceptance of our obligations to one another.

Raúl Porras Barrenechea, a noted Peruvian intellectual and historian, spoke once of the failure of civil charity in Peru. This expression may refer to the belief that our mutual obligations are what is missing from our collective life; that is, the belief that we are all passengers in the same boat and that to enforce the rules and moderately seek the common good is more than a favor we do for one another; it is a moral obligation whose achievement fulfills our condition as rational and sensible human beings.

Conclusion

It is not difficult to see the relationship between the conception of democracy that I have outlined and the memory work that has been undertaken in societies affected by violence or authoritarianism. If the dynamic core that generates democracy is the experience of citizenship, and if such experience is in its most basic sense a cultural lived experience and moral reality, it is clear that in such societies citizenship can only be based on a shared memory of the unjust and traumatic past. This memory, as has been suggested, is neither utilitarian nor vengeful. If the collective practice of memory comes to be impregnated with the ethical content that has so far been mentioned, then it will be basically true. People will not look to construct an interpretation of the past based on a distorted picture of what happened, nor will they yield to the desires and interests of the powerful. On the contrary, theirs will be a memory built on a genuine search for the truth about the past.

In addition, this memory will not be restored and recovered simply to keep us frozen in the past but rather, through its moral character, its preoccupation with the human question of "what to do" on an individual and collective scale, it will always be a "protective" memory, a memory that dips into the past but only in order to achieve some critical clarity about the tasks of the future. Finally, in being a memory with such ethical dimensions, it will be necessarily bound to intersubjectivity. It will not only be an inclusive web of memories that dialogue with one another but also a memory that speaks of the reciprocal compromises that unite those who share in a mutual political community, a territory, a certain historical circumstance. In these qualities of truth, of critical reflection about what to do and of compromise with others, the promise of citizenship in the memory of the violent past is to be found. In becoming fertile ground for a citizenship that is borne out of the critical recognition of a tragic past, memory can begin to be, as well, the indispensable—although insufficient—foundation of democracy in a society that is looking to leave behind violence, terror, abuse, and the arbitrary exercise of power without turning a blind eye to them.

PART

II

The Challenges of "Capturing" Memory

6

Operation Memory: Contemporary Argentine Novelists Wrestle with History

Marguerite Feitlowitz

How can you hide something you don't even know? Escape an inherited pre-disposition to live under cover?

How do you recount collective experience in a way that is personal, if those who lived through the dictatorship have been unable to do so?

How do you resist the imposition of vicarious memory without betraying your parents and their ideals? How do you resist the alienation that comes of honoring ideals you never lived and politics you find hard to grasp?

The questions that serve as my epigraph were all posed by literary figures. But variations on these problems run through every chapter in this volume. Citizens living under military dictatorships whose definitions of wrongdoing are so sweeping as to include unsupervised *thought*, develop mechanisms to dull, even paralyze, the mind. What, then, does it mean to *bear witness* if one has internalized the official language of a repressive regime? How can a language born of trust in a social contract be recovered, after it has been perverted and violated by a murderous junta? How does a society recuperate the practices of participatory democracy, when institutions have been lain waste, not just by the military but also by complicit elected and civil officials? The historians and scholars, political scientists, journalists and activists in this volume have all investigated these dilemmas, according to their own bents and priorities.

Returning to the realm of literature, the questions above torment the motley protagonists of the latest novels by Luis Gusmán, Alicia Plante, and Patricio Pron, which home in on civilian complicity with the last military dictatorship (1976–1983), which "disappeared" some 30,000 individuals in a secret network of over 600 torture centers and death camps. All of the characters—minor as well as major, marginal as well as central—shed light on the secrets of the past hidden in the lacunae of the present. Among the common themes in these and many other recent Latin American novels, we find: enforced forgetting and self-preserving oblivion; the need for testimony and documentation and the accompanying imperative to be skeptical of same; official and alternative histories; as well as the simultaneous need for collective (particularly heroic) narratives and individual resistance to collective (particularly heroic) memories. The respective ages of the characters are of high importance, as generational connections to the "years of lead" make for a deep fount of conflict.

In Gusmán's 2002 *Ni muerto has perdido tu nombre*[1] (Not Even in Death Have You Lost Your Name), Federico, the twenty-one-year-old son of *desaparecidos*, will dare everything, in the face of amnesty for the "Dirty War" repressors, to solve the mystery of his parents' fate. The sweet thirty-something screenwriter of soft porn in Plante's *Una mancha más*[2] (Murder of Another Stripe) is at once the anti-hero and tragic victim in his own sordid campaign for truth and justice, between 2004 and 2006. In Pron's *Mis padres siguen subiendo en la lluvia*[3] (My Fathers' Ghost Is Climbing in the Rain), which covers events from 1972–2008, "children are the detectives of their parents, who cast them out into the world so that one day the children will return and tell them their story so that they themselves can understand it" (Pron 4). That Pron himself figures so prominently in the fiction makes the very act of writing part of the drama.

Each of these novels is, in its way, a homage to Rodolfo Walsh, the great investigative journalist and documentary novelist who redefined the literary mystery, which in his hands became a coldly analytic but deeply felt quest for justice. Walsh was gunned down on March 25, 1977—one year and a day after the coup—immediately after he posted his famous "Open Letter from a Writer to the Military Junta." His mutilated body was taken to the Navy Mechanics School concentration camp and displayed to the *desaparecidos* there as a "trophy," yet another act of torture for those prisoners, who revered him for speaking truth to power since the early 1950s. Walsh's books are tightly written; nouns are so precise they obviate the need for adjectives. Atmosphere is evoked by specific material elements; tension and suspense are created by the exact calculation of the passage of time. His characters' ways of speaking arise from particular neighborhoods and professions, from shared political battles; yet every character has a voice that is recognizably his own.[4]

Each of the novels I consider here is a kind of Walshian thriller, though on different levels and to different ends. They offer a timeline for the ways in which the impunity of the 1980s and 1990s seeped into almost every aspect of Argentine life, and for the unfolding consequences of impunity's judicial end in the early 21st century. They uncover a host of crimes and criminals that, in unexpected ways, form the poisoned back of the democratic tapestry.

Gusmán: Dead Letters and *Desaparecidos*

Ni muerto has perdido tu nombre opens with an act of memory: "Varelita scrolled through his mind for whom he could call that night." We're out on the street in a phone booth with a man who "likes to work alone . . . according to his own *modus operandi,* that's how he put it, using that anachronism" (Gusmán 11–12).[5]

He is methodical in his choices, his mind being "a file of murky things," and only seeks out those who will not denounce him, "even after all these years. In any case, most of them didn't show up to meet him, yet even now, he was able to do a little business" (Gusmán 12). At first he thought he would try to sound like an actor on the phone, but he quickly understood that it was better to sound like himself: it enabled him to gauge the terror provoked by his voice.

Varelita (not his real name) was one half of a kidnap-torture-extortion duo called Varela-Varelita, which took the moniker from a jazz band of the 1950s. Whatever happened to Varela (not his real name), he wonders, as he dials one Ana Botero (not her real name, but one given her, back in the day, by Varela-Varelita). Her machine picks up, and just as he's remarking that her voice hasn't changed one bit, he notices where his booth is located: in front of Varela-Varelita, a real-life old café (Scalabrini Ortiz, corner of Paraguay, in the heart of the Palermo district of Buenos Aires), also named for the band. He has a moment of nostalgia, wishes he could go in and have a chat, over vermouth, with Varela, but then finds he doesn't like this moment one bit: it's pouring cats and dogs, with great booms of thunder, which seems a very bad omen. He has always been superstitious of this kind of weather.

In this single compact scene, Gusmán establishes that this will be a mystery of mistaken identity, indeed multiple mixed-up identities; that there is both magnetism and tension between that which is dislocated ("anachronistic," to quote Varela) and grounded ("Varela-Varelita" is often touted as one of the last authentic *porteño* bars); and that the very elements have a role to play in the story. If this all sounds very high-flown, we shouldn't forget that the goings-on are sordid.

Gusmán leaves Varelita out in the rain to introduce us to twenty-one-year-old Federico Santoro, whose parents disappeared when he was an infant, and who was lovingly raised by his grandparents, who routinely said, "One day Ana Botero will come and explain to you what happened." Hers was a name that has always haunted him, and maybe now more than ever, in the immediate aftermath of his grandmother's death. Ana Botero had saved his life, but that's all they would say. When he asked if they had a picture, they replied that they'd burned all her photos. Federico has been raised to be reverent toward, and guided by, the unknown. Each day his grandmother would light a candle before the pictures of his missing parents; Federico learned the days of the week by the color of the candle, Thursday being the color of the couple's disappearance. Following his grandmother's death (his grandfather died much earlier), he honors this ceremony, for in his grief he has no other way to tell the days apart. But then he finds the letter his grandmother left him, in which she writes that his father last communicated with them from a distant family property called Colina Bates, saying that "the package" (by which he meant his baby son) would be delivered by one Ana Botero. Suddenly it seems he doesn't need this woman, he will go instead to Colina Bates. He will get off the "treadmill" that has been his life—the sense of moving in place, without destination or point of origin. The meaning of his life will no longer be held in abeyance.

Federico's development has been arrested in part owing to his deference to his grandparents' terror of politics. He has stayed clear of public action and socially minded peers. Interestingly enough, this is a profile more often associated with children born in captivity and raised by parents who falsified their biological origins. That Gusmán assigns this trait to Federico is intriguing; in his case, it suggests an almost mystical conception regarding sources of information. After all, why would Ana Botero be more reliable than a human rights organization? Why would she necessarily be an honorable witness? Blackmail is a current that runs through the novel; among its forms, Gusmán seems to be saying, may be love itself, the searing protective love that comes of criminal loss.

Gusmán's text is tight (almost a novella), with chapters alternating between Federico and Ana Botero, and shifting among Buenos Aires, Córdoba, and Colina Bates, in the province of Entre Ríos. Gusman spins the web among these characters in prose so skeletal it approaches poetry. The technique is shrewd, because there is a great deal of coincidence in the action, and explanation might strain credulity. That said, Argentine reality has always been stranger than fiction.

For the first time in his life, Federico goes to a march of children of *desaparecidos*; as he is striking up a conversation with a young man named

Juan, Varelita is on the phone with Ana Botero, saying he has information about her husband, whom she believed to have been killed in a shoot-out in 1977. It would "cost a great deal" to learn more, and he'd only take dollars. She is thrown back in time: her nightmares and sunlight terrors return; the sound of an approaching car is almost more than she can bear; the ensuing silence is even worse. As she did during the dictatorship, she takes to walking for hours on end through the streets of her native Buenos Aires, where there was no safe place to settle. Varela-Varelita had finally got her, in the Plaza Congreso, two blocks from where she was born. She has money saved up, but not enough for Varelita. A girlhood friend who had refused to help her in the "years of lead" now offers as much as she needs. Varelita, whom she eventually meets in a city square, says her husband is in a mental hospital, in the far province of Córdoba. "I swear I'd rather he be dead than insane" (Gusmán 49), she confides to her friend, for isn't a madman a kind of *desaparecido?* Why does she believe this story? Varelita has presented her with a letter in her husband's hand (she had first fallen in love with his beautiful penmanship) saying he is alive and needs her help. So she embarks on the course laid out by her former torturer: ask for a Doctor Farías who will take her to a patient called Pablo Díaz (her husband's name was Iñigo), and say he was kidnapped in 1977.

The choice is provocative: "Pablo Díaz" is such a common name, Ana could be said to be looking for "John Doe." In the world outside the novel, Pablo Díaz is the name of one of three survivors of the infamous "Night of the Pencils" (*La noche de los lápices*), a military-police raid which began on September 16, 1976, and lasted until September 21, and whose aim was to destroy the high-school student association in La Plata that was advocating for lower school-bus fares. Díaz was a key witness at the 1985 trial of the ex-commanders and has testified in subsequent courts and human rights venues. Héctor Olivera based his 1986 film *La noche de los lápices* on the incident, with the charismatic Alejo García Pintos in the starring role of Pablo. It won the Oscar for Best Foreign Language Film, in addition to many other domestic and international prizes. I find it hard to believe that Gusmán's choice of name is casual or coincidental. It could be that Varelita (who would certainly know about the Night of the Pencils) is making a hideous joke. This small detail is vintage Gusmán, unsettling both the fiction and the documented history.

As Ana Botero is driving halfway across Argentina, then looking desperately into the vacant faces of one madman after another, Federico is consulting files in the offices of human rights groups. He learns from a lawyer that a third person, identity unknown, had disappeared from

Colina Bates with his parents. Ana Botero meanwhile realizes only one person can tell her if her husband is alive, and that is Federico's grandmother. She returns to Buenos Aires and telephones, catching Federico as he is preparing to leave for Colina Bates; he agrees to meet her at the Café Británico, like Varela-Varelita an iconic porteño bar but in the neighborhood of San Telmo. Never having seen her picture, he yet knows her as soon as he sees her—"fine, elegant, very thin . . . not very different from the other women" (Gusmán 65). She tells him the story: she had not met his parents in the context of shared political activity (*militancia*); rather, it was Iñigo, her estranged husband, who called her from the hiding place at Colina Bates, asking her to bring money so that he and his comrades could leave the country. She arrived. But the trio couldn't agree on an escape plan, and finally Federico's parents retreated to a bedroom, consulted, and came out with their baby, asking her to take him to his paternal grandparents. A local mechanic drove Ana and the infant to the next village where they caught the bus for the capital. To Federico, the strangest thing about the story is that she abandoned her car. You don't understand, she explains, we'd be dead, we needed the cover of public transport. The detail is significant, for it shows the young man's innocence, and it sets up the return of the mechanic a little later. Ana begs Federico not to make the trip, but he won't be dissuaded. Before leaving, however, he asks for her photograph; at once touched and a little embarrassed, she gives him one she has in her purse, showing her as considerably younger than she is today.

Federico puts up at the Hotel Excelsior, far less grand than its name, and asks about the present owners of Colina Bates. The place looks at once friendly and hermetic in a small-town sort of way. Colina Bates is located just outside of Tala, a town in a lunar landscape whose signature feature is a towering derelict quarry. "In spite of having been exploited, an enormous wall of white granite was yet majestic, with all the erosion and its open veins. The quarry erupts as though alien to the landscape, suddenly opening like a wound in the earth. It functions like the gate to a walled city, beyond which one finds Tala" (Gusmán 73). Great booming explosions were a defining part of the region's atmosphere—how else to extract the granite that, one way or another, was everyone's livelihood, and how better to dispose of so-called "subversives"? As Federico is told by the elderly editor who first published news of the "operation" at Colina Bates:

> Here, sooner or later, everyone knows everything. And it was a Sunday
> and the quarry wasn't working; but on that day too you could hear

explosions. When the quarry was active, you couldn't breathe. If there was a lot of wind, wind from the north, we tied handkerchiefs around our faces, as though they were surgical masks. That obliged us to talk with the handkerchief in our mouth. So everyone had a strange voice. On the weekend, when the quarry wasn't working, everyone went around with their face uncovered. One Saturday I went to a dance and found everyone unrecognizable. Even their voices were different. It was strange: I didn't know who was who. (Gusmán 84)

Or was it that, in a deeper sense, he'd never known "who was who"? This lack of consciousness, like the quarry itself, would seem to be a defining element of Tala.

On fire with his mission, Federico returns to the quarry. "The first thing that made an impression were the rabbits' red eyes. 'As though they were crying blood'" (Gusmán 87). "Under this mountain of stone must be whatever remains of my parents," Federico thinks (Gusmán 89). He is drawn to "one white rock that seemed brighter than the others" and proceeds to spray-paint their names—Marta Ovide / Carlos Santoro—in large black letters on the pale rock face. Walking away, he realizes, "Iñigo. Iñigo's name is missing" (Gusmán 90). He doesn't know the man's last name, and neither do we.

The present owner of Colina Bates is not there when Federico comes to call. Instead he meets the wife, Gloria, who knows the original owners were called something like Santoro, and is quick to say they intend to sell. Federico is certain she's no local; she has a big-city haircut and a *porteño* accent. As Federico is consulting with the son of the notary who handled the property, a terrified Ana Botero is racing to Tala, in order to rescue young Santoro for the second time. The notary tells Federico that while the young man has the original deed, he, the notary, has a credible bill of sale, made out to one Juan Garnero, dated November 26, 1977. One day prior to his parents' disappearance, Federico says. Defending his father's transaction, the notary yet promises to consult the Registry of Deeds and Properties, which will take a few days. Enough time for the powers-that-be to make the whole problem (including the young man) go away.

Tala is proving to be a magnet: Varelita arrives, not only because he misses Varela (now known as Aguirre), but also to claim his half of the money someone paid for Colina Bates (the phone-call business has really not been adequate). It's the second time Varela skunked out on the deal: Carlos Santoro had turned the property over in exchange for their lives and for years he's been holding out on his partner.

The only person glad to see Varelita—even though he threatens to expose Varela/Aguirre as a thief—is Gloria, who has been desperate to leave this backwater and return to Buenos Aires. Her hospitality extends to a poisoned bottle of whiskey, and that's the end of Varelita. In the dead of night, she and Varela bury the poor sod in the quarry. They get home, and realize they had forgotten to deal with his suitcase, which is full of letters. "He made them write them while they were alive. That was the game. Look at these . . . They're from that Iñigo, Ana Botero's husband" (Gusmán 156).

As if she hadn't even heard him, Gloria closes the valise. "Get in bed. Tomorrow we have to be up with the sun" (Gusmán 156). These are the novel's last words, spoken by its clearest thinker and most efficient actor, who stands for all that is sordid, banal, and greedy, and who gets exactly what she wants. Gloria is ultimately a horrifically refracted version of Ana: she actually saves her husband and engineers a whole new chapter in their lives.

What really happened way back when? What will happen now? Some things will never be cleared up: Varela had told Ana Botero that she'd been given a pill and had "sung the whole song" about the hiding place at Colina Bates. Varelita says that it wasn't true. Ana Botero can never know, and will always live with that existential vacuum. The young man who had waited most of his life for Ana Botero to illuminate the mysteries of his parents' lives is also left hanging. Even as Varelita is visiting Varela-Aguirre, she tells Federico, "The story of Ana Botero is over," and asks him please to use her real name, Laura Domínguez. "It doesn't fit with your face," he replies (Gusmán 151). In an effort to persuade him, she makes a perfect, yet misdirected, confession, telling Federico that under drugs and torture, she might have given up Colina Bates, she truly does not know. The young man, who had long suffered at the thought that his parents had been tortured to death, is on one level relieved to learn that they had been shot in the quarry. His instincts had been right about their blown-up remains. Yet if Ana Botero was seeking some sort of forgiveness, or even mere understanding, from Federico, she was mistaken. Here Gusmán's title takes on a darker level of meaning: Laura Domínguez will always be Ana Botero. Even in death, she will never lose this name. And Federico has the photo she gave him, to prove it.

> "My grandmother told me that one day Ana Botero would come and tell me things. What she didn't say was that others would come and tell me things about Ana Botero. . . . "

> "Who am I then for you? What did I do? Save you, and or condemn you?"

"You had something to tell me and now you've done it. Don't tell me anything more." (Gusmán 151)

It is hard to believe that the story of Ana Botero is over, either for her or Federico. But we'll never know. This is the last we see of them.

This slim, tense, elliptical book reveals an extensive web of repressed fact, disguised reality, disappeared persons, and identities that will be forever unknown.

The kindly mechanic and his wife knew about the young *militantes* at Colina Bates, thought they had found safe harbor, and only wished them well. The husband actually saw them being shot in the quarry, but withheld this horror from his wife. All of Tala knew about the "subversives" but no one ever denounced Varela-Garnero-Aguirre, who became a local power broker. The disappeared persons are, in addition to Carlos Santoro, Marta Ovide, and Iñigo, also Ana Botero, who will never know if she gave up her husband and comrades; the young Laura Domínguez, who was re-baptized Ana Botero; the many inmates of the insane asylum, among whom, the orderly tells Ana, are likely some political *desaparecidos*. We shouldn't omit Varela and Varelita, who had prior names and identities (and will likely have others), which are missing from the world of the text. We might also add Colina Bates, once a cherished family property and safe haven turned into a place of terror and then of ill-gotten gain, resented by Aguirre's efficient, citified wife, who turns it into a site of murder, an act she views as her own liberation. "They were a pair of subversives," she says, "who knows what shit they believed?" Federico is so irreparably changed by the long-awaited Ana Botero that he refuses to participate any more in the story.

Because Gusmán has grounded his fiction in material detail, rural and urban geography, and in the uncanny reach of history, it is hard not to wonder about the post-novel future of the characters. Aguirre has every reason to stay away from Federico and Ana Botero. But, as has happened to a number of actual survivors, they could meet by chance. "It's a peculiar kind of anguish," I was told by one survivor, "spatial violation and temporal dislocation all at once. You feel totally unprotected."

Gusmán at once utilizes and subverts the Walshian mystery. The criminals are exposed, but no justice is done. There are no well-earned second chances, not even for the woman who once *may have been* broken under drugs and torture, and who consciously risks her life to save another. Walsh's rigorously lucid fictions provide a model for investigative thought, for how to sift evidence, how to weigh competing versions of a single event. He is a master at conveying the simultaneity of socially and geographically distant events, forcing us to keep multiple timelines clear and dynamic. And yet for all his analytical stringency, he emboldens us to *feel*, to value solidarity, not for sentimental reasons, but because it can be powerful, affect political change. In the world of Gusmán's novel, the question of solidarity is rendered moot. There is a dullness of feeling at the end: what happened, happened; and now it's time—as Gloria says—to catch forty winks and move on.

Gusmán also uses, and undermines, the traditional *bildungsroman*, in which the young protagonist leaves home, grows through adventures and ordeals into his authentic self, earns his rightful name, and becomes part of a larger group or project. Our pleasure and edification come from witnessing the protagonist's development, and the gratification it brings to those around him. Gusmán doesn't allow this. After laying out the basics of the genre in his portrayal of Federico, he shows us how, in such a climate, the *bildungsroman* is impossible. Federico turns his back—on Tala, on Ana Botero, and on us readers. The knitting-together of the social fabric, the emotional unity that crowns the *bildungsroman*, does not happen. The traditional genre requires a society, and in particular an older generation, that is morally stable but not stultified, forgiving of the impetuosities of youth, and welcoming to those who would contribute to the greater good. It is also possible that Gusmán is giving Federico what the established genres (and official history) do not: time to search out his own course (as opposed to the treadmill), and privacy (as opposed to secrets).

But that may be more optimistic than this rigorous novel can allow.

Plante: Mysteries within Mysteries, the Sordid Tragedy of a Poet Manqué

"Qué le importa al tigre una mancha más?"
"What does one more stripe matter to the tiger?"

Or, as Alicia Plante's translator Andrea Labinger, has it, "What's one more crime to the criminal?" It isn't the only question at the heart of the novel; we may also asks: What *is* a "crime" in a society that is profoundly criminal? In a society shot through with fear and hatred, betrayal and failure?

Murder by Another Stripe opens at the beginning of 2004, at the tail end of decades of legal challenges to the amnesty laws. (In 2001, a federal judge ruled the amnesties unconstitutional; in 2003 both houses of Congress voted the laws' repeal; on June 14, 2005, the Supreme Court declared the amnesties null and void.) Although democracy returned to Argentina in 1983, the narrator lets us know that "it suited the military to let civilians deal with unemployment and uncontrollably rising prices: they had been true to their principles, and withdrew with a clear conscience. In any case, abandoning government didn't mean abandoning power: they would be there, behind the scenes, preventing any reversals in the transition" (Plante 104).[6] This background is so ingrained in her characters that Plante can afford at times to be subtle, or offhand, knowing her readers will pick up on the references. But I should like to offer some landmark specifics: 1989 saw hyperinflation, with prices rising by the hour; the 1990s were a time of fevered privatization and the disastrous dollarization of the peso; in 1999, the economy collapsed, and bank accounts, wages, and currency exchanges were frozen; by the beginning of 2002, 52 percent of Argentines were living below the poverty line while 20 percent could not afford enough nutritious food; needless to say, resources for health, education, and social services were severely curtailed.[7] Older generations have seen their ideals trampled and their careers lain waste; many young people, notably the protagonist, Raúl, have grown up with a bitter sense of limited prospects. There have been marches and uprisings, neighborhood mobilizations for mutual aid, and notably the *cacerolazos*, the spontaneous banging of pots and pans as a form of political protest. Many ex-military worked in private security firms, which, "with today's crime wave, are multiplying like rabbits" (Plante 103).

In terms of plot, the central crime is baby-stealing, which was never covered by the amnesties. This is the crime that gives rise to every other crime in the novel, and it has much to do with dramas of masculinity, patriarchy, and power; with motherhood, nurture, and the fortress of domesticity; with the debts, allegiances, and secrets that both bind and strain the generations. These submerged dynamics are intensified by the politics surrounding the amnesties' impending nullification, which trigger suppressed memories, and actions at once bizarre and logical, from unlikely characters.

The novel opens in the month of January at a post-funeral gathering in Vicente López, a Buenos Aires suburb. Seemingly out of the blue, Raúl, the thirty-eight-year-old protagonist, has the enraging sense that the new widower and neighbor, García Mejuto, is staring at him with suspicion and suppressed hatred. An émigré from Franco's Spain with a thriving construction business, he has a handsome blond son named Daniel who teaches physics at the University of Buenos Aires and who espouses the kind of progressive teaching that could have got him killed during the dictatorship. To Raúl, who gets by writing screenplays for pornographic films, Daniel is rich, cossetted, and gracious—way out of his league—and Raúl leaves the gathering in a sour mood. He ruminates on how he hated his own bitter and violent father, how he'd still like to kill him, even though he's dead.

Then suddenly an image comes back to him: the rainy winter night in June 1978 when a taxi pulled up to the house across the street, García Mejuto got out "carrying a large package," and he, Raúl, heard the unmistakable crying of a baby. Raúl's mother, the daughter of Sicilian anarchists (whose father detested her husband), wanted to file a report; she'd heard about the children stolen from *desaparecidos*, but her husband (who sometimes hit her) would have none of it, and then, as she said, "the moment passed." Mother and son would stand behind their blinds, watching the same four *milicos*, as they contemptuously call the military men, arrive regularly for barbecues in the García Mejuto backyard. The quantities of food and wine, loud music and raucous laughter added to their disgust, fear, and fascination. Everyone in the neighborhood knew that Dani was adopted, but somehow over the years "the information was rendered inert in the collective consciousness, a real but deactivated part of neighborhood folklore: nearly thirty years had passed and even though the kid no longer lived with his parents he was unquestionably part of the block" (Plante 16).

Was it really natural for everyone to let the facts fade? The social presence of *milicos* had to have exerted some pressure. And then, too, Ramona, Daniel's adoptive mother, had from the start what her husband called a "disturbing passion" for the child, insisting that he was *hers:*

> [The birth mother] didn't deserve him, she thought, and the thought dilated in her mind as though someone else had said it. She didn't deserve him . . . A kid, pregnant from sheer irresponsibility, so typical of youth, nothing easier at that age . . . , and on top of it, in times like those, with the fucked-up ideas they had, crazy, stupid, all of them crazy, shit-eating kids, she shuddered to think of Dani taking milk from that woman, being raised by her . . . what would have become of him, the ideas they would have put in his head! (Plante 110)

Of course Ramona never spoke like this to Dani or to the neighbors. The official story was that she and her husband had agreed to the adoption while on holiday at Iguazú, saving a poor chambermaid and her baby from disgrace and further hardship. That Dani was a physically "golden child" implies the possibility that the chambermaid was seduced, or even raped, by a foreign tourist. For Ramona, the narrative was entirely self-affirming, and lined up with a larger discourse of the regime: she had rescued the baby, and brought him into the bosom of upright *criollo* culture. Cherished and raised with every advantage, Dani grew up to be sweet, devoted, and exemplary. For the world to see, it's a lovely little family.

"Well, I talked at length with that 'baby' today," Raúl reflects, after Ramona's funeral. In an access of energy, he comes up with a plan, which he is ready to execute by February 2005: he will extort ten thousand pesos a month from García Mejuto, threatening to reveal the secret about Dani. Like Varelita, he gives his orders from a phone booth or call center, always making contact on the first Monday, but from a different Buenos Aires neighborhood. He wants the money to buy his own apartment in the desirable, bustling neighborhood of Palermo Viejo. He has clearly dreamed hard and longingly about this, for he knows exactly where he wants to live: "between Honduras and Nicaragua, in those blocks, and as far as possible from Juan B. Justo because that's where it floods like crazy in heavy rains, and especially when the wind blows in from the river." But then, why not also a little house in the tranquil Tigre Delta? (Plante 69) Information, he realizes, can be converted into hard currency. But unless he knows enough to terrify García Mejuto, the old guy will eventually stop paying. So he digs in and ultimately identifies the *desaparecidos* who were Dani's birth parents. Plante's embittered, grasping pornographer provides a textbook lesson on how to go about such a search, what organizations to consult, what questions to ask, how best to corroborate evidence (Plante 77–83). That he is utterly unsentimental, feels irritation at the blurriness of 1970s photos, and makes fun of the human rights groups' acronyms adds to the irony. Plante is so detailed in these passages she must believe that literature is a necessary source for such information, that novels, perhaps more than politics, have the potential to reach and persuade a wide audience, one that may be on guard against anything having to do with the left, given the pitched battles of the last dictatorship. In the context of economic strife, any backward-looking rhetoric of "human rights" has been tarred by many beleaguered Argentines as a bourgeois luxury.

Increasingly adept at blackmail, Raúl parcels out gradually the information he finds—dates, a selection of three possible birth mothers, and then, finally, the whole accurate background: Dani's father taught physics at the National University in Rosario, his mother looked to be fair, light-eyed, and blonde. Raúl takes some furtive photographs of Dani, and sends them, along with images of his biological parents, to García Mejuto: "SO YOU WON'T BE A WISE GUY!" (Plante 96).

Raúl's dreams start to come true—he buys the apartment and the house, he happily fattens the monthly support for his mother—and then suddenly he is dead. According to the Tigre police, it's a murder-suicide, in which he first shot his live-in girlfriend (the actress in the movies he wrote for ElMacho Films) and then himself, leaving a note that they "couldn't take it anymore."

The near-universal distrust of police ushers in a new cast of characters with emblematic connections to the 1970s. For Julia, an *ex-militante* and longtime resident of the Tigre, the so-called crime and its solution are "too perfect," suggesting that the police are in on a cover-up. (Raúl's builder, a boatman, and other trades people are also skeptical that this young man, obviously delighted with his house and passionately involved with renovations, would kill himself.) Julia is part of a triumvirate—her lover, Gerardo, and dear friend Leo Resnik, a magistrate. Plante goes back and forth in time and among characters and their respective motivations: there will be a cascade of further crimes, some in the service of justice.

The first transgression is committed by Julia, who surreptitiously enters Raúl's house, where she finds two pages printed out from the website of the Grandmothers of the Plaza de Mayo. With these documents and impassioned pleas for the ideals so many of their friends died for, she will wear down Leo's resistance, "who has worked behind the back of the police before" and will do so again now. Gerardo, an ex-political prisoner, burdened with survivor's guilt, throws in with these investigations, though not so much to satisfy Julia as to honor the friend whose name was found in his datebook on the day of his own arrest, and who died during torture, perhaps believing that Gerardo had given him up.

Armed with his back-channel research, Leo eventually approaches another judge, with the impeccably Spanish surname González Saavedra, who reflects, "In my day, Jews [such as Resnik] didn't enter the judiciary." The elderly judge finally agrees to take the case, not for legal reasons (he has objected to democracy's judicial reforms) but because he is terrified of his looming retirement and determines to keep the case going for as long as possible, dotting every *i* and crossing every *t*. Moreover, this could be his crowning achievement.

> Nothing, he reflects, not even the thirty thousand *desaparecidos*, has generated such critical reaction as that of the babies; it must be the emotional image of the pregnant women, the idea of "the mother" turned into a martyr, waiting to be killed as soon as they give birth . . . All that touched a very sensitive fiber, and for many persons, especially women, perspective on the dirty war and the repression had changed when [the Grandmothers] began finding dozens of children of *desaparecidas*. This at least was his daughter's opinion, that women found it easier than men to identify with them; psychologists were saying the same thing now. (Plante 296–297)

So it looks like there will be a domestic pay-off for the judge as well: the appreciation of his daughter, with whom he has apparently debated, if not argued. One generational rift, it appears, is about to be healed.

For all this, Plante doesn't want us to forget that "dirty warriors" still have their own networks. García Mejuto, running of out of money and scared out of his wits, will attempt to bring things full circle by appealing to the man who gave him Daniel. He reasons that it wasn't a sentimental gesture, but rather a transaction between men, nothing to do with friendship or esteem: there had been free construction work on one side of the deal, and a baby on the other. No debts hanging, which should guarantee his protection. Mario Heriberto Cecchi, a "hard case," had risen fast and high in military intelligence: he was famous for his interrogation techniques and for never losing a prisoner under torture until "the right time." Cecchi has recently returned to Argentina, after fifteen years in Chile, Uruguay, and Brazil, on "matters of joint security" (clearly a reference to the CIA-backed Condor Plan). He finds civilian life "trivial" and "anarchic." He has no recollection of the rattled man sitting before him, until García Mejuto reminds him of the extensive constructive projects he'd done for him at no cost (and for which he kept the paperwork). "And that, not to mention the baby, could be a problem, *mi capitán* . . ." Cecchi lets García Mejuto believe he will protect him, then proceeds, illegally, to have the intelligence service tap his phones so he can put a tail on Raúl, whom he will kill along with Silvia. Under cover of a friendly visit, Cecchi will also murder García Mejuto and make it look like a household accident, and no one will suspect anything different.

The final scene finds Cecchi getting drunk in an airport bar, waiting for the first plane out to Barcelona, Madrid, wherever. He has lots of cash in Montevideo and can get to it whenever he wants. As for leaving home, Cecchi couldn't care less: "elegant, his brown uniform impeccable, his moustache heavy and dark, his sunglasses in one hand, and car keys in the other, [he] left his house each morning, in a halo of proud virile beauty" (Plante 160). But, as he knows, it's an illusion. "His fragile-seeming wife" has raised the kids, managed the home, and kept him (not that he minded) from idling in bed; it's she who wears the pants in the family. "Decades ago, twenty years for sure, he made a mistake. He's tempted to march into the prosecutor's office and ask, where did he go wrong, how could he not have realized?" (Plante 316).

They're closing in from all directions: González Saavedra; two survivors who recognized his photo from the papers; and Raúl's mother, who, on May 3, 2005, officially reopened the entire case, following interviews with Julia, Gerardo, and Leo. Even if Cecchi manages to get on a plane, any number of countries will be pleased to extradite him. What Cecchi really hates is "having been wrong," twenty years ago. In 1985 (in a trial that opened in April), the ex-commanders were convicted in a civilian trial of crimes against humanity—is that the mistake he means? Or is it that, even earlier, he set his sights on stardom for the losing team? One way or another, his game is up. But for Cecchi this provokes no moral dilemma.

Plante carefully manipulates her characters' presence on and behind the scenes. In addition to the ironies mentioned above, she holds off bringing back Raúl's mother, so that the right-wing judge functions as a foil to the left-wing camaraderie at the end. But he is absolutely necessary, and that seems to be her point: confronting crimes against humanity shouldn't be relegated to one political stripe or another. And how rare it is that a person's motives are totally pure.

One of the saddest ironies in the book concerns Raúl, who twenty years earlier won a coveted prize for student poetry. He hadn't written verse, or anything lyrical, since high school. But on a day when García Mejuto is telling him he can't pay, and when it all seems to be falling apart, Raúl "unexpectedly had the impulse to find pencil and paper and describe the pitiful images that bubbled up and surrounded him, something like a poem perhaps: he laughed bitterly as he put his cigarettes, lighter, and a little money in his pocket" (Plante 147). He had wanted the house in Tigre as a tranquil place to write.

Pron: Questing for Truth, or The Terrors of Authorship

"He would have to think of an attitude, or a style that would turn what was written into a document."

My Fathers' Ghost Is Climbing in the Rain is obsessed with the act of writing. The above epigraph from César Aira introduces the second of the novel's four sections, and it well describes the central drama of Pron's protagonist and the author who so closely resembles him. As Pron says in the digital addendum to the novel, it is "a story about certain things that happened to me and to my family in the period spanning 1972 through 2008."[8] Most of the events are true, or "mostly true," even if not in the testimonial or autobiographical sense. The membrane between fact and fiction in this elliptical novel is extremely fine, and has the porous luminosity we associate with poetry.

Unlike Gusmán's Federico, who ultimately needs to escape the story, Pron's first-person narrator is, like the prodigal son, fighting his way back in. And yet, like Federico, he will say, "You don't ever want to know certain things, because what you know belongs to you, and there are certain things you never want to own" (Pron 49). Unlike Raúl, a debased hack, "I" is a published author, who dreamed of becoming part of an international republic of letters. Like Federico, "I" is obsessed with finding the keys to the mystery of his parents' lives, and by extension, to that of his own. Like Raúl, "I" will investigate a series of crimes-within-crimes, assembling an archive of documents; unlike the criminal Raúl, benevolent "I" is so morally uneasy with his rights to these documents—that is to say, with his right to recount the past—that he proposes a deeply unsettling abdication of authorship.

Pron immediately establishes the ways in which the genesis of the novel was "impossible." Having left Argentina in 2000 to live and travel in Germany, the "consumption of certain drugs made me almost completely lose my memory . . . of the last ninety-five months" (Pron 3). And then he announces the project:

> I suppose at some point all children need to know who their parents were and they take it upon themselves to find out. Children are the detectives of their parents, who cast them out into the world so that one day the children will return and tell them their story so that they themselves can understand it . . . they can try to impose some order on their story, restore the meaning that gets stripped away by the petty events of life and their accumulation, and then they can protect that story and perpetuate it in their memory. Children are the policemen of their parents, but I don't like policemen. They've never gotten along well with my family. (Pron 4)

The mere mention of "police" shuts everything down. In the next line (which opens a new chapter), the narrator tells us that his father has been hospitalized and is unable to talk. No one will tell him what has happened. This informational blackout—and the possibility of losing his father—has two immediate effects: it impels the narrator to tell us that he had recently given up his own apartment, not because he was in financial straits, but because he sought the "irresponsibility" that comes of being rootless, of parting with one's belongings, of sleeping uncomfortably on other people's sofas and looking with distaste at their bookshelves. He had come to Germany fleeing

> a literature I had tried and failed to escape . . . [that] of a writer, let's say who is not the author of *The Aleph*, around whom we all inevitably revolve, but rather the author of *On Heroes and Tombs*, someone

who spent his whole life believing that he was talented and important and morally unquestionable and who at the very end discovers
that he's completely without talent and behaved ridiculously and
brunched with dictators, and then he feels ashamed and wants his
country's literature to be at the level of his miserable body of work so
that it wasn't written in vain and might even have one or two followers. Well, I had been part of that literature, and every time I thought
about it, it was as if in my head an old man was shouting *Tornado!*
Tornado!, announcing the end of days . . . (Pron 8)

It's a portrait of the young artist as a kind of refusenik, not of the
old repressive order of the generals, nor of the aesthete in the figure of
Borges, but rather of the *engagé* novelist and public intellectual exemplified by Ernesto Sábato.[9] The narrator is adrift, having lost the only home
he'd ever known, that of books, which he tries to replace with pills. From
this point on, continuity is broken, and numerous chapters will be missing. We go for example from Chapter 7 to Chapter 9, where we get the
first image of his father, "sleeping with a book in his hands . . . dropped to
cover his face as if he were a dead man found on the street during some
war" (Pron 11).

While disjointed, the essential details of Pron's "impossible to create"
novel are here, and they equally implicate father and son. Reading, writing,
and war: he catalogues the authors in his parents' library: Sarmiento, Che
Guevara, Cortázar, Walsh, Viñas, but not Bullrich, Ocampo, Sábato; recur-
ring words are *tactic, strategy, struggle, Argentina, Perón, revolution* (Pron
29–31). "Once again" this catalogue is repeated in the subsequent chapter; the chapter after that one is missing, and then we are returned to the
narrator's listing of medicines that support his regime of oblivion. In one
of his father's books a passage is underlined: *I have fought the good fight, I*
have finished the race: I have kept the faith. The narrator slices through layers of self-imposed forgetting to recall biblical chapter four, verse seven of
Paul's letter to Timothy (Pron 33). He thinks that possibly it consoled his
father, or maybe it was intended as an epitaph; and he thinks that if "the fog
of pills dissipated for moment so [he] could know who [he] was," he too
would select that verse for his gravestone.

But then I thought that I hadn't really fought, and that no one in my
generation had fought . . . my father's generation had been different,
but, once again, there was something in that difference that was also
a meeting point, a thread that went through the years and brought

us together in spite of everything and was horrifically Argentine: the feeling of parents and children being united in defeat. (Pron 34)

These reflections on collective shame give way to the narrator's first performed action in the novel, which takes place as he watches his mother prepare dinner. In exhaustive detail, he writes out the recipe—"a relic of a time of procedures, of a time of precise and punctuated steps, so different from those days of pain that blunted us all" (Pron 35). This emphasis on action over nomenclature is sustained until the end, when finally he says, "meat loaf," comfort food to be sure. The recipe is the first important document in the novel. But any expectation that his mother will be a repository of memory is quickly dashed, for later while they are watching a film—a Grade B horror/crime movie hinging on induced amnesia—she suddenly blurts out that she'd seen it before, "when your father left me hiding" (Pron 40). This shock impels the narrator to write down everything he remembers of his family life—details of childhood sicknesses, ephemeral vegetarianism, and so on, which arise out of chronological order. Again, chapters will be missing. The first part of the novel culminates with the narrator's entry into his father's study, where he will find an item that he describes with spot-on precision: his young father playing a guitar next to a young woman—not his wife—with an expression that evinced impatience with sitting for a picture; "she had to fight and die young." He has no idea what that's all about, but he has seen into the heart of the story he is trying to both to tell and not tell: "*certain things you never want to own*" (Pron 48–49).

Part II abounds in documentary evidence, much of it from *El Trébol*, the local newspaper of record (we are in the province of Santa Fe, the nearest city being Rosario, which for some unexplained reason Pron calls *osario). The narrator's father, a longtime investigative journalist, has written many of the articles in the carefully assembled folders the narrator examines. The narrator goes through the materials slowly and often repetitively, piecing together the oddments and clues that I will summarize here: one Alberto José Burdisso, "a Faulknerian idiot" who cleaned the pool at the local sports club, went missing, as was reported in early June 2008. The father is obsessed with the case—it turns out Alberto's sister, Alicia, is a *desaparecida,* indeed she is the impatient-looking girl in the photo. The media run pieces on Alberto—will he show up? Is he dead? Did the poor simpleton just wander off? Three years ago, he'd received a government indemnity for the disappearance of sister, bought a shabby little house in the country, a small place in town, and an old car—maybe he was just starting over? The town isn't so much afraid for Alberto as for itself: "what emerged was a collective fear, the fear of a recurrence and the fear of losing the almost proverbial tranquility of El Trébol" (Pron 74). Citizens stage a march in the main plaza: "No to Impunity and Yes to Life" is their (traditional human rights) slogan. The search for Alberto goes national; finally, after twenty days, volunteer firemen, acting on a tip from a man out gathering firewood (the narrator's father, it will later be revealed) find Alberto's body. The events are perhaps even more sordid than those in the novels by Gusmán and Plante: a woman, her lover, and her brother had seized on the poor "man with the mind of a child," and, under guise of love and friendship, stripped him of everything he had been able to acquire with his indemnity. Then they brutally murdered him. The town's reaction is notable: for the first time the citizens organize an act of remembrance for Alicia, who went missing, we learn, on June 21, 1977, from the province of Tucumán, a leftist-guerrilla stronghold. Taking its cue from the Mothers of the Plaza de Mayo, the town as an entity signs on as plaintiff in the trial of Burdisso's killers. The prosecutor is a member of H.I.J.O.S. The narrator's father speaks at both Alberto's funeral and at the ceremony for Alicia. We learn that Alicia Burdisso was held in *La Escuelita* (the camp that Alicia Partnoy wrote about so movingly in the novel she wrote about her own experience there.[10] We also learn that in June 2010, the notorious General Benjamín Menéndez was convicted in Alicia's disappearance, his fourth *prisión perpétua* for crimes committed during the dictatorship.

But for the narrator, the case is far from closed. Puzzlingly, he chooses as the Part III epigraph, *Parents are the bones children sharpen their teeth on,"* a quote from Juan Domingo Perón, who betrayed his young leftist followers, letting them be mauled by the party's right-wing "gorillas." There has been no evidence that the narrator's father harbors such violent bitterness. Is it, rather, that the son is calling into question his parents' political touchstone? Or is he circuitously expressing his own guilt? Or does he vent an abiding pessimism that he is trying, against the odds, to defeat? The novel lends credence, but no definitive support, to each of these possibilities.

Why, the narrator wonders obsessively, was his father so obsessed with the case? His sister tells him to visit the city museum on the history of their local press—he watches his father on screen with a mixture of pride and disillusionment at the inability of his own generation to rise to that of their parents. There is a missing chapter and then he remembers that his father used to talk about writing a novel:

> Brief, composed of fragments, with holes where my father couldn't or didn't want to remember something, filled with symmetries . . . the

novel my father would have written wouldn't have been an allegory or domestic fiction or an adventure or a romance, it wouldn't have been a ballad or a coming-of-age novel, it wouldn't have been a detective novel or a fable or a fairy tale or historical fiction . . . It probably wouldn't have been a mystery or a horror novel either, even though those would cause the right amount of fear and grief. (Pron 144–45)

This is the very form of the novel being written by the son. The narrator's resistance to the forms catalogued above and attributed to his father comes from his refusal to betray his parents' idealistic struggle against the conventions of an established genre. The important crime is the social crime, needing a narrative "in the shape of an enormous frieze or with the appearance of an intimate personal story that held something back" (Pron 153). This, perhaps, is the narrator's real inheritance—mysteries within mysteries, crimes within crimes, and no clear way forward.

After these reflections following the trip to the museum, the narrator falls sick, dreaming wildly in fevers that take place in chapters whose numbers are all mixed up.

He wakes, in Part IV, to the rain that gives the novel its title. Bit by bit—and of course all out of order—some crystallizing details emerge from repressed memories. Why, he asks his sister, did their father always go out alone to start the car every morning before letting his kids hop in? Because in those days, she says, amazed that he's forgotten, journalists were finding bombs in their cars; he didn't want us to get blown up. He recalls the elaborate instructions his parents drilled into them: always walk facing traffic, have alternate routes to every destination, never stomp on cardboard left in the street, never repeat anything that was said at home, never talk about the Peronist coat-of-arms painted by his father. He recalls the card he had to wear around his neck with his name, blood type, contact phone numbers; and if anyone tried to pull him into a car, he was to throw this card to ground, and yell his own name as loudly and as long as possible. It dawns on him: his parents' lives were devoted to protecting them in a time of constant terror. He realizes that even in Germany he always walked facing traffic, and wherever he went, he imagined alternate routes. Across oceans and continents and decades, practices and forms remain, even if one doesn't know why. And then there is his parents' lesson in how a story correctly told could save one's life: "Anyone who told his story from beginning to end was doomed because the ability to speak without hesitation—which is so rare in people—was, to their persecutors, much stronger evidence of the story's falseness than if it was about aliens or ghosts" (Pron 180). The way this novel is being written is more than an aesthetic legacy: it's the manifest labor of staying alive.

The final part of the novel is by turns tender and appreciative, benighted and cruel. The narrator tells us he was born in March 1975, less than a year after the death of Perón (on July 1, 1974), whose funeral was marked by torrential rains. Having lost its "father," the Peronist left failed to bring off its revolution. His parents' organization crumbled into nothing. Children, he says, were our parents' "consolation prizes"; they also provided the cover of a normal life, potentially a form of protection under the generals. The statement feels extremely unfair, given what we know of the narrator's parents. It is also extremely immature, which, to his credit, the narrator seems to know, because he keeps delving into his father's papers, finding more and more evidence of a morally admirable and professionally cogent life. He realizes, looking out at the rain, that he *can* tell this story, that he *will*, "because what my parents and their comrades had done didn't deserve to be forgotten, because I was the product of what they had done, and *because their ghost—not the right or wrong decisions [they] had made but their spirit itself—was going to keep climbing in the rain until it took the heavens by storm*" (italics added, Pron 198).

The narrator is rewarded for the feeling, and for the lyricism of its expression. In one of the three final chapters (37, followed by 40 and 41), the narrator's mother has a moment of revelation as she and her son sitting looking at a family album:

> Your father isn't sad that he fought the war: he's only sad that we didn't win . . . Your father would have liked for the bullets that killed our comrades to have traveled a long distance, not just a few meters, a trajectory that could be counted in thousands of kilometers and in years of journeying, so that we all could have had more time . . . to live and write and travel and have children who wouldn't understand them . . . Your father would have liked for the bullets that killed them to have given them time to live and to leave behind children who wanted to understand and would try to understand who their parents had been and what they'd done and what had been done to them and why they were still alive. . . . Your father would have liked not to be one of the few who survived, because a survivor is the loneliest person in the world. . . . Perhaps he thought, as he sometimes did: "At least it's in writing," and that whatever was in writing would be a mystery and would make my son search for his father and find him, and also find those who shared with his father an idea that could only

end badly. That in searching for his father he would understand what happened to him and to those he loved and why all that makes him who he is. (Pron 201–203)

What I find so extraordinary about this passage is that it is not offered as an epiphany; it is an ordered recitation of the facts of this couple's quietly valiant life.

The best of the detective, documentary, family, and social novels are all present in Pron's book, as are elements of the *bildungsroman*, and the tale of the prodigal son. For all of his resistance, Pron has found a way to satisfy many of the conventions he rails against. The father survives; everyone in the family gets to speak. The immediate crimes in question are solved, the perpetrators are brought to justice in civilian courts; personal and public archives have been kept and made available; individuals and communities get a second chance to rise up in the face of fear and make their appeal to the law.

And yet, as I wrote earlier, the generic tensions get resolved in a way that raises yet more questions. The narrator certainly matures over the course of the novel; he returns to the fold without disowning his professional and personal base in Germany. And yet Pron concluded that the only way to solve the problems he encountered in making this book was to submit it to his parents for their corrections and permission for publication in Argentina (it was originally brought out in Spain).

"Setting the Record Straight: My Father's Version" is a careful, tactful, and interesting text: Pron *padre* is a stickler for Spanish grammar; he corrects small details; he is philosophical: "That a generation thinks it lost—or won—a battle implies an adolescent arrogance that falls away in adulthood, when you understand that *Homo sapiens* has been on this planet for thousands of years." He clarifies that he *did* read Silvina Bullrich, Victoria Ocampo, and Sábato, but wouldn't give them space on his bookshelves. He clarifies certain political positions, and supplies some of the slang used in their organization. He wholly rejects the notion that children were their consolation prize, and suggests, "out of respect to all parents who went through those historical circumstances, that the contents of section 13 be reformulated and section 14 consequently adapted." But he also appreciates the need for a fictive form, and the potentially distorting dynamics of that form, as a foil for the hard truths that need to be purveyed. The father's tone is one of adult cooperation, and it is established by the father, whose son who had deferentially requested "correction."

Pron *hijo* continues the Addendum through May 2013. His work did indeed lead to other discoveries: it turns out that El Trébol had three activists disappeared for political reasons. The Addendum suggests that the history of this small, tranquil, neighborly place is far richer, more complicated, and perilous than a single book could communicate. While I remain uncomfortable with Pron's relinquishing the responsibilities of authorship, I certainly agree that no one book should aspire to tell the whole story.

To Set the Record Straight

For all their differences, the novels by Gusmán, Plante, and Pron have a real kinship. They arise from the same political/social substrate, though each is situated in its particular moment (c. 2000, 2004–06, 1972–2008, respectively); they take place outside of Buenos Aires, in locations that are fairly unusual in urbane literary Argentina; they have roots in the same body of literature; they are explicitly aware that the reader has either lived through much of the history in play, or has indirect, communal, or imposed memories of the events in question. In Gusmán's novel, which takes place in the years of impunity, the suppression of history and the triumph of evil seem all but predetermined, until we remember that a son has courageously turned the quarry where his parents were murdered into an accusatory grave. Plante and Pron demonstrate that issues of major moral and historical importance go dormant, and explode, in ways that seem almost random: had Raúl's life not been stunted by forces beyond his control, Dani's origins would have gone undiscovered. Had her poor defenseless brother not been murdered, Alicia's case would never have come to trial; had the elected government not tried to "make amends" by paying indemnities to the relatives of *desaparecidos*, Alberto would likely be alive. Each of these novels is quite specifically focused; reading them together both widens and deepens our field of vision. And they remind us: "history" cannot be reduced to the raw data of isolated events or even to the patterns of events, though these, of course, must be registered and documented to the extent possible. The ways in which we think about what happens is also part of history: our anxieties, dreads, and dreams; the precepts, categories, and genres that help us organize our thoughts and feelings; the ways in which we both resist and seek to recover individual and collective memories. "History" is the play of rupture and continuity: we struggle to articulate happenings whose depth, complexity, and horror strain effability. And that agon is the battle for life.

Notes

1. *Ni muerto has perdido tu nombre.* Buenos Aires: Sudamericana, 2002.
2. *Una mancha más.* Buenos Aires: Adriana Hidalgo, 2011. The English translation, in preparation by Andrea Labinger, will be called *Murder of a Different Stripe.* A fine interview with Labinger is found at: *http://wordswithoutborders. org/dispatches/article/the-translator-relay-andrea-g.-labinger.*
3. *Mis padres siguen subiendo en la lluvia.* Madrid: Literatura Mondadori, 2011, and New York: Vintage Español, 2011. *My Fathers' Ghost Is Climbing in the Rain,* translated by Mara Faye Lethem, New York: Alfred A. Knopf, 2013.
4. Walsh's work is terribly under-represented on these shores. The first English edition of Walsh's *Operation Massacre* was published in Daniela Gitlin's fine translation in 2013. See my essay on the book at: http://lareviewofbooks.org/ essay/el-nuevo-periodismo-and-the-dirty-warhttp://lareviewofbooks.org/ essay/el-nuevo-periodismo-and-the-dirty-war
5. Translations from Gusmán's novel are my own. Page numbers refer to the Spanish edition.
6. Labinger's translation is not yet published; the English renderings from Plante's novel are my own.
7. Feitlowitz, *A Lexicon of Terror: Argentina and the Legacies of Torture* (2011), 303, and Note 7, 370: David Rock, "Racking Argentina," *New Left Review,* no. 17 (Sept.–Oct. 2002), 55–86.
8. Pron, "Setting the Record Straight: My Father's Version (English)," http:// patriciopron.blogspot.com/p/setting-record-straight-my-father's . . .
9. Sábato was appointed by President Alfonsín to chair the National Commission on the Disappeared, which researched and published *Nunca Más,* which facilitated the 1985 trials of the ex-commanders and served as a model for investigations elsewhere in Latin America.
10. Partnoy's novel about the experience was published as *The Little School,* 1986.

7

Acts of Opening, Acts of Freedom: Women Write Mexico 1968 (Roberta Avendaño's *On Freedom and Imprisonment*)

Susana Draper

I would like to start by suspending for a moment the common consensus that memory is necessary for democracy to work, in order to point to a less intuitive observation: that is, the link between memory and democracy can become extremely complex and problematic, especially when obsessive remembrance is sometimes seen as a duty that cannot be questioned. In some cases, such overabundance leads to a peculiar form of amnesia or else, as Walter Benjamin has shown, it keeps alive the memory created by the oppressors—memories that do not interrupt or unsettle the present status quo in which people imagine, construct, or whitewash the past. As Peter Winn argues in his chapter, a necessary effort that we need to make when creating our cultural historization of the past consists of turning the idea of a politics of memory into a *memory of politics*. In order for memory to be linked to rethinking democracy, we need to accept that images of the past can "suspend" the normal logic of the present in which they emerge, interrupting and questioning it. The recurrence of the past is always tied to a labor of re-creation that, following Marjorie Agosín's powerful images, weaves the old pieces and threads anew, creating the *arpillera* of a present. However, there is a problem when a society dwells obsessively on major massacres, since the power of interruption they represent produces a sense of impotence—although these recollections uncover a problem in the past, their effect is to freeze or paralyze the present. As the editors state in the introductory chapter, "coming to terms with history is a difficult task, fraught with ambiguity, uncertainty, misunderstanding, and the potential for failure" (Grindle). At the same time, there is a liberating force in taking ambiguity, uncertainty, misunderstanding, and failure as essential components of any form of remembrance. This approach would leave the idea of a pure and original past aside; instead, we would come to understand that the past can only be actualized through the new, different forms that emerge from an *agon* of the life of the past and the present, to borrow the idea posed by Marguerite Feitlowitz in her analysis of literature. Therefore, I propose here to approach the relationship between memory and democracy from the viewpoint of a remembrance of the events of 1968 Mexico that focuses on a desire for social justice—a memory of politics that cannot approach democracy without problematizing persisting forms of social inequality.

In *May 68 and Its Afterlives*, Kristin Ross writes that the memorializing boom that has taken place in recent decades has meant that "we automatically associate memory of the recent past with memory of atrocity (trauma). This makes the idea of people working together to take charge of their collective lives sound unfamiliar. It also makes us wonder how to 'figure' a memory that brings pleasure, power, excitement, happiness, disappointment—instead of trauma" (Ross 2). Indeed, when we talk of processes of remembrance in Latin America, we often automatically assume that they involve memories tied to horror. So how can we think *also* about movements for social change, about the joint efforts of a group of people, about their conflicts and ambiguities? We need a form of remembering that is capable of moving beyond the realm of spectacle to include memories that are more communal and collective, of less epic moments.

Thus, I am interested in exploring whether the excessive insistence on remembering atrocity can sometimes cancel out the transformative potential of a notion of democracy. As Friedrich Nietzsche argues in his essay on the use of history for life, the overabundance of a certain kind of memory destroys the possibility of linking it either to a demand in the present or perhaps to a different way of relating to the past.[1] I propose that the link between memory and democracy must transcend both to connect with that which was-not, that which is still unfulfilled in the past and the present. In bringing the possibility of "opening up" the past to other figurations, I wish to perform a temporal displacement, de-centralizing the role that the spectacular massacre of Tlatelolco in Mexico has had in the historization of the movement. So, I pose the question of what happens if we approach '68 and its promise of democracy by suspending the primacy of that event. By that I don't mean suspending belief in its existence, which is and was absolutely real and terrible. But precisely because it was a great massacre, the state that committed it in effect succeeded in creating a certain dominant memory of '68 for future decades, one that blocks the radical questioning of politics involved in that historical event—which was above all a moment of challenge to and problematizing of democracy. That is to say, in the history of Mexico's social struggles the state seems to define a domain of activity punctuated by the persistence of massacres. What happens is that in the end, even though it is in negative terms through association with death, horror, fear and sadness, the state is the one to frame and teach what was, in the words of philosopher José Revueltas, the most important political event of the 20th century in Mexico.[2]Thus, by determining the predominant social memory of the Tlatelolco massacre, the state maintains its control and surveillance of the '68 movement. In this context, opening up a space of freedom in terms of rethinking the historical event involves a struggle to extend, stretch, and counter-position the calendar.

The Sixties in the Nineties

What memory is generated by such a leap in time, what image of '68 appears, and in what sense does it involve overturning official memories and counter-memories?

The thirtieth anniversary of 1968 generated a series of "after-images" of '68. One is the classic text by one of the most important leaders of the movement, *La estela de Tlatelolco* by Raúl Alvarez Garín, perhaps the best-known book published in connection with the anniversary; it was accompanied by other texts that remain marginalized, two of which drew my attention because they focused on female figures.[3] I refer to *Amuleto* by Roberto Bolaño and *Sobre la libertad y el encierro* (*On Freedom and Imprisonment*) by Roberta "Tita" Avendaño.[4] Both have for one reason or another been displaced: *Amuleto* has been seen as problematic for focusing the memory of '68 Mexico on the character of Auxilio Lacoutoure, an Uruguayan poet with no published work and no immigration papers.[5] The novel narrates the work of imagination of Auxilio composed while she hides in the bathroom of the UNAM (national autonomous university of Mexico) in September 1968, for over ten days, during which the facility is constantly besieged by the riot police. She confesses that she is obsessed with thinking about encounters that had never taken place, engaged in the impossible task of imagining what would have happened if . . . (instead of contemplating that which actually occurred). History emerges in this literary form as an open process of imagination that opens possibilities and forces us, readers, to keep expanding on this exercise. Bolaño seems to suggest the idea of a relationship between the promises of truncated pasts (that which never took place) *and the task of imagining the structure of a historical moment from there.*

Avendaño's work, *Sobre la libertad y el encierro,* has dropped out of print and has become a ghost text (to the point where Avendaño's own son is asking for help locating a copy). She links 1968 to 1998 in a text that reconstructs her experience in a women's prison two months after the Tlatelolco massacre and one month after the end of the university strike. What is intriguing is that the text does not limit itself to the year 1968, but points to a problem that was current at the time it was written, in the 1990s. Clearly, the problem we are considering here is how to evaluate these ways of constructing the past three decades later. What are the subterranean struggles in these texts and how do they defy the logic of society that conserves or maintains "a" memory (the one belonging to the males, the leaders, the accepted parties, etc.)? How does Avendaño's text serve to link memory and democracy? How do we pass from memory to democracy? Or, in other words, how does this construction affect how we think about "democracy"? How do we examine the call for democracy that characterized the student movement from the point of view of one of the few women to write about its history?

Why are these textual memories important?

In 2002, one of the few women on the National Strike Committee, Ignacia Rodríguez, remarked in an interview with *La Jornada*: "Discrimination against women in '68 was truly massive. Our participation was crucial (. . .). But even so, *it was only the men who spoke for the movement.*"[6] There is a sense of ownership or monopoly of the word-memory that persists decades after the fact, and which makes it important to explore the role of these women in order to combat the inequality that still persists. By doing so, we un-focus the dominant counter-memory and problematize the ownership of meaning that we see in the memories of the leftist male students and leaders, in order *to hear questions that did not emerge in that register.*[7]

In these pages I explore the question of what happened when the first generation of women to arrive *en masse* on the political scene *wrote about* that experience. This is a question that is barely raised in mainstream scholarship on 1968, which usually mentions women as part of an overall model in which many "minorities" were claiming their rights. But what form does 1968 take when it is seen from the perspective of those who were not seen to be there?

This is a point made by Sheila Rowbotham in the introduction to her book *Promise of a Dream: Remembering the Sixties* (2001) in which she states:

"Many obvious questions about the left in the sixties have simply never been asked and many areas of political and social experience have been curiously ignored. For example, amidst all the words expended on the sixties, women make very limited entrances, usually as legs in miniskirts. Radical young women suddenly arrive in the record during the seventies as the Women's Liberation movement emerges. But what of us in the sixties? Where did all those ideas about reinventing ourselves come from after all?" (Rowbotham, xii)

There is a basic air of impropriety at work, because women were entering a space that did not belong to them and this provoked a discomfort that shows up in some texts.

On Freedom, the Text

Roberta Avendaño was a schoolteacher and a law student. Although she was involved in grass-roots social movements prior to 1968, it was only then that her name started becoming better known, as she was one of the very few women to act as spokesperson on the National Strike Committee.[8] In January 1969 she was arrested and held in various clandestine centers until she was incarcerated, first in Lecumberri and then in the Women's Prison along with common prisoners. Sentenced to sixteen years in jail, she was paroled two years later in 1971 under a special amnesty (although the charges were not dismissed then).

Her text says almost nothing about the university or the massacre. It starts with her arrest and is mostly devoted to describing life in the women's prison. Unlike the classic '68 prison memoir *Los días y los años*, by Luis González de Alba, in Avendaño's text there is absolutely no trace of a militant poetics or images of the heroic nature of life in jail. Instead, most of the text consists of stories about the lives of the common prisoners she lived with, talked to, and befriended. The student movement is mentioned at the beginning, when she is detained along with other women for participating in the protests, and in the final pages, when she analyzes the six points in the student manifesto and reaffirms their validity.

This matches other narratives by middle-class women prisoners at that time, such as *Oblivion* by Uruguayan writer Edda Fabbri (also published decades after she was freed), which speak explicitly of the need to distance themselves from the militant prison epic of the dominant (male) memory. As Graciela Sapriza notes, usually the women's testimonies feature figures that focus more on daily life and the affects. These alternative descriptions are powerful, because by avoiding social stereotypes, they create an alternative, more nuanced "figure" or model for analyzing the political struggles of the past. At the same time, though, it is hard not to fall into the usual narrative of women in their domestic environment, taking care of others, which reproduces another stereotype (men as politically active and women being devoted to domestic concerns: the epic versus the common). However, we need to take a closer look at what these micro-political memories imply and state. By "micro" I mean not "little" but texts that pose zones of ambiguity, ones that are less easy to categorize.

At this level, the omission of politics in terms of the "main events" of the movement could make for a more difficult task for us, the readers, who may wonder: where is the political in this text? How can we read "1968 politics" from within a very specific situation of non-political imprisonment? By "reading" I mean a task of interpretation such as Avendaño undertakes when she takes the life in prison as a complex system of signs that make her, a teacher and a law student, feel that she is totally unprepared to "make" sense of the situation. There is an interaction and a reality that *exceed* not only her experience as a political activist but also as someone who was being trained to impart knowledge (as a teacher) and to practice law (as a lawyer). In this text, displacement triggers a different experience of the political by problematizing freedom, that is, what we understand by freedom and how we experience it.

This problem relates to the central role played by the common prisoners in Avendaño's text, which is striking, and which makes an interesting contrast with another account given by Ignacia Rodríguez, who says that when she was in prison she was petrified, shut up in her cell, afraid of being sexually abused, and constantly schemed about how to escape with Avendaño. However, Avendaño herself only mentions the idea of a possible escape in passing, saying: "we live in a country that's like a great big prison. Where would I go?" (*Sobre la libertad,* 133). In a way, in *Sobre la libertad,* we go from a way of thinking about those "other" women as "abject" in words that project fear and disgust (prostitutes, criminals, lesbians), to a text that starts getting closer to that "other" side, that seems to function as a bridge to another place, a bridge being built through words and affects.[9] There is an emphasis on creating dialogues, using language to construct a way of communicating with that otherness that is beginning to constitute the everyday. *The women who live in jail open up a universe that had no place in the democratic demands of '68, as if they were an underworld in which the "common" had nothing to do with the "political."*[10]

At the same time, *it is necessary to search for the ways in which the micro-political accounts Avendaño uses connect to a bigger, motley picture (a fragmentary totality) in order to avoid reading them as just "anecdotes."* Here I feel that Avendaño is talking about the key element that most of the critics mention about 1968: the moment in which connections among the groups that were not connected took place. This is something that does not happen in the male narrative accounts, and José Revueltas's "The apando" is one of the best examples of such a mind set, depicting the common prisoners as criminals without hope. In Avendaño the issue is not hope, but *establishing a net that links specific stories, names, lives, to a situation* (producing a figurative diagram). Free women suddenly found themselves in their own little prisons of racist, classist and sexist idealism. However, the strength of *Sobre la libertad* is that it does not fall into mere melodrama, or end by showing us a simplistic liberation in which barriers are broken down and justice assumes a comforting textual shape.

The present from which Avendaño writes, the late nineties, is presented as almost worse. As we go with her, now a lawyer, to visit prisoners in jail, she says that there are more and more detention-containment centers, and more inequality: ". . . just like everything else in our country, things in the jails have gotten worse; now there are multiple buildings for 'containing' criminals. How many more will they have to build? . . . They're happy just to lock people up, but they don't care about the conditions. They pompously call them Re-adaptation Centers, but readapting to what?" (143). In dwelling on the facts of prison life, the text problematizes what was once assumed to be "given" and revolutionary about the movement in the world of public politics. Such assumptions were contested and resisted in different ways in the personal reflections of the leading figures of the movement. As the initial division between "political prisoners" and "common prisoners" started to blur, this blurring is at once shown, expressed and processed in Avendaño's narrative.

This dual scheme (political–common) can be seen in the very structure of the text, in the organization and problematic unfolding of the prison experience: Avendaño begins with her kidnapping, clandestine detention and interrogation, her transfer to Lecumberri, the prison in which most of the men in the student movement were held, and her transfer, along with other women friends, to the Women's Prison. She then talks about the first "common" women prisoners she saw and the visit from her parents, who were indignant and in tears because they could not understand how the first woman in the family to go to college could be in jail (25). After her parents' visit, she describes the spatial separation between the "politicals" (who were all on one floor) and the "common prisoners" (in the rest of the building) and recounts the first dialogue that took place, about cleaning. A common prisoner, Martha, comes up to tell them what part of the prison they are supposed to clean, whereupon Avendaño writes: "I gave her the spiel, but she couldn't have cared less that we were Political Prisoners, so we had to come to an understanding of something like 15 or 20 pesos a week, to pay whoever did the cleaning for us. Once this conflict was resolved we went up to the cell to sleep" (29). The reference to "the spiel" in the text implies that people in the movement had talked about the issue of cleaning and that the "politicals" had decided that they were not obliged (qualified) to do such basic tasks. Here, the fundamental distinction between "common" and "political" is staged in terms of a division of labor in the prison, as manual and mental labor.

Another issue is the fear of being raped by a group of lesbians. The writer then describes her first nights as "pandemonium," little hells that show up again and again the division between her kind of prisoners and the others. The tone of the text lightens: the escape of a common prisoner, "Sharon," emerges, in Avendaño's words, as a "moment of relaxation and diversion" that distracts from the monotony (40). After this incident the text becomes more fluid. Dialogue with the "common" prisoners starts to displace the "political" prisoners entirely from the rest of the text, to the point that almost all the following chapters are organized in terms of the names of different "common" friends that Avendaño makes in prison, and whose stories she tells.

What does this textual displacement tell us? How should we read this gradual erasure of the protective distinction that created fear and political shame? After Sharon's escape, Avendaño proceeds to talk about Tlatelolco for the first time. The massacre re-emerges in the context of the prison by way of a common prisoner who was kept in the isolation area for "crazies." She heard that some political prisoners had arrived and wanted to see them, so Avendaño and her companions were asked to go to that area. The woman asked:

> "Are you the students?" "Yes," we answered, and then she said to us, "Haven't you seen my daughter then? She's a brunette, with short hair . . . she's a college student, haven't you seen her? No? You must have! She went to the demonstration and hasn't come back, tell her it's time to come back now . . ." I couldn't say yes to her question, I couldn't bring back that poor mother's daughter . . . and tell her where she was; does anyone know? Do the people who massacred her on October 2, 1968, even know? That mother went crazy with pain at the loss of her daughter . . . (41)

After this little story Avendaño starts to focus on the other prisoners, as if something unsaid had happened to cause a complete shift in the way the text is organized. It goes from an "I" who is separate and protected by the distinction "political" to a person who experiences a connection to the "others"—those who, like this woman, were animalized by the police (a perception that Avendaño herself had held, as seen in her depiction of the "common" prisoners at the beginning). There is a curious split in the text in which the beliefs of a university student full of ideas about emancipation collide with her inner view that coincides with that of the police who imprisoned her/ them. At the same time, the "crazy" mother who was confined and isolated for searching for her daughter who died in the massacre may resonate with Avendaño's own story, since her own mother died shortly after she was incarcerated. Thus, affects starts to take precedence over the *a priori* distinctions, putting to the test the whole "lesson" that the movement had tried to teach society, without seeing that they were reproducing the stereotypes they were supposedly trying to eliminate.

A complex system of splits takes place in the text, dramatizing in the organization of words and chapters a reflections about two separate worlds that are gradually getting closer. As time passes, a gap opens up between the political experience and the experience of life in jail. Visits become more sporadic and the funds sent by the movement start to dwindle. Avendaño writes how after a while she starts looking for ways to work because she has run out of money: she bakes bread to sell on Saturdays, and she makes stuffed monkeys, flip-flops, and necklaces in order to earn money. This generates a time frame in which the student "movement" is stopped, everyone returns to normal life, and those who remain in jail have to learn to deal with life in that context.

In another chapter, Avendaño begins to tell us about the friends she was starting to make and the solidarity they felt at times, as well as the support that many of them provided when she received the news of her mother's death. She confesses that before prison, her friends were mostly other people "like her" (middle-class students) and she had no friends outside that milieu, so her jail time opens up another world of social relations that changes her understanding of friendship: "I met many friends in jail, it was a new world for me" (63).

A second split occurs in the middle of the text, as this dynamic emerges. It is also related to a story of freedom when Amparo, a common prisoner, is set free after serving a 15-year sentence. This causes the writer sadness-happiness because once women are freed, the outside world "swallows" them up and they do not stay in contact, making the ones who remain imprisoned feel betrayed or abandoned. At the same time, as the text advances, we can also sense a shift in the way *temporality is* described and experienced when she narrates the lives of the other prisoners. Here, a certain form of cyclical rhythm characterizes the non-political prisoners' life-scheme, a sort of common pattern: they are in jail; they are freed; they go outside but then eventually they go back to prison, with guilt and shame. The prison seems to work like a destiny and the only real form of freedom seems to be the moment of death.

This relates to what I see as the third split in the text, which is also connected to freedom, but this time, a freedom that is related to death: it involves a tragic case of an old woman who was unjustly imprisoned because she lived in a shanty town and had altars with candles that set off a fire. Her house burned down and so did the lamp post next to it, which belonged to the state. The woman was put in prison for committing a crime against state property. After years in jail, she died and nobody came to claim her body. The prisoners carried the coffin, which was paid for by the state, to the main door and when they got there they yelled, according to Avendaño: "She's going out free." This rather chilling image evokes a freedom that does not coexist with life.

This image points to a division of space both in and out of prison, as if they were two almost incommensurable realities. The story of the little old woman who dies and is mourned and carried to the prison outer door by prisoners proclaiming that she is "leaving free" communicates a sentiment that forces us to question what freedom means in this text that uses the word as its title. What does freedom "en-title"? What experience is "en-titled" in this way?

On Freedom "and" Imprisonment

The book's title mentions freedom and imprisonment, but it seems as if the text describes only of the experience of imprisonment. What is the role of freedom in this act of remembering? How is it linked to the 68 movement and its re-formulation of the theory and practice of freedom outside the monopoly of liberalism? How is it possible that memories of prison should be the most intense expressions of a movement that was characterized by its passionate defense of freedom and its attempt to redefine the meaning of democracy? If the sixties involved a widespread takeover of the public and private spaces (the street and the universities, factories and workplaces), what is the metaphorical role of the prison?

An answer may be found in one aspect of the 68 movements in different parts of the world: the possibility they raised of an encounter between groups and classes that did not generally interact. As Ross points out, one of the keys to '68 lies in a "crisis of functionality" in the logic of social place (25); that is, a case of dislocation that involved finding power in unexpected places, instead of following the script of one's given social identity. Along these lines, Alain Badiou adds: "if a new emancipatory politics was possible, *it would turn social classifications upside down. It would not consist in organizing everyone in the places where they were, but in organizing lightning displacements, both material and mental*" (60; my emphasis).

A political practice of this kind involves questioning social roles and the meaning of knowledge in a social context, in other words, the way in which "communication" between unequals is managed, at once possible and impossible. It is interesting that there has been a lack of attention to the ways that this relationship is configured in terms of gender. When Revueltas and Eduardo Valle, Ross, and Badiou discuss how the key to '68 lies in the desire for encounter between unequals, they provide only general categories involving class and social place, such as workers, students, peasants, metropolis, colonies, etc., but they show no interest in examining anything *beyond those categories*. Thus, in the theory about '68, analysis of dislocation has not managed to dislocate the way in which social classification as such operates (that is, the configuration of the categories themselves). We need to examine *the multiple, unequal and hierarchical composition of each category*, and how proximity of people in categories that were not normally close began to emerge via the forging of a language that was generally made up of fragments of unequal experiences. (Does this "communicability" affect men and women, homosexuals and heterosexuals, working-class women, peasant women and students equally?) I am intrigued by the fact that although theoreticians of '68 have stressed the mingling of unequals, there is very little interest in analyzing the specific ways in which these encounters took place, or in how a common language was starting to be created.

To Avendaño the prison exposed a sense of the "unreality" of her earlier perception of the university as a privileged source of knowledge; this sense may be related to the fact that it was in prison (and not in the activist life outside of it) that class and sexual differences were perceived in such proximity, as part of the everyday life. The obsession of marking the difference between "political" and "common" prisoners that permeates the first pages of the text may be related to the class difference that was masked by the theoretical concept of a comfortable struggle for egalitarian politics. While the different '68s sought to produce egalitarianism or social leveling at both the micro- and the macro-level, this became more feasible at other equally important levels: "the personal is political," young versus old, the new way of living and political organizing versus the traditional form of left and right. *However, this leveling is perhaps the most vital form of interpellation in prison.*

Still, the question that remains involves the first part of the title *Sobre la libertad,* "On Freedom," about which little is said explicitly in the text, although it suggests a way of thinking about freedom: not as a "goal" (getting out of jail) but as a type of experience. When she talks about escaping, Avendaño says that since the country is one great jail, there is nowhere to escape to. Thus she differentiates between freedom as something that occurs in space (getting out, being free, being freed, literally "put into freedom" in Spanish), and freedom as a non-permanent mode of experience. There is a paradoxical element in this freedom that emerges from the experience of dispossession and exposure to what is outside the language of political emancipation. There is the freedom that we associate with the ability to exercise one's own will (I'm free because I can decide/determine), and then there is a freedom that she finds in the experience of not "being" who she usually is.

In Avendaño's text we perceive a shift of position from abjection to a sense of the oddness of life on the outside, which makes the prison space look like a distortionof the "ideal" that '68 sought to construct: in the mingling of classes and of different people. In this context, freedom seems to have less to do with willpower (sovereignty, property) and more with the development of the ability to connect that emerges from being exposed to different women, to being that is not symmetrically similar to oneself— exposure to non-analogous others without essentializing their otherness. At the same time, freedom that comes from an event that was not supposed to happen in a "normal" life has little to do with the experience of freedom as something "nice" or happy. In a way, it involves learning from the enforced necessity of connecting and communicating with the other. But what can be learned from the exposure of what is "outside" of socially legitimized knowledge?

At the end of the book, Avendaño talks about two types of knowledge: the knowledge learned in formal education and the knowledge acquired by living through this peculiar form of '68. She says: "Experiences that are enriching, that you get when you start searching for truth, for integrity, when you start trying to put into practice *what they told you at school,* and you get a painful awakening to reality (. . .) not the one in the speeches and on TV, but *the one people live in, the one you live in, the one that tears you apart and beats you up; those realities don't match up and then you've got a dilemma: which do I choose? The one I was given or the one I find?* And your life is decided, and what they gave you as a punishment to discourage you *becomes your strongest support*, it's true, it's true! (. . .) Here, next to injustice, I've grown strong, although I've also despaired of finding an echo in people, [a recognition] that they shouldn't permit this" (144, emphasis mine). Following up from this quote, can we say that this was Avendaño's singular university of '68?

Here, I am interested in the role played by the encounter in these narratives and how freedom follows from there, as if it were related to a dislocated form of knowledge (a knowledge transposed to an "improper" place). This form is not internal or personal but results from an alternative form of communication that emerges in the final text as another "school" of learning. Reflecting on it three decades later, it is still a space of forced encounters that creates friendship among those who are not *socially related (the relationship between subjects who coexist in society without seeing, speaking to, or connecting with one another)*. Thus, the '68 that emerges in this text has less to do with the student movement as such—as something that began in August and ended in December. Perhaps for Avendaño this no longer made sense in 1998. But the question about democracy that was the basis for the movement arose out of a problem of inequality that is still unresolved, and which makes it increasingly difficult to create links or bridges among people, languages, and struggles.

When Avendaño articulates the promise of the past within the context of a present, she confronts the meaning of exposure to what remains distant—outside the university, outside the law. Memory, in this case, helps to bring (once again) the problem of democracy within the context of social injustice, re-elaborating an image of 1968 that insists on one of its most singular elements within the history of Mexico—the beginning of a conversation among unequals, the ones who had remained outside both the discourse of the state and the dominant memory of the male leaders.

Notes

1. I refer to the idea of memory for life and action that is discussed in "On the Utility and Liability of History for Life," in opposition to a form of antiquarian memory that accumulates data and leads to a paralyzing hypertrophy of memory.

2. On the idea of 1968 as a moment that divided history into a before and an after, see the series of voices that emerged in Elena Poniatowska's work, essays by José Revueltas (*México 68: Juventud y revolución*), Gareth Williams' book *Mexican Exception* and the voices compiled by Héctor Aguilar Camin and Hermann Bellinghausen in *Pensar el 68*, among others.

3. For now I will only mention *Pensar el 68*, an anthology of testimonies edited by Hermann Berlinghausen and Hugo Hiriart that was published in 1998. Its memory work is similar to *La noche de Tlatelolco* in that it collects recollections of different participants in the student movement at different times, pre- and post-Tlatelolco (*Pensar el 68*. Mexico: Cal y Arena, 1998).
4. The number of studies of the role of women in Mexico in 1968 is not large, but there is a growing interest in the topic, as shown by articles and doctoral theses. See in particular "La participación de la mujer universitaria en el Movimiento estudiantil de 1968 en México" by Karina Lvone Cruz Flores and "Otra Mirada al 68: Mujeres universitarias en Puebla" by Gloria A. Tirado Villegas.
5. Auxilio emerges in parts of *La noche de Tlatelolco* and also in a diary entry by José Revueltas, who promised to write something about this figure, whom he saw as the incarnation of a unique form of love.
6. Interview of Ana Ignacia Rodríguez, "La Nacha," conducted by Blanche Petrich: "Pelearé hasta que se castigue a los culpables del 68" (*La Jornada Virtual* 22 julio 2002). http://www.jornada.unam.mx/2002/07/22/009n1pol.php?origen =politica.html
7. By counter-memory I mean memories that contest the official, state version.
8. Before the student movement started, Avendaño had taken part in Othón Salazar's teachers' movement in 1958, in the movement at the Normal School in 1960, and then in the protests against the Law Faculty director César Sepúlveda and Chancellor Ignacio Chávez.
9. Also, it's strange that Avendaño does not mention the same activities as Ignacia Rodríguez—the workshops and courses, etc.—and that she emphasizes instead the moments when emotional connections were being made with the "commoners." Her text focuses particularly on the relationship between jail and poverty, and the inability to find, as she says at the end, an "echo" of that concern among her colleagues, her equals, her political peers on the "outside." The temporal distance acts on that distant past in an interesting way.
10. The common appears as a horizon that I propose to read from a materialist feminist stance, in which gender appears, following Christine Delphy, as "a new perspective, not a new object" ("For a materialist feminism," 62), one that links freedom to those categories that were virtually imprisoned also, like the women themselves, in the ideological framework they came with.

References
Alvarez Garín, Raúl, *La estela de Tlatelolco*. Mexico DF: Editorial Grijalbo, 1998.
Avendaño, Roberta, *Sobre la libertad y el encierro*. México: La idea dorada, 1998.
Badiou, Alain, "We Are Still the Contemporaries of May 68," *The Communist Hypothesis*, London: Verso, 2010.
Bolaño, Roberto, *Amulet*. New York: New Directions, 2008.

Delphy, Christine, "For a Materialist Feminism," in *A Materialist Feminism: A Reader in Class, Difference, and Women's Lives*, edited by Rosemary Hennessy and Chrys Ingraham. Routledge, 1997.

Fabbri, Edda *Oblivion*. La Habana: Casa de las Américas, 2007.

González de Alba, Luis, *Los días y los años*. México: Era, 1970.

Nietzsche, Friedrich, "On the Utility and Liability of History for Life," *Unfashionable Observations*, trans. Richard Gray. Stanford: Stanford UP, 1995: 83–167.

Petrich, Blanche, "Pelearé hasta que se castigue a los culpables del 68," *Entrevista con Ignacia Rodríguez, "La Nacha," La Jornada Virtual*, 22 julio 2002. http://www.jornada.unam.mx/2002/07/22/009n1pol.php?origen=politica.html

Revueltas, José, *México 68. Juventud y revolución*. México: Era, 1978.

Ross, Kristin. *May 68 and Its Afterlives*. Chicago: University of Chicago Press, 2004.

Rowbotham, Sheila, *Promise of a Dream: Remembering the Sixties*. London: Verso, 2001.

Sapriza, Graciela, "Memorias de mujeres en el relato de la dictadura (Uruguay, 1973–1985)," *Deportate, esuli, profughe. Rivista telematica di studi sulla memoria femminile*, no. 11, 2009: 64–80.

Valle, Eduardo, *Escritos sobre el movimiento del 68*. Sinaloa: Universidad Autónoma de Sinaloa, 1984.

8

Preserving Maya Oral Literature Through Recorded Memories

Ava Berinstein

Maya oral literature is a rich source for considering the concepts of democracy and memory in the past, present, and future. Yet Maya verbal art is at risk of extinction. Currently, the translation of ancient texts and the art of story telling help to convey Mayan language and culture. Moreover, the transmission of these stories through Indigenous community radio stations plays a central role in community life and the revitalization of Mayan language and culture.

The pages that follow are organized in sections: the first describes a general prehistory of the Mayan people with an introduction to the Q'eqchi' Maya; the second discusses the historical significance of oral literature to Mayan life and thought, tracing its origin to pre-Columbian times; the third examines the variables contributing to the endangerment of the Maya oral tradition. Historically, these variables lead to language shift and ultimately, language death and cultural endangerment. The translation of the pre-Hispanic Q'eqchi' legend "The Dance of the Deer" explains why the ritual Deer Dance is (still) performed and provides an illustration of a rich, poetic oral literature. In the next section I look at modern-day oppression and the continued marginalization of Indigenous peoples in Guatemala, despite the signing of the Peace Accords in 1996. Violence, repression and injustices continue to threaten the Indigenous Maya while limiting their access to the freedom of expression. Here, we consider measures to counter this oppression and propose utilizing community-based radio to help prevent the threat of language ethnocide. In the last part I examine the role of memory in language and cultural preservation and the obstacles that Mayas face to be heard and to have a voice. In particular, community radio and Maya cultural identity are intimately linked to the meaning of democracy. The chapter concludes with future directions for Q'eqchi' research and Indigenous activism.

The Q'eqchi' Maya People's Language and Culture at Risk

The Q'eqchi' Maya are descendants of the ancient Maya civilization that flourished in pre-Columbian times in Mexico and Central America from 1000 B.C.–1500 A.D. Q'eqchi'[1] is the language of the Eastern Mayan K'ichean (formerly spelled Quichean) branch, one of 29 Mayan languages spoken in Guatemala. The formal classification is Proto-Maya/Eastern Mayan/K'ichean-Mamean/Q'eqchi' (Campbell and Kaufman 1985). They are the predominant Maya groups in the central highlands and northern lowlands of Guatemala. There is an estimated population of 400,000 in Northern Alta Verapaz and the southern Petén departments of Guatemala (Lewis 2009), with a total population in all countries including Belize and El Salvador of 423,500. However, population estimates vary widely. According to a UNESCO 2002 census, the Q'eqchi' population in Guatemala and Belize was estimated to be 716,101.

Dialect differences are very slight among regions where Q'eqchi' is spoken, and the "prestige' dialect is spoken in Cobán, Alta Verapaz, where research for this chapter was carried out. The Spaniards founded Cobán in 1543; the town is allegedly named after the Indigenous *cacique*. In this area, Q'eqchi' Maya is the primary language, and few speak Spanish in the villages of the region. The modern history of this region as well as other parts of the country is one of cultural tragedy. In 1954, Guatemala's democratically elected president, Jacobo Arbenz, was ousted by a military coup. A military dictatorship held power during 36 years of civil war. Government troops committed genocide against the largely indigenous Maya rural villagers in an attempt to eradicate support for the opposition guerilla movement. Entire villages were wiped out—men, women, children, and even infants—and some 200,000 Maya were killed (G. Garvin and E. Hegstrom 1999). By 1996, when the Peace Accords were signed, the countryside was impoverished, and people who had been poor before were far poorer. Livestock was decimated; fields neglected; and of the terrorized rural population, few were literate or aware of their rights.

Today Guatemala is a young democracy, and the peace is holding, to a degree. There are, however, large disparities between the five percent of the population who control 80 percent of the country's wealth, and the large, rural, mostly Maya population. Among Guatemala's Maya, 65 percent have a third-grade education or less, and poverty is widespread. Many elderly citizens do not speak or understand Spanish. There are only a few newspapers and a small independent press. Large radio and television stations are owned by a few wealthy organizations that generally hold conservative, business-oriented viewpoints and broadcast only in Spanish.

Mayan Ethnopoetics

Mayan literature is among the oldest in the world. The beautiful and often prosaic verbal expression of the Mayas that has persevered for an astonishing two millennia from pre-Columbian antiquity to the present day (Tedlock 2011) is an archaic footprint of oral literature. The lines are not defined by a systematic meter. Instead, when legends are narrated, there are distinct intonational patterns (Berinstein 1991) used to indicate whether the poetic line is part of a verse. Woven within the verse structure are couplets, triplets, and other alliterative stylistic, and mnemonic devices that define the unique structure of Maya oral literature.

The documentation of Mayan languages and texts helps to elucidate Mayan oral literature, life, and thought, both ancient and modern, including, for example, the study of Proto-Mayan and the study of hieroglyphics (Hull 2002). Indeed, as Tedlock (1985: 202–201) demonstrates through his English translations of the *Popul Vuh* (the K'ichee' Mayan Book of Creation), the codices teach us about Mayan poetics through the different rhythms of words and phrases and the use of pauses. The *Popul Vuh*, originally written in hieroglyphs and transcribed into K'ichee' using the Latin alphabet in the 16th century is a rare example of literary survival from the Spanish Conquest's mass destruction. As translations of the *Popul Vuh* and hieroglyphs illustrate (Tedlock 2011, 1985, Hull 2002), couplets were the primary poetic device used in all varieties of hieroglyphic inscriptions deciphered in scripts and codices dating back to the Classic and post-Classic periods (A.D. 250–1500). This poetic structure continues to be used in modern-day narratives (Schele and Freidel, 1990). And one might hypothesize that the use of such poetic phrases, alternating rhythms, and parallelism (both grammatical and semantic), is what facilitates the memorization of these rich narratives so that they may be recited with the same authenticity today.

Maya Verbal Art: An Oral Tradition at Risk

Today, many factors contribute to the endangerment of the Maya oral tradition. First and foremost, the elders are dying and legends aren't being passed down to the next generation. Another contributing factor is that the younger generation isn't using the native Mayan language. Maya parents are speaking in Spanish to their children rather than in their first language in the hope that this will provide better opportunities for them to succeed in the world. These instincts are reinforced by the fact that "bilingual" education classes are taught in Spanish. Sadly, the message for "success" is: speak Spanish; listen to Spanish radio stations; go to school and receive an education in Spanish; forsake your Mayan culture; forsake your Mayan first language; and, often, forsake your traditional Mayan clothing.

Over time such language shift leads to language death and, for the Maya, despite the vast population, the extinction of verbal expression puts the documentation of this culture at risk. Strengthening signs of language shift that threaten the vitality of Maya spoken language have been observed by England (1998) and others (Bricker 2004, Maxwell 1996), suggesting that Mayan languages be classified among the world's endangered languages.

"The Dance of the Deer," narrated in 1978 by Francisco Choco'oj Paau, demonstrates the role of an oral culture in reviving a cultural history. In the text translation, couplets (and repeating refrains within a verse) are italicized and indented for ease of reference.[2]

What is the meaning behind the Dance of the Deer? The Deer Dancers here in the region of Alta Verapaz, Guatemala, are appointed to carry out a tradition.

According to our ancestors, there was a time when there was a massive drought in our land.

The sacred plants. The sacred trees.
Each of the bushes began to dry out
Each of the animals began to die because of the drought.

All of the animals—the tigers, the monkeys, the raccoons, and the deer saw how it was. They noticed that it was terribly dry and that some among them were dying. They thought that they would petition the divine Tzuul Taq'a, the one who judges in the world,

that he might do us the favor,
that he might grant us our water, our drink.

All of the animals did it. They gathered together. They elected the deer to represent their commission to San Pablo Xukaneb[4] so that he might do the petition before Lord Tzuul Taq'a,

the one who might grant us our drink.

That's the way they did it. The deer represented the animals and they pre-pared themselves for their journey to San Pablo Xukaneb to ask that he consider their petition.

When they were halfway there, the deer found themselves in danger when the tigers blocked their path. The deer needed to do their errand in San Pablo. They realized that they were in the tigers' grasp. They thought, "Who should they ask to help them there in the mountains?" They called the monkeys who lived nearby in the hope that they might come to their rescue.

The monkeys came. In their agility,

they began to tease the tigers.
They began to pull on the tigers' tails.
They began to grab them on the path to confuse them.
They began to trick the tigers

so that there would be time for the deer to escape and go to petition before Tzuul Taq'a.

That is what they did. They arrived at San Pablo Xukaneb in good time. They made their petition. Tzuul Taq'a came.

He granted the water.
He granted the animals their drink.

All of them were saved there.

That is the reason why the symbolic Deer Dance was created in our community.

This free translation introduces the readers to Maya life, customs, and beliefs, as told by "our ancestors" (literally, "our-root our-tree"), for the narrative is the "root" that bridges past and present. The ancient ones (the elders) have passed these legends to each generation. It is the connecting root.

As the legend unfolds and the drought begins, all of the animals understand the significance of this punishment. They understand that they must petition Tzuul Taq'a, the one who judges in the world, for only Tzuul Taq'a has the power to grant us our water, our drink. Tzuul Taq'a is the world; it is "Mother Earth," or the ancestor—or creator—of the world. In this spirit traditional Maya keep the traditions and practices found in literature before they plant their crops, or harvest them, or disturb Mother Earth in any way. Oral literature helps us to understand the past and protect the future. It examines language within a broader context—one that captures the cultural, spiritual, and intellectual life of a people.

Often, historical re-enactments of legends are celebrated through dances; the Dance of the Deer, the Dance of the Moors, and the Dance of the Conquest are performed at the annual celebration of the patron saint. The dances are rooted in a tradition. The ancient Maya commemorated dancing on the monuments (Grube 1992; Looper 2009). The Deer Dance, as it is practiced today, with marimba music, fully adorned dancing deer, dancing monkeys, and dancing tigers, comes alive in local festivals. From the narrative, we learn how important it is to value earth's elements and all of life's living creatures. Animals and plants are revered (*loqlaj:* "holy, sacred") and words that express nature's symbolism are woven into Q'eqchi' language and culture. Indeed, every Mayan legend has a life-lesson, a way to live: practice goodness; be grateful for what you receive; and never take anything (from nature or the earth) without first burning incense and asking for permission. As one Maya educator, Luis Cucul, explained, "Stories always have morals. They always have morals. It's a way of teaching us how to live better; how to live with Mother Nature."

The Maya are mindful. In their legends, when one is mindless and acts without thinking (or acts for himself), there are always consequences. These legends were passed down for hundreds and thousands of years, and it is by word-of-mouth that we have come to learn about Qawa' Tzuul Taq'a, God (Lord Mountain-Valley), the divine lord of the valleys and the mountains (and everything in between), the Creator. And it is by word-of-mouth that the tradition and rituals for planting corn still survive today, are still practiced today, in the way that the ancient Maya described.

Turning the Tide toward Cultural Revival

Building on over 20 years of linguistic documentation with a focus on the grammatical analysis of Q'eqchi' Mayan, my dissertation (Berinstein 1985) was based on a corpus of Mayan oral histories that were collected between 1978 and 1981, primarily in Alta Verapaz, Guatemala. This collection of folktales, legends, and ancestral customs is now fully digitized, transcribed, and translated into English, Spanish, and Q'eqchi'. These memories record ritual Maya practices and reflect thought and cultural values; they now form the corpus for collaborative work with a not-for-profit organization, Cultural Survival, to broadcast folktales on local, Indigenous-led, community-based radio stations in an effort to revitalize the Q'eqchi' oral tradition, language, and culture.

The need to document and disseminate Q'eqchi' Mayan narratives orally is critically important. Only few collections include Q'eqchi' folktales in Spanish (Ajmac Cuxil 1975; Osborne 1965; Shaw 1972). Those written in Q'eqchi' with English translations include Burkitt (1920), Eachus and Carlson (1971), and Freeze (1976), and there is an English-only collection,

Danien (2005). Even if these translations were readily available in Guatemala, how many people could read them?

Instead, imagine the impact on cultural inheritance if Maya legends could be heard on the radio, reaching hundreds or thousands of homes, accessing and connecting with children and their parents together, reminiscent of a time when people gathered together to hear a shaman, priest, or elder of the community convey narrative wisdom, teachings, and rituals practiced by their ancestors. Imagine an Indigenous-led radio story-telling program.

Indeed, radio has the potential to impact change and language revitalization as it is the one medium that binds Guatemalans together. All strata of society listen regularly. The most popular broadcasts are *radionovelas* (radio soap operas), beloved throughout Latin America. In urban areas, large Spanish-language pop stations dominate the airwaves. In the backcountry, however, the need is served by small, local, community-owned and volunteer-operated radio stations. These humble stations are generally housed in a tiny cement-block structure with a single light bulb, the most basic broadcasting equipment, and a low-powered transmitter and radio tower outside in the yard. These tiny stations are the hubs of their communities, broadcasting information provided by non-governmental organizations (NGOs), government agencies, and local sources. These stations offer news about local initiatives, such as the building of a new school, and other events of importance to the local audience.

Community radio stations also foster civic engagement and civil society. As a catalyzing voice, community radio plays many roles, promoting democracy, civic engagement, literacy, and cultural identity. Indigenous community stations are uniquely qualified to choose content to represent their interests and cultural concerns. Often the radio station is the only available instrument to convey critical information about violations of Indigenous peoples' human rights, health, the environment, and ongoing events. Coupled with educational efforts in native communities, community radio story-telling programs have the potential to revitalize language and culture through broadcasting oral literature. Language revitalization refers to the ability to turn "around the decline of language use in particular communities," rather than try to resurrect a language that is little used (Henderson et. al. 2014:76).

When Indigenous Maya narrate and broadcast folktales, legends, and other speech genres on their community-based radio stations, memories are rejuvenated and this encourages local residents to participate in the restoration of customs and traditions. The radio also transmits a shared voice, a shared cultural identity.

Indeed, non-profit community radio plays a critical role in the daily lives of hundreds of thousands of Indigenous people in Guatemala. Francisco Xico, a Mayan priest who volunteers at his local community radio station, says, "The radio helps keep our culture and language alive." Others agree, such as Ancelmo Xunic, a Cultural Survival staffer. Local radio "is by the community, for the community," he commented. Angelica Cubur Sul, a radio volunteer stated, "As an Indigenous woman, I can say that the community radio is the only place that I can express my views and opinions and be sure that they will be heard by the entire town. The Mayor expresses his opinion on our radio, so do the police, and so do I."

Sadly, Indigenous Maya still face many obstacles that prevent them from starting a community-based radio station. First and foremost, the Guatemalan Telecommunications Law does not allow special licenses for non-profit community radio. Because the stations must compete for licenses at public auctions, it would be too expensive for non-profit community stations to procure one. Only commercial radio and government-run radio can operate legally. Representatives of Guatemala's community radio movement have commented on the government's restrictions on community radio, calling it a sign of "monoculturalism, discrimination, and racism," in the words of Alma Temaj, a Maya radio volunteer. Despite hearings at the Inter-American Commission on Human Rights (IACHR) about the freedom of expression of Indigenous peoples in Guatemala, and despite a request that the IACHR urge Guatemala to stop persecuting community radios and close the office of the Attorney General for Radio, whose sole mission is to prosecute unlicensed community radio operators, the Guatemalan Congress has not yet passed legislation to make it possible for Indigenous Maya to operate community radio stations.

Cultural Survival's community radio partners in Guatemala are currently fighting for their right to freedom of expression through community radio. A new bill in the Guatemalan Congress, Bill 4479, proposes a provision in the criminal code that would sanction the imprisonment of individual actors and representatives of unlicensed stations, effectively criminalizing community radio with a penalty of up to 10 years in prison.

Bill 4479 threatens the vitality of dozens of community radio stations that base their existence on the promises made in the Guatemalan Peace Accords and the United Nations Declaration on the Rights of Indigenous Peoples. Since 1996, when the Peace Accords were signed, community radio has become vital for Indigenous groups around Guatemala, and often serves as a communication lifeline. Although the right to this means of communication is clearly defined by the Guatemalan Peace Accords, the

Guatemalan Constitution, and organizations like the United Nations and the International Labor Organization, access to community radio remains restricted. Worse yet, Indigenous community radio stations are frequently targeted in police raids during which expensive equipment is confiscated and radio personnel are arrested.

Recently, Cultural Survival staff visited Radio Damasco in San Pablo, San Marcos, which was raided by the police in mid-November of 2012. Justo Momzom Sali, a member of Radio Damasco, spoke of the raid and what it meant to him, and his feeling of powerlessness in the face of official repression. "Radio Damasco is a necessity for the community. We need to stress how important it is that a space be made for our voices, for the voices of our community." Victor Angel, Director of Radio Damasco, was arrested and imprisoned after the community radio station was raided by police. Similarly, when the police raided the community radio station Doble Via in San Mateo, Quetzaltenango, in October 2012 and confiscated its equipment, it put an end to programming aimed at the construction of peace, protection of the environment, historical memory, Mayan *cosmovisión*, citizenship, community leadership, disease prevention, and much more.

Some organizations, such as the Asociación Mujb'ab'l yol, play an important role in building awareness and in supporting community radio in Guatemala. After the raid, they issued a press release that read: "They can steal the equipment from community radio stations, but they will never be able to silence the voice of the children, youth, men, women, and elders who urge this movement forward. No one is giving up" ("Upside Down World," October 16, 2012). In June of 2014, over 20 Maya community radio representatives gathered at Asociación Mujb'ab'l yol headquarters in San Mateo, Quetzaltenango, to participate in a two-day workshop. Rigoberto Juárez, an Indigenous rights activist and community radio founder of the "Voz Popular," the radio program of the guerrilla movement that provided critical news during the civil war, proceeded to ask all those present what they believed the mission of community radio to be. The consensus was that: "community radios are the voice of the people . . . an instrument of justice and equality . . . a means not an end . . . a tool to the service of the community . . ." With the support of such communities and their leaders, community radio can also help to reverse the impact of language shift and potentially help to revitalize Mayan language and culture.

What Can Be Done?

Let us ask ourselves, what if no one could tell the legends? The consequences would be dramatic, endangering cultural practices, linguistic genres, historical reconstruction, memories, shared histories, religious and ritual practices, folklore, and legends. The roots would be broken and the link between generations severed. And, if no one is narrating, how will memories be formed? How could we preserve the vitality of the linguistic community? How could we help prevent language and culture loss, restore collective memory, and promote cultural identity and community leadership?

In Guatemala, despite vast numbers of Mayan communities that are relatively vital, Indigenous populations remain marginalized with limited access to health, social, educational, cultural, and human rights. The constraints that Maya people face impact the vitality of the language community and cultural identity. This is what contributes to language shift and eventually to language death. The freedom to speak and be heard in one's own language should be an inalienable right; not something that is repressed or subject to political context. Recently, Daniel Pascual, a 42-year-old K'ichee' defender of Indigenous rights and the current president of the Comité de Unidad Campesina (CUC), had to appear at the Constitutional Court of Guatemala accused of libel, slander, and defamation as a result of his work in pursuit of the promises of the Peace Accords; he has been a key supporter of the right to free expression and the legalization of community radio in Guatemala, among other things. Speaking to Congress to demand equal treatment of the Indigenous community and the legalization of the Community Media Bill, Pascual said:

> I consider myself a defender of human rights, and we are all aware that there are constant violations of economic, cultural, social, and environmental issues in our country. In this sense I am firmly convinced that the Universal Declaration of Human Rights of the United Nations recognizes the freedom of expression as a universal right of every person, likewise this is recognized by Article 35 of the Republic of Guatemala. Therefore I've done nothing more than exercise this right over the past 20 years. (www.CulturalSurvival.org/news, July 23, 2014)

While the situation remains difficult for the Q'eqchi' in Guatemala, a more positive story is emerging for the Q'eqchi' in Belize.

Radio Ak' Kutan is a community-based radio station located in Blue Creek, Belize. The station broadcasts in three languages: Q'eqchi' Maya, Mopan Maya, and English. Radio Manager Aurelio Sho is fluent in all three languages and is determined that the Maya voice be heard. This non-profit radio station caters to the needs of all of the communities in the surrounding area. It involves local community members and leaders and broadcasts content overlooked by commercial or mass media broadcasters. It is owned, operated, and driven by the communities served, and it provides a forum for sharing diverse stories and experiences. It is unique in that it ensures unrestricted opportunities for members of the community to produce programs. In fact, the community participates in formulating plans and policies, defining objectives, principles of management, program content, and the administration and financing of the radio station. The community is free to comment and criticize. In essence, the radio promotes cultural identity through cultural agency. The goal of community radio as a cultural agent is to reflect and promote local identity, character, and culture, provide a range of programs with a diverse set of voices and opinions, encourage open dialogue and democratic process, promote development and social change, and encourage sharing of information, innovation, and participation by all.

The Berinstein collection (2013)[3] of Q'eqchi' legends and customs has been digitized and MP3 files have been created. One set of MP3 files was offered to Ak' Kutan Radio for broadcast on their weekly storytelling program in Q'eqchi'. The impact on the community was immediate. Listeners have called in and texted the station, asking for more stories. Others are now sharing stories that they remember their parents and grandparents telling them. Survey results of 300 community members and community leaders from 19 communities indicate that 100 percent of listeners want to hear more stories. Aurelio Sho said: "When I hear you speak in my language, it means that you are talking to me. It means, I value it."

I spent time working with Aurelio Sho at Ak' Kutan Radio and at Tumul K'in the school that is dedicated to serving Q'eqchi' and Mopan Maya high school students in the neighboring communities. While there, I had an opportunity to work with the students. In one of the classes, they listened to the original Q'eqchi' recording of "The Dance of the Deer." All of the students were already familiar with the dance, as they have seen it and heard about it from their parents. Two boys in the class had performed as deer dancers in the Maya Festival that was held in Belize that summer. While everyone knew about the Deer Dance, no one had heard the legend that explained why it was performed.

After the students heard the legend, I asked them if they would like to draw pictures to illustrate the story so that we could create a book with their original artwork. The first question asked was, "Can we have a copy of the book?" They worked on their illustrations with great enthusiasm and when they completed their depiction of the story, each student went to the front of the class and presented it to the others. There was great pride in their voices as they talked about the story. Some drew pictures of a rain god; others drew pictures of deer masks and jaguars; others drew pictures of a waterfall and a rainbow with birds flying in the sky, others drew a variety of animals drinking water from a river after Tzuul Taq'a saved them. All looked forward to the day when the book would be printed with their names, their artwork, a picture of the class, and of course, a CD, so that their parents could listen to the story while they read it.

In Belize, the relationship of community radio and a cultural heritage is intimately linked with the meaning of democracy. Luis Cucul, a local educator, defined democracy clearly in personal terms. "Democracy is really a word that means that everyone should be a part of it; having a right to say anything; to have a voice. The kind of education that was given to us (as Maya) failed us. We were not taught to be outspoken people. Now, my children are outspoken. It's us, we are the ones not making it work. We are afraid to take risk and say it's wrong." Aurelio Sho had a similar definition. "Democracy means bringing people together . . . You have the right to fight for what is right; to have a voice."

Having a voice seems to be intimately linked to the possibilities for community radio in Belize. For Tumul K'in teacher Victor Cal, "Radio is an important instrument to reach the home, to reach the family. The radio can bring it from the elders and give it to the younger generation, the younger members of the community." For Aurelio Sho, "Radio is a very powerful tool and to use it to preserve culture means a whole lot to me. The native language that you speak in delivering content . . . having your audience understand the language being spoken on the radio means a whole lot. It means a sense of ownership. . . . This opens the door to the communities for participation, giving voice to the voiceless."

Future Research and Direction

Building on the model in Blue Creek, Belize, where Q'eqchi' stories are broadcast on the Ak' Kutan story-telling radio program and students in the Tumul K'in high school are being exposed to Mayan literature and culture, our goal is to build a similar model in Izabal, Guatemala, and eventually in Alta Verapaz, where Q'eqchi' is widely spoken. We seek to broadcast oral histories on Indigenous radio stations, collect oral histories from men and women, elders, and the younger generation, disseminate CDs of narratives in schools and libraries, create radio-theatre dramatizations, illustrate the stories with original Indigenous art involving students and adults in the community, distribute illustrated bilingual booklets of the folktales in the schools, and thereby rejuvenate memories and revitalize Mayan languages and culture. The road ahead, however, is a long and difficult one, particularly in Guatemala.

Remembering the past is a task for scholars in collaboration with Indigenous Maya. It is critical to continue recording legends and fortifying an archive of diverse memories and speech genres to revitalize the oral tradition; it is equally important to continue the interpretation and analyses of recorded texts and transcripts. Another way of bringing the past into the present is to bring into current use, through community radio, the languages that define a culture.

Recently I have had the privilege to record personal stories from Maya (Mam and K'ichee') men living in Somerville, Massachusetts. Their diaspora experience and the challenges they faced as they left Guatemala and traveled by foot through Mexico to seek refuge in the United States represent another genre of recorded memories. It is our hope that one day community-based radio stations in Guatemala will serve as a bridge between the diasporic communities in the United States and the homeland.

Notes

1. Alternate names and spellings over time include: Cacche', K'ekchi, Kekchí, Kekchi, Ketchi', Q'eqchi', and Quecchi'. I have adopted the orthography of the new ALMG (1996) standard orthography for Mayan.

2. As pointed out, if the couplets are sequenced as simple phrases or sentences within a paragraph, it obfuscates the pattern of symmetry and parallelism. For illustrative purposes, I use indentation. This "free" translation of The Dance of the Deer is primarily focused on demarcating the verses (roughly corresponding to a paragraph) and demonstrating the role of couplets. It does not reflect the intonational phrasing of each line within the verse. For more information on the role of intonation in discourse structure, see Berinstein (1991). It is important to note that while indenting the couplets has the positive effect of demonstrating the clear parallelism, it has a negative effect that may suggest to some that one of the lines in the couplet is separated by a pause, when there is not necessarily one. For this reason, in Berinstein (1991) I marked the end of a couplet line that did not have a pause break with a # sign. In this way, the parallelism was clear, but it was also clear that prosodically, the two (or more) lines were linked as a single intonation unit (without pausing). In The Dance of the Deer I include multiple phrases of the couplet on a single line if it is a single intonational unit so that there can be no confusion.

3. The Berinstein narrative collection (2013) is representative of the "prestige dialect" as spoken in Cobán, AV, Guatemala. The narratives were recorded between 1978–1980 in Cobán. In 1981, I continued fieldwork with Carlota Yalibat who immigrated from Cobán to California. Transcription and translation was supported in-part by a Smithsonian, National Museum of National

History post-doctoral fellowship and by a David Rockefeller Center for Latin American Studies Visiting Scholar award.

4. There are 13 divine mountains that the Maya might call upon to petition for a specific purpose. Xukaneb is the highest one of the mountains located in Alta Verapaz, Guatemala. As we see in the translation of "The Hills and the Corn," below, these13 mountains are summoned by Lord Xukaneb when his daughter is stolen from him.

References

Academia de Lenguas Mayas de Guatemala. 1996. Norma del alfabeto del idioma Maya Q'eqchi'. Guatemala: ALMG

Ajmac Cuxil, Concepción. 1975. Cuentos, leyendas y casos recopilados en la región indígena de Guatemala. Tradiciones de Guatemala 4: 205–20.

Berinstein, Ava. 2014. "Q'eqchi' Mayan Language Revitalization through Verbal Art," Cultural Survival, https://www.culturalsurvival.org/news/qeqchi-mayan-language-revitalization-through-verbal-art, May 13, 2014.

Berinstein, Ava. 2013. "Q'eqchi' Mayan Narrative Collection." A digitized and documented collection of 21 Q'eqchi' Mayan narratives translated in Q'eqchi', English, and Spanish. Unpublished. (See Appendix 1.)

Berinstein, Ava. 1991. The role of intonation in K'ekchi Mayan discourse, In Texas Linguistic Forum 32: Discourse, Cynthia McLemore (ed.), The University of Texas at Austin, Austin, Texas: 1–19.

Berinstein, Ava. 1985. Evidence for Multiattachment in K'ekchi Mayan, Garland Publishing Inc. New York & London.

Brasseur de Bourbourg, Charles Étienne (ed.) 1861. Popol vuh. Le livre sacré et les mythes de l'antiquité américaine, avec les livres héroïques et historiques des Quichés. Paris: Bertrand.

Bricker, Victoria R. 2004. Linguistic Continuities and Discontinuities in the Maya Area. In Pluralizing Ethnography: Comparison and Representation in Maya Cultures, Histories, and Identities. John M. Watanabe and Edward F. Fischer, (eds.), Santa Fe: School of American Research Press: 67–93.

Bricker, Victoria Reifler and Helga-Maria Miram (translators) 2002. An Encounter of Two Worlds: The Book of Chilam Balam of Kaua. Middle American Research Institute, publication 68. New Orleans: Tulane University.

Brody, Jill. 1986. Repetition as a Rhetorical and Conversational Device in Tojolobal (Mayan), International Journal of American Linguistics, Vol. 52, No. 3:255–274.

Burkitt, Robert. 1920. The hills and the corn. Anthropological Publications of the University Museum, Vol. VIII, no 2. Philadelphia: 181–227.

Burkitt, Robert. 1918. The hills and the corn. Museum Journal 9, 3–4, Philadelphia: 273–89.

Burns, Allan. 1980. Yucatecan Mayan Ethnopoetics: The Translation of a Narrative View of Life. Nora England (ed.), Journal of Mayan Linguistics, Vol 2. No. 1:3–12.

Campbell, Lyle R. & Terrence Kaufman. 1985. Mayan linguistics: Where are we now? Annual Review of Anthropology 14: 187–198.

Campbell, Lyle. 1977. Quichean linguistic prehistory, University of California, Publications in Linguistics 81, Los Angeles.

Crystal, David. 2000. Language Death. Cambridge University Press, United Kingdom.

Cultural Survival Website–News. "Protecting Freedom of Expression in Guatemala: The Case of Daniel Pascual," https://www.culturalsurvival.org/news/protecting-freedom-expression-guatemala-case-daniel-pascual, July 23, 2014.

Cultural Survival Website–News. "Community Radio Volunteers Analyze and Discuss Indigenous Rights Violations," https://www.culturalsurvival.org/news/community-radio-volunteers-analyze-and-discuss-indigenous-rights-violations. June 23, 2014.

Cultural Survival Website–News. "Another Community Radio Station Raided by Guatemalan Police," https://www.culturalsurvival.org/news/another-community-radio-station-raided-guatemalan-police. November 28, 2012.

Danien, Elin, C. 2005. Maya Folktales from the Alta Verapaz. University of Pennsylvania, Museum of Archeology and Anthropology, Philadelphia.

Eachus, Fran and Ruth Carlson. 1971. Kekchi texts. According to our Ancestors: Folktales from Guatemala and Honduras, Mary Shaw (ed.), SIL Publications, no. 32:151–66; 389–410.

Eachus, Fran and Ruth Carlson. 1966. Kekchi. In Marvin K. Mayers (ed). Languages of Guatemala, Summer Institute of Linguistics, Mouton & Co., London: 110–124.

Edmonson, Munro S. (translator) 1986. Heaven Born Merida and Its Destiny : the Book of Chilam Balam of Chumayel. Austin: University of Texas Press.

Edmonson, Munro S. (translator) 1982. The Ancient Future of the Itza: the Book of Chilam Balam of Tizimin. Austin: University of Texas Press.

Edmonson, Munro S. (ed.) 1971. The Book of Counsel: The Popol-Vuh of the Quiche Maya of Guatemala. Publ. no. 35. New Orleans: Middle American Research Institute, Tulane University.

England, Nora. 2009. To Tell a Tale: The Structure of Narrated Stories in Mam, a Mayan Language, International Journal of American Linguistics, The University of Chicago Press. Vol. 75, No. 2: 207–231.

England, Nora, 2007. The influence of Mayan-speaking linguists on the state of Mayan linguistics, Linguistische Beriichte Sonderheft 14: 93–111, Special edition Endangered Languages, Peter K. Austin and Andrew Simpson, (eds.), Hamburg: Helmut Buske Verlag.

England, Nora, 2003. Mayan language revival and revitalization politics: Linguists and linguistic ideologies. American Anthropologist, American Anthropological Association. Vol. 105, No. 4: 733–743.

England, Nora C. 1998. Mayan efforts toward language preservation. In Endangered Languages, Lenore Grenoble and Lindsay Whaley (eds.), Cambridge: Cambridge University Press: 99–116.

Freeze, Ray. 1976. K'ekchi' texts. International Journal of American Linguistics, Native American Texts Series. Louanna Furbee-Losee (ed.), University of Chicago Press. Vol. 1 no. 1: 21–31.

Garvin, Glenn and Edward Hegstrom. 1999. Report: Maya Indians Suffered Genocide, The Miami Herald http://www2.fiu.edu/~fcf/reportmaya.html

Grube, Nikolai. 1992. Classic Maya Dance. Evidence from Hieroglyphs and Iconography. Ancient Mesoamerica 3:201–218.

Gubler, Ruth, and David Bolles (translators) 2000. The Book of Chilam Balam of Na. Lancaster (CA): Labyrinthos.

Henderson, Brent, Rohloff, Peter, and Robert Henderson. 2014. "More than Words: Towards a Development-Based Approach to Language Revitalization," Language Documentation & Conservation, Vol. 8: 75–91. http://nflrc.hawaii.edu/ldc.

Hull, Kerry M. 2003. Verbal Art and Performance in Ch'orti' and Maya Hieroglyphic Writing (Doctoral Dissertation). University of Texas, Austin, Department of Anthropology, Austin.

Hull, Kerry M. 2002. *A Comparative Analysis of Ch'orti' Verbal Art and the Poetic Discourse Structures of Maya Hieroglyphic Writing.* FAMSI Report: http://www.famsi.org/reports/00048/index.html.

Lewis, M. Paul (ed.), 2009. Ethnologue: Languages of the World, Sixteenth edition. Dallas, Texas. SIL International. Online version: http://www.ethnologue.com/.

Looper, Matthew G. 2009. To Be Like Gods: Dance in Ancient Maya Civilization. University of Texas Press, Austin.

Luxton, Richard N. (translator), 2010. "The Book of the Chilam Balam of Tizimin." California: Aegean Park Press.

Luxton, Richard N. (translator), 1995. The (Chilam Balam) Book of Chumayel; The Counsel Book of the Yucatec Maya. California: Aegean Park Press.

Maxwell, Judith. 1996. Prescriptive Grammar and Kaqchikel Revitalization. In Maya Cultural Activism in Guatemala City. Edward F. Fischer and R. McKenna Brown, (eds.) Austin: University of Texas Press: 195–207.

Maxwell, Judith. 1987. Some aspects of Chuj discourse. Anthropological Linguistics Vol. 29. No. 4, Mayan Languages and their Speakers:489–506.

Osborne, Lilly de Jongh. 1965. Folklore, Supersticiones y leyendas de Guatemala. Comision Permanente de Folklore, Etnografía y Etnología de la Sociedad de Geografía e Historia de Guatemala.

Paxton, Merideth. 2001. "Books of Chilam Balam," in: Oxford Encyclopedia of Mesoamerican Cultures Vol. 1. Oxford: Oxford University Press.

Roys, Ralph L. (translator), 1967 [1933]. The Book of Chilam Balam of Chumayel. Norman: University of Oklahoma Press.

Schele, Linda and David Freidel. 1990. A forest of kings: The untold story of the ancient Maya. William Morrow, New York.

Shaw, Mary, editor, 1972. Según nuestros antepasados: Textos folklóricos de Guatemala y Honduras, Summer Institute of Linguistics.

Sommer, Doris, 2005. Cultural Agency in the Americas. Duke University Press, Durham, NC

Tedlock, Dennis. 2011. 2000 years of Mayan literature. Berkeley, University of California Press.

Tedlock, Dennis. 1985. Popol Vuh: The Mayan Book of the Dawn of Life. (revised edition) Simon & Schuster, New York.

Thompson, J. Eric S. 1967. Maya Creation Myths, II. Estudios de Cultura Maya 6: 15–43.

Thompson, J. Eric S. 1930. Ethnology of the Mayas of southern and central British Honduras, Chicago Natural History Museum, Anthropological Series, Chicago. Vol 17. No. 2:132–34.

Upside Down World. "Community Radio Station Doble Via Raided by Guatemalan Police," http://upsidedownworld.org/main/news-briefs-archives-6 8/3917-community-radio-station-doble-via-raided-by-guatemalan-police. October 16, 2012.

Weeks, John M. and Elin C. Danien. 2008. The lost notebooks of Robert Burkitt: Maya linguist. Edwin Mellon Press. New York.

Winn, Peter (this volume). "The Memory of Politics: Pre-Coup Democracy & Chile's Democratic Transition."

Ximénez, Francisco. 1857. Las historias del origen de los indios de esta provincia de Guatemala. Introduction, paleography, and notes by Carl Sherzer. Vienna: Academia.

PART

III

Citizenship and Democratic Futures

9

The Weight of the Past, the Politics of the Present, and the Future of Democracy in Brazil and the Southern Cone

Frances Hagopian

In the opening passage of the *Eighteenth Brumaire of Louis Bonaparte*, Karl Marx famously wrote that the past—the "tradition of all the dead generations"—"weighs like a nightmare on the brain of the living." Latin America's recent experience with dictatorship and democracy suggests otherwise: memories and experiences of a recent, dark past have served not to constrain contemporary democracies but to transform them in ways that were previously unimaginable. In some cases, democratic citizenship forged in the crucible of authoritarianism may have even enabled countries to come to grips with their pasts and to create more participatory, inclusive, and stronger democracies.

Pre-authoritarian democracy in Latin America was limited even by "realistic" standards (Dahl 1971). Militaries played a tutelary role; elected governments lacked transparency and mechanisms by which to hold them accountable; political representation was state-controlled and hierarchically organized; and avenues for popular participation were few and far between. Justice institutions served the "somebodies."[1] Most Latin American democracies look different today, in large part because of the experience of authoritarianism, the forces unleashed by it, and the perspectives political actors carried away from it. Most apparent is that political elites learned to value not merely tolerance and moderation, but also democracy's institutional rules for dividing power. Less widely recognized is that participants in popular movements learned to organize in a sphere outside state control, developed non-hierarchical, participatory norms, and recognized the potential of a broad gamut of institutions—representative, accountability, and justice—for confronting their pasts and imagining new futures. Where independent social movements were dynamic, they gave birth to a democratic political culture and stronger democratic institutions.

The aim of this chapter is to shed light on how the central elements of democratic citizenship—including the democratic principles and practices of tolerance and compromise, participation and deliberation, and accountability and representation—were formed during the years of authoritarian repression and how they, in turn, transformed democratic institutions. It focuses primarily on Brazil, where social and political change was profound.

The first section reviews the focus on balancing the short-term risks and benefits of pursuing a policy of truth and justice that political actors and political scientists brought to the subject of memory and democracy soon after the transitions from authoritarian rule. After making the case that the impact of authoritarianism was both broader and deeper than the memories of the repression such regimes unleashed, the next three sections focus on the multiple channels through which the past influences contemporary Latin American democracies: section two on the ways in which elites' understandings of the past changed their perceptions of states and moderated their behavior toward other social actors; the third part deals with the emergence of new actors and movements in the sphere of civil society. In part four I examine the establishment of a more genuinely democratic political culture, stronger democratic institutions, and ultimately, coming to terms with the past. With an eye toward highlighting the causal mechanisms of political change, the fifth section contrasts the Brazilian experience with those of the other countries of the Southern Cone of Latin America, particularly Chile, where, as Sergio Bitar and Peter Winn contend in other contributions to this volume, the transformative effect of social change was more limited. The final part concludes.

"Transitional Risks" against Coming to Terms with the Past

In what was without exaggeration the most widely read volume on the democratic transitions, O'Donnell and Schmitter (1986) asked whether democrats should offer amnesty to military officers implicated in egregious human rights violations in order to hasten their exit and safeguard democracy in the present, or whether they should instead seek justice, thereby improving the prospects for a high-quality democracy in the future but perhaps risking an authoritarian regression in the present. The case for offering militaries such assurances was compelling. After the Argentine government put top military officers on trial, other Latin American militaries, fearing a similar fate, extracted from civilians commitments of impunity, or worse, clung to power as long as possible and rejected any concessions to the democratic opposition (Weyland 2014, 176). In Chile, so fearful were military officers of retribution Argentine-style that they dug in behind Augusto Pinochet in the mid-1980s to stay in power at all costs (Weyland 2014, 208–209).[2] Moreover, the case against upending self-proclaimed amnesties was strengthened by the *carapintada* barracks rebellion in Argentina during Easter week in 1987 protesting the Alfonsín government's policy of allowing middle-rank military officers to face civil trials for human rights abuses.

These debates about how to "settle past accounts [without upsetting present transitions]," as O'Donnell and Schmitter (1986) characterized this high-stakes game, thus initially took on the quality of a cost-benefit analysis in which the gains of prosecuting and punishing perpetrators of egregious violations of human rights were weighed against the risks of imperiling the democratic transitions inherent in bringing the thugs to trial. Despite their initial, single-minded focus on completing the difficult transition from authoritarian rule and keeping new democracies safe from authoritarian regressions, O'Donnell and Schmitter's sober recommendation to resolve an immensely difficult dilemma, even in those cases in which the military was heavily complicit in crimes, was *not* to try to ignore the issue; that would be "the worst of bad solutions" not only because some horrors were too unspeakable to ignore, but also because forgoing justice to mitigate short-term risks to democracy might actually incur the long-term risk that the nightmare could be repeated (1986, 30). If perpetrators believed they would never be brought to justice, then covering up military crimes could contribute to a sense of impunity on the part of the armed forces, especially its most sinister elements. Burying such a past would also bury the very ethical values a society needs to make its future livable, and the possibility of transforming the messianic self-image of the armed forces as *the* institution ultimately interpreting and ensuring the highest interests of the nation (1986, 30–31). Although it was paradoxically much "more difficult and dangerous" to attempt to collect past accounts "of greater weight and more recent origin" involving a wide spectrum of persons in places where memories were "more intense," and "victims (or their survivors) and victimizers are still present," this was precisely where and when it was more important not to bury the past (O'Donnell and Schmitter 1986, 30).

However compelling such arguments, future presidents, cabinet ministers, and their political advisers including those who participated in the Transitions project, instead followed Santiago Carillo's advice "not to dig around in the past."[3] They coalesced around the view that there could be truth, perhaps reconciliation, but not justice, and that securing democracy was worth the price of impunity.[4] Their actions had the effect of postponing justice. In Uruguay, the agreement by civilian politicians to a deal approving military amnesty in the Naval Club Pact of 1985 was decisive for restoring civilian rule and electoral democracy (Gillespie 1991), but it also proved difficult to overturn in a referendum forced by the human rights movement. In Brazil, no such deal was formally uncovered, but civilians tread lightly in the 1980s. Not until late in the first term of the Cardoso presidency would the government open the archives of military repression and compensate the families of 265 victims who had been killed or disappeared under the military regime (and not until 2012 did it impanel a Truth Commission).

Yet decisions made and deals struck during transitions did not become permanent constraints on the design of democratic institutions and policies, as both advocates of compromise and confrontation—myself included—assumed they would (Stepan 1989; Karl 1990; Hagopian 1990). The impact of transitional pacts was limited in part for the reasons scholars have already offered—that such bargains constrained only the signatories, not future actors (Przeworski 1989), and that the electoral logic of democracy leads civilians eventually to privilege social over military interests (Hunter 1997). Less well recognized is that the lessons a broad range of actors drew from democratic breakdowns and authoritarian repression may have strengthened their commitments to democracy, and that the emergence of inchoate movements seeking freedom and justice ultimately influenced how societies came to terms with the past.

Elites Learn from the Past

The logic of the claim that memory has an impact on democracy is that those who remember "learn" from and are changed by what they remember. Traumatic authoritarian experiences qualify as the type of severe crises from which political actors may draw lessons from their errors and adopt new attitudes, behavior, and tactics that make possible transitions to stable and enduring democratic regimes (Bermeo 1992, 274). Societies and individuals most often learn from these crises in their own past, but they can occasionally also learn from the pasts of near and more distant neighbors (Weyland 2014).

Though the concept of learning applies to all actors, leading scholars emphasize the influence the role of elites in the process of democracy. Seen as the heroes who steered democratic transitions through turbulent waters, their ability to judge the risks and rewards of replicating other transition models and to restrain their less well informed rank-and-file was seen as critical to exiting autocracy (Weyland 2014). Seen as the villains responsible for having destabilized democratic governments and backing coups in the "extraordinary times" of interwar Europe and Latin America in the 1960s and 1970s, their reassessment of the "relative effectiveness of democratic institutions for the fulfillment of group goals" was essential for successful democratization (Bermeo 1992, 275; 2003). Crucially, elites "learned" not merely to respect democracy and not to mobilize for revolution or knock on the barracks door, but also not to cling to policy preferences that their opponents could not abide. Whereas policy "radicalism" was associated with the breakdown of democratic regimes in Latin America, policy "moderation" in combination with normative commitments to democracy helped to ensure democratic regimes across Latin America (Mainwaring and Pérez-Liñán, 2014).

Although elites of both left and right lacked an appreciation of democracy in the period immediately preceding the military coups of the 1960s and 1970s, many scholars heralded in particular the "taming" of the left—or what Katherine Hite (2000) has called "the end of the romance." In a narrative that evokes the lament of Gaetano Mosca, Benedetto Croce, and Gaetano Salvemini, each of whom in the early 1920s admitted that their indifference toward and criticism of the "better" parliamentary regime in Italy had led to the loss of liberty under the Fascist dictatorship (cited in Dahl 1971, 18),[5] the left in Chile, Uruguay, and elsewhere confessed later in the century to having undervalued democracy as irreparably flawed due to its "bourgeois" nature. Jorge Arrate, a leader of the Chilean Socialist Party who had extensive contact with Eurocommunists while in exile in Rome, reflected in 1982 that "The loss of democracy and its denigration in the official discourse [of the dictatorship] induce a more profound appreciation of the value, meaning and contents of political democracy" (cited in Bermeo 1992, 278). His Socialist colleague Carlos Altamirano was "shocked by the absence of liberty" in Communist East Berlin, where he had taken up residence (cited in Bermeo 1992, 285). Among the ranks of the former Uruguayan Tupamaro guerrillas made famous by Costa Gavras's *State of Siege* is current Uruguayan president José Mujica (of center-left *Frente Amplio* coalition), who served fourteen years in custody after the 1973 military coup. In a sign of how far he and his colleagues have travelled, the *Economist* (2013) named Uruguay "country of the year" in 2013, in part due to its "man at the top."

The emphasis of this narrative has been on the sobering effect of the harshness of repression and the scale on which it was conducted, and on the lessons to be drawn from responding to popular demands that might frighten elites. In his chapter in this volume, Peter Winn is appropriately critical of the leaders of Chile's Concertación for demobilizing their bases as part of an obsessive strategy of not upsetting the economic model at any cost—for essentially drawing the *wrong* lessons. Such a focus on the effects of repression and dampening popular demands, however, is too narrow. The memories of authoritarianism inculcated in the tragic actors of the democratic breakdowns bring not merely an appreciation for democracy, but also a healthy suspicion of the too-strong state. As Francisco Weffort (1989) has written so eloquently, in Brazil, the traumatic reality of dictatorship during the government of Emílio Garrastazu Médici (1969–1974) showed many democratic liberals on the left and socialists—who had been convinced of the usefulness of the state as an instrument of greater economic development, the "democratization" of the economy and society, and greater social equality—that their dream could turn into a dictatorship that "promoted simultaneously the growth of the economy and the misery of the masses" (Weffort 1989, 346).

The emphasis placed on moderation of the left—both by those who welcome such moderation and those who are troubled by it—presumes, moreover, that the left were the only actors who needed to learn lessons. The right too, having previously welcomed the removal of nettlesome presidents with threatening agendas by force, found authoritarianism was not all it was cracked up to be. Again in Brazil, those "liberals" who opposed João Goulart and welcomed the coup in 1964 in the name of a democracy that to them meant less state intervention in the economy, instead discovered that the regime they got featured a state every bit as interventionist as the one they had helped to overthrow. Finding themselves on the outside, marginalized from the power they had helped to create, they saw "the monstrous fruit of the seed they had planted" (Weffort 1989, 346). In 1975, they launched an *anti-statism* campaign to protest state regulation (Stepan 1985, 335). More boldly, two years later, a group of eight leading entrepreneurs ("elected" among the "ten most representative spokesmen of the business class" in a poll conducted by the *Gazeta Mercantil,* Brazil's most influential daily newspaper within the business community) signed a highly critical "Manifesto of the Eight" (Stepan 1985, 337) that voiced open criticism not only of "statism" but also of the technocratic management of the economy and the regime itself (Martins 1986, 90–91). Now allying themselves with civil society in favor of political liberalization, business leaders learned the importance of weaning themselves from dependence on the state for economic as well as political support and developing a stronger, truly *private* sector.

In Argentina, the story followed the same plot line, even more dramatically. In an essay with the marvelous subtitle "Or, Why the Future Is No Longer What It Used to Be," Carlos Acuña evinced great optimism about the future of democracy in Argentina because the horrific military regime of 1976–1983 and the systematic exclusion of the economic elite from policy-making had finally convinced the elite of the folly of knocking on the barracks door to promote its interests. After the economic collapse of 1981 and the Malvinas fiasco of 1982, the business elite had proof that the military had "ceased to be predictable" and had become a "risky actor" (Acuña 1994, 59). Even the long-standing custom in the elite circles of Buenos Aires of inviting uniformed military officers to chic dinner parties was abandoned. Temporarily, at least, business elites even invested in a political party to represent their interests (Gibson 2001).

Politicians and business leaders, moreover, were not the only elite actors to experience a change of heart. Notably, leaders of some key intermediate institutions also came to reevaluate democracy and its alternatives. The new leadership of labor unions in Brazil eschewed the corporatist bargain their predecessors had struck with populist-era governments to gain benefits they could not win in the marketplace by accepting state intervention and restraints. When corporatist institutions ceased to provide inducements and imposed only constraints (Collier and Collier 1991), this new generation of labor leaders, the most prominent of whom was Luiz Inácio "Lula" da Silva, embraced a "new unionism." With their authority resting not on having friends in high places in the Labor Ministry and Social Security Institutes but on the support they drew from the shop floor, union heads soon discovered they could go it alone, raise their own dues, and fight for wages via collective bargaining rather than in state labor courts (Tavares de Almeida 1987; Keck 1989). Labor's transformation upended industrial relations and a system of interest representation that depended on mediation through state-sponsored channels. By embracing the legal right to free association—enshrined in Article 8 of the 1988 Constitution—and by unyoking itself from the protection of state labor courts, the new unionism freed labor associations to act as pressure groups in a democratic society, created the possibility of political autonomy, and represented an important crack in a hierarchical political culture.

Perhaps even more dramatic was the impact of authoritarianism and violence on the Roman Catholic Church. In 1964, the church in Brazil sponsored women's marches against the "godless" Goulart government, and in Chile in 1973, it called upon the military to intervene. But once the full force of state violence became manifest, the hierarchy of the Catholic

Church in both countries, as well as in Peru and El Salvador, was transformed by the regimes they had helped to bring forth (Fleet 1985; Mainwaring 1986; Mainwaring and Wilde 1989; McDonough et al 1998). The church hierarchy defended the human rights of protection from abduction, torture, and death; gave voice to struggles for economic survival, civil freedoms, and ultimately democracy; and hastened the change of regimes at the top. For Huntington (1991, 77), "this repositioning of the Catholic Church from a bulwark of the status quo, usually authoritarian, to a force for change, usually democratic," was one of the most critical variables in explaining the third wave of democratization worldwide. Along with other scholars, Huntington attributed this change in large part to the doctrinal shift of the Second Vatican Council, which stressed the legitimacy and need for social change as well as the rights of individuals (Huntington (1991, 78). This doctrinal shift took root on Latin American soil at the second meeting of Latin American bishops at Medellín, Colombia, in 1968, and inspired the Catholic Church in Brazil to confront dictatorship and renew its evangelical mission by ministering to the poor (Holston 2008, 238). Not all Latin American Episcopates opposed authoritarian rule; in the face of violence and torture, bishops in Argentina, Uruguay, Guatemala, and elsewhere were silent, perhaps because they did not face religious competition (Gill 1994), were not directly threatened (Smith 1982), or because the hierarchy in those countries had a different understanding of mission (Mainwaring 1986). But where churches did act, the effects were profound.

New Actors Emerge in New Spaces

The emphasis on the importance of elite learning during the period of democratic transition and consolidation may have been well placed for the reasons underscored here, but such a focus understated the transformative potential of *mass* memories and lessons learned on the region's democracies once they were released from the intensive care unit. The mobilization of ordinary people in a stronger and now autonomous sphere of civil society set in motion political transformations that led to more representative, participatory, and accountable democracies. To fully grasp the significance of the social movements authoritarianism unleashed, we must recognize civil society as not merely the *terrain* on which a diverse, dynamic set of civic associations organized to make demands on the authoritarian polity, but also as the *target* of collective action, in Cohen and Arato's (1992, 504, 509) compelling formulation. When new actors organized in new associations and movements, they democratized social relations and institutions, norms, collective identities, and cultural values. Thus the *social* transformation that collective action unleashed ultimately reshaped power relations and facilitated more democratic regimes with deeper roots in democratic societies.

In his brilliant essay "Why Democracy," Francisco Weffort (1989) observed that before the coup, Brazilian parties of all stripes saw the state as the place to "do" politics, and society as something amorphous and supposedly incapable of becoming organized. The left in particular saw seizing the state as an expedient path to political change, but under the dictatorship state terror reduced all regime opponents to the common denominator of unprotected and frightened human beings. In their most difficult moments, lacking parties and courts in which they could have confidence, the persecuted had to make use of what they found around them. Their primary recourse was the family, friends, and in some cases fellow workers (Weffort 1989, 347). From such fear, a civil society was born.

What began as a retreat into private life by those who had once been organized, eventually gathered momentum as they and new actors were mobilized in new spaces of civic engagement. State repression that "eviscerated" workplace organizations, fractured civic organizations, "militarized" the "public domains of citizenship" (Holston 2008, 238), and rendered political parties symbolic government supporters paradoxically created the possibility of new spheres of association that were safe, remote, and independent of central authority. In Brazil, those spaces were first protected and supported by the Catholic Church, which strengthened several existing associations, notably urban labor unions in the industrial suburbs of São Paulo; fostered an "unprecedented growth of rural unions" with a surprising degree of autonomy from state authorities (Stepan 1985, 332); and organized several new grass-roots initiatives. Brazilian bishops established a National Labor Pastoral for workers and a Pastoral Land Commission to support the rural poor and the struggles of landless peasants and, when the judicial system failed to do so, document their murders.[6]

Perhaps the most transformative of the new grass-roots initiatives of the Roman Catholic Church were the Christian Base Communities (CEBs). CEBs were small, relatively homogeneous, grass-roots groups of ten to forty people who gathered regularly to read the Bible and reflect on their daily lives in light of the Gospel. Brazil's bishops actively promoted their creation in the spirit of the Vatican II reforms aimed at energizing the Church by making participation less ritualistic and more meaningful. CEBs engendered among some participants leadership skills that were portable and eventually carried over into other organizations and even into politics. At their peak there were about 100,000 of these grass-roots church communities across Brazil. Although CEBs are no longer in vogue, in part because more conservative bishops have withdrawn their support, their members have migrated to Black, Land, and Marginalized Women's Pastorals; human rights organizations; movements of the landless and Afro-descendants; and groups advocating for the indigenous and that prepare students to take college entrance examinations, all of which continue to be shaped profoundly by liberationist ideas and views (Burdick 2004, 9–10). Numerous scholars have drawn a direct link between the ideological, organizational, and human resources built up in the base communities and the invigoration of other organizations of civil society in a sphere independent of state control, confirming the Catholic Church's ascribed role of "midwife of civil society."

The poor were also inducted into politics during authoritarianism via neighborhood associations. As people turned away from the ballot box, clientelistic Societies of the Friends of the Neighborhood, the halls of state-sponsored unions, and factory life, they turned toward domestic life in the urban neighborhoods and in the distant peripheries. The focus of working-class commitment became the social life of residence, and beyond immediate state, party, and employer sanction, "new spaces of civic participation and collective evaluation" emerged (Holston 2008, 238). Once politics moved to the neighborhoods and rural areas—precisely the places where state agents and political parties had previously been absent—the rural and urban, informal poor who had not previously been politically active, in no small part because they had been left out of corporatist and most other organizations, could now engage and participate politically not where they worked but where they lived. During an authoritarian experience in which the state "intervened deeply into the everyday lives of the poor"—removing slums from the central areas of Brazilian cities and encouraging a huge migration from the countryside to the cities where health care, education, and infrastructure were inadequate (Avritzer 2009, 27–28), new urban voluntary associations that "thrust the poor into politics" grew prolifically to fill the void and offer means for the poor to claim access to public goods, with several important effects. They provided a venue for workers in the informal economy to organize and have their interests represented; created avenues for securing land rights and delivering local government services to their "autoconstructed" neighborhoods (Holston 2008); and laid the groundwork for new institutions of participatory democracy.

Once the space for civil society spread across Brazilian territory and expanded to incorporate previously excluded sectors of Brazilian society, other organizations followed. Some mobilized new political identities.

Like in neighboring Argentina, Chile, and Uruguay where women organized to seek information about the whereabouts of their children in brave confrontations with state authorities, Brazilian women organized against political repression. In Brazil, however, political and economic repression fueled a powerful, cross-class women's movement (Alvarez 1989). Afro-descendants also organized as such not merely, as in the past, to celebrate African contributions to Brazilian culture but also to protest police violence, with important consequences for the reform of justice systems.

Most remarkably, when life and politics returned to "normal" and the political conditions that gave rise to them no longer held, social movements did not recede. Organizers might have abandoned them once political parties were once again open for business, and the rank-and-file could have returned home, content to allow intermediaries to represent their interests. But they did not. Rather, new patterns of organization in civil society outlasted the authoritarian regime, spread into existing organizations, and created new links to old and new democratic institutions. These organizations were critical to changing Brazil.

A New Democratic Citizenship: Fostering a Culture of Participation and Strengthening Democratic Institutions

One of the major themes of this book is the importance of democratic citizenship *and* institutions for creating effective democratic societies. In the case of Brazil, the deepening of democratic citizenship was set in motion by a cultural transformation born of authoritarianism that enhanced personal capabilities, reordered elite and mass beliefs about what to expect from a democratic state, invigorated channels of political participation, and inspired new ways of organizing and doing politics. The new democratic citizenship, in turn, was instrumental in strengthening institutions of representation and accountability. The former were important in enhancing democratic governance, and the latter in protecting rights in the present and coming to terms with the past.

A More Democratic Political Culture

Changes in political culture may take many forms. One is a change in basic attitudes and beliefs about politics. In this respect, Brazilians have grown less tolerant of authoritarianism. In 1972, the public generally accepted the military's role in politics; 73 percent believed that "the people do not know what is best for Brazil" (Rochon and Mitchell 1989, 309). A decade later, Brazilians expressed a clear preference for democracy over dictatorship, but differed over what democracy meant. Whereas those higher up the ladder of occupational prestige opposed a role for the military in politics and supported greater autonomy for unions and a stronger Congress, working-class respondents favored universal suffrage and the enfranchisement of illiterates (Rochon and Mitchell 1989, 315).

Support for democracy has solidified even more since then, with growing numbers espousing the belief that democracy is the best form of government and rejecting the notion that democracy can exist without political parties. Brazilians also reject the plebiscitarian variant of democracy that has appeal elsewhere in Latin America: clear majorities disagreed that the people should govern directly (and not through elected representatives); that the voice of opposition parties should be limited; and that those who do not agree with the majority represent a threat to the country. Moreover, they resoundingly support government checks and balances; in a 2012 poll, 85 percent opposed the hypothetical ability of the president to limit the authority of Congress and the Supreme Court when the country is facing hard times. Brazilians have also grown less tolerant of corruption. In 2002, 65 percent of respondents to the National Election Study disagreed with the assertion that "it doesn't matter if a politician robs, as long as he gets done things that the population needs," and 85 percent disagreed that a politician who delivers good government should be able to divert public money to finance his electoral campaign. Popular skepticism of politicians, political parties, and hierarchy more generally has grown in recent years, but such skepticism is generally considered healthy for a democratic political culture to the extent that it supplants deference.

The transformation of political culture in a more democratic direction was inspired by personal transformations and new habits of discussion and participation born of repression. The role of the CEBs was critical. Although CEBs may be best known for the content of the theology—liberation theology—discussed in those weekly meetings in the 1970s and 1980s, ultimately more important was their organizational form, which was aptly characterized by Levine (1993) as congregational in much the same way that Weber understood the essence of Puritanism—self-managed communities of believers who eschewed sin rather than rely on "priestly chicanery" to absolve one of it. In handing the study of the Bible directly to the people who had previously relied on priests to interpret the message of the Gospel for them, CEBs transformed the attitudes of their members toward hierarchy and authority, within and outside the church. There is, moreover, every reason to believe that the transformation of Brazilian political culture is real and enduring. Although ordinarily culture is assumed to change only very slowly, a wrenching regime change can provoke rather abrupt changes in political attitudes toward democracy (as they did in Germany in the 1950s; Verba 1965, 154). Such attitudinal change can be enduring when it habituates the next generation in the norms of democracy. With ever-stronger mass support for democracy's norms and institutions, arguably such a pattern has taken hold in Brazil.

A More Engaged Citizenry

A second manifestation of change in the political culture of Brazil is in the way citizens behave politically, associate and participate, and engage with formal political institutions—in how people behave *as citizens*. In this respect, change has been palpable. The sheer number of Brazilians participating in politics today is staggering, especially compared with earlier in the twentieth century when fewer than five percent of adults voted in presidential elections, and even as recently as 1960, when only a third of the voting age population turned out to vote for president.[2] In 2010, 82 percent of registered voters cast valid ballots (in the United States, just over 58 percent of the age-eligible population participated in the 2012 presidential election). Although voting in Brazil is mandatory and there are potential penalties for non-compliance, these are rarely enforced, and no more so than in other countries with compulsory voting and lower participation rates.

Brazilians have been among the most participatory citizens in Latin America and join civil organizations at higher rates. Brazilians also show interest in politics, sign petitions, protest, participate in community events and political campaigns, and attend party and neighborhood association meetings at comparatively high levels relative to other Latin American countries, as well as other advanced and emerging democracies around the world. In 2012, 15.4 percent of respondents to the Latin American Public Opinion Project (LAPOP) survey had signed a petition and 10.8 percent had used social media such as Twitter or Facebook to circulate political information. Moreover, in 2013, more respondents to a São Paulo survey (77 percent) supported the millions of demonstrators who took to the streets in the wave of June protests than favored direct elections in 1984 (71 percent) or advocated the impeachment of President Collor in 1992 (43 percent), the subjects of the two most important prior waves of protest in Brazil.

Brazilians also manifest a more active citizenship by associating in the realm of civil society in ways that outlasted the authoritarian regime. In a 1993 survey, only about one-third of Brazilians did *not* belong to a voluntary association, one-fifth belonged to three or more, and 40 percent of women and 31 percent of men reported, in a mass survey, membership in a grass-roots community (McDonough et al 1998, 925). The pervasive stress on self-expression and discussion in the CEBs helped to develop the norms of political participation, which were transferable to other organizations.[7] Indeed, there was evidence of a strong, uniform, reciprocal relationship between religiosity and neighborhood ties: the more numerous such ties, the more religious the community, and vice versa (McDonough et al 1998, 938). These patterns have persisted. Today levels of civic association and political participation are high in Brazil by comparative standards. The 2012 LAPOP survey found that 26 percent of Brazilians had participated in a neighborhood or community association in the past year, and that 63 percent had participated in a church or religious organization.[8]

Stronger Democratic Institutions
New civic associations, especially those that arose to protest authoritarian abuses and neglect, arguably helped to produce stronger, more representative, and more accountable democratic institutions. But because tracing the impact of political learning and associability on the design of institutions presents a considerable methodological challenge, in this section I eschew causal claims in favor of providing three illustrations of such a path: the impact of citizen movements on achieving constitutionally hard-wired rights and strengthening the channels of political representation; the impact of local associations on local governance institutions; and the impact of human rights groups on the reform of national institutions of law, justice, and accountability.

Rights and Representation
At the time of the transition from military to civilian rule in 1985, Brazil was still governed by an authoritarian constitution decreed by the military regime in 1967. The Congress elected in 1986, which doubled as a Constituent Assembly, organized itself with rapporteurs, committee chairs, and editors to fulfill its charge to frame a democratic charter. But the process of writing a constitution in Brazil was not limited to notables. Due in no small part to popular pressure for a channel for popular participation into drafting the constitution, the Assembly passed Article 24 allowing "the presentation of proposals to amend the draft Constitution . . . as long as subscribed by 30,000 or more Brazilian electors."[9]

During the convention, mobilized citizen organizations generated a total of 122 qualifying popular amendments, a process that required petition drives to secure the required signatures (Holston 2008, 251). The 122 proposals were backed by more than 12 million documented signatures, representing a broad cross-section of Brazilian society (about 12 percent of the electorate); only approximately 14 percent of the 288 different plenary organizations that sponsored these initiatives were employer associations. Citizen initiatives were surprisingly successful in shaping the constitution. One of the most important policy achievements of democratic Brazil, the right to and provision of universal health care, for example, came about as a result of a grass-roots effort and the mechanism of the citizen petition that proposed the creation of the Sistema Único de Saúde (SUS) and eventually enshrined the right to health care for all in the Constitution of 1988.

Such mobilization did not end with the Constituent Assembly. The Movement to Combat Electoral Corruption, an umbrella movement of more than 50 organizations, successfuly mobilized to pass the 1999 law against vote buying, "Your vote does not have a price, it has consequences" (*Voto não tem preço, tem consequência*) and the "Clean Record" (*Ficha Limpa*) law of 2007, which makes a candidate who has been impeached, who resigned to avoid impeachment, or was convicted of a crime, ineligible to run for office for eight years. Citizen movements, in short, have also thus changed expectations of elected officials, created and reinforced accountability institutions, and created broad incentives for local and national political parties to offer policy proposals, effectively provide public services, and deliver security and prosperity. They have also snapped traditional Latin American systems of interest mediation—notably corporatism and clientelism—in favor of substantive political representation.

From Neighborhood Associations to Institutions of Participatory Democracy

A second important effect of the dense web of neighborhood associations that organized the urban informal poor was the emergence of the quite remarkable institutions of participatory and deliberative democracy in Brazil. The foundations for the institutions of participatory democracy were laid in Article 29 of the 1988 Constitution, which instructs municipalities to adopt charters that incorporate the "cooperation of the representative associations in municipal planning" (clause 12) and "public initiative in the presenting of bills of specific interest to the municipality, the city or the neighborhoods, by means of the manifestation of at least five percent of the electorate" (clause 13).

Since the 1990s, one of the most important forms of citizen political involvement has been through participatory budgeting. During this process hundreds or thousands of citizens meet in a series of open assemblies in order to establish spending priorities before the legislative budget cycle begins. Elected delegates negotiate the budget with municipal bureaucrats and monitor the previous year's spending and investment priorities. The idea is to allocate a share of public resources to reflect citizen priorities, not the political criteria of a notoriously clientelistic political system. Where civil society is strong and allied with local authorities, as in the emblematic case of Porto Alegre, the capital of Rio Grande do Sul, public investment has risen and public services and local public goods have been extended for the first time to informal neighborhoods and residences. Moreover, remarkably, local democracy and governance institutions have been strengthened through the transparency and accountability of the budgeting process as well as through popular participation and deliberation (particularly among the poor), which have infused meaning into local democracy.

Participatory budgeting institutions are only one, if the most notable, among a number of other councils, conferences, and other venues for citizen participation. Health councils, another "power-sharing" institution in Avritzer's (2009) typology of participatory institutions, bring together representatives of the state, service providers, and representatives of the population with the legal mandate to formulate and implement health policies. By 2002, such councils were in place in 98 percent of Brazil's cities. Citizen participation in these participatory institutions is, of course, uneven, and not all function as Tocquevillian "schools of democracy." Yet even the weakest community organizations have the right to veto city master plans that govern urban land use and development.

Perhaps the most salient question to ask is whether citizen engagement with and the effectiveness of these institutions will wane, or whether they will spread, deepen, and influence governance at the local and higher levels of government. One indication that their incidence and importance may be spreading is the growth of an intriguing initiative of civil society that scales deliberation up to the national level, the National Public Policy Conference. The conferences—large-scale participatory and deliberate experiments—begin with open municipal conferences, which deliberate policy proposals and elect representatives to state conferences, which, in turn, may endorse, modify, or reject municipal popular preferences. Their input becomes the basis for national conferences, which bring together societal representatives and government officials. In the past decade or so, eighty-two national conferences have mobilized millions of people to provide societal inputs into the design and implementation of public policy in such areas as health, education, women, and violence (Pogrebinschi 2013, 222–223, 228). Although participation has been uneven across Brazilian territory, as one might expect, local conferences were held in as many as

2,160 municipalities in preparation for the 2011 Third National Conference on Policies for Women. It is hard to imagine that without the participation of veterans of the neighborhood associations and CEBs "born of fear," and without the local participatory political culture they engendered, institutions such as the NPPCs would be as vibrant as they are. Citizens' groups, in short, have increased the transparency of government and expanded avenues for popular input into public policy.

Coming to Terms with the Past: From Human Rights Campaigns to Institutional Reform

Historically, inequality was layered onto the fabric of political and state institutions, and in practice meant unequal access to the law. As embodied in the classic Brazilian expression attributed to Getúlio Vargas, "for my friends, everything; for my enemies, the law," the wealthy and privileged could circumvent the law, whereas the poor and Afro-descendants could not.

By clamoring for overdue justice, police reform, and judicial reform, human rights campaigns have altered this picture. Justice for the disappeared that seemed so elusive in 1990 is on the horizon, in part because political contexts have changed. A powerful human rights movement pressured presidents who were not part of grand bargains. In Argentina the iconic Mothers of the Plaza de Mayo, once labeled by the military and its supporters as "Las Locas" (the crazy ones) and whose cause was flouted by Carlos Menem in pardoning top military officers, ended up as welcome guests of Nestor Kirchner in the Casa Rosada twenty-six times (Fernández-Anderson, 2011, 1–2).[10] But also critical was the transformation of legal systems from the 1980s and 1990s, when they upheld amnesty laws barring prosecutions against former state officers responsible for perpetrating human rights violations (sixteen countries had passed such amnesties, González-Ocantos 2012). What has enabled judiciaries to take bold jurisprudential steps against impunity has been a sea change in the guiding norms of the judiciary itself—from the formalist, positivist legal cultures that historically protected conservative interests in Latin America to one guided by a juridical vision committed to the defense of human rights that applies doctrines derived from international human rights law. González-Ocantos (2012) attributes this change to committed activists— victims and human rights lawyers—who mounted informal pedagogical interventions to familiarize judges and prosecutors with complex and previously unknown juridical doctrines derived from human rights law. Thus litigants succeeded in overturning amnesties and bringing perpetrators of human rights abuses to trial.

While equal access to the judicial system and equal protection under the law are still more aspirational than real, progress has been made. Human rights groups that have called for an end to impunity not merely for generals and admirals and even paramilitary captains but also for corrupt mayors and local police officers who moonlight for criminal gangs and local businessmen have made progress toward the reform of judicial institutions and regimes of accountability for those who abuse them. The Brazilian Public Prosecution (*Ministério Público*), for instance, which became independent of the executive and judicial branches of government with the 1988 Constitution, is charged with defending the constitutional interests of citizens and society at large, safeguarding the environment, protecting consumers, guaranteeing minority rights, and monitoring public administration at both the federal and state levels. It has the authority to take to court any person or entity for any breaches of collective rights or the artistic and cultural autonomy of the nation, including mayors and members of Congress. Courts have gained autonomy from the other branches of government through recruitment, tenure, and financing, and exercised it on such critical occasions as declaring major government policies unconstitutional. Citizen movements in Brazil have even been influential in creating three new special secretariats (whose heads have cabinet rank) to promote human rights, women's rights, and the inclusion of Afro-descendants: the Special Secretariat for Human Rights, the Special Secretariat for Women's Rights, and the Special Secretariat for the Promotion of Racial Equality. Finally, with the presence of every living president, Brazil launched a Truth Commission twenty-seven years after the military left government. In sum, these movements of those who remember are bringing the rule of law and the concept of equal access to the law in Latin America into the twenty-first century.

The Southern Cone and Beyond: Comparative Perspectives

The monumental changes described in the transformation of political culture and institutions in Brazil did not unfold in quite the same way or produce quite the same results in Argentina, Uruguay, and Chile. Although all three have retained democratic regimes for decades, and elite and mass political actors in each have learned to embrace the normative tenets of democratic competition, none has matched Brazil's record of achieving new spaces for citizen participation and safeguarding of citizen rights through the creation of new institutions and the reform of old ones. If memory serves to stimulate new forms of grass-roots association and participation, why are they not visible in the neighborhood? At least three factors stand out as critical: the role of the Catholic Church, the role of the business community, and the relationship between political parties and civil society.

Numerous witnesses and scholars have attested to the special spaces created by the Catholic Church for self-defense, civic organization, and eventually, pro-democratic political action. The Brazilian hierarchy led what was probably the most progressive Roman Catholic Church in the world (Levine and Mainwaring 1989, 214). The connection between the positions adopted by church leaders and political participation on the individual level has been drawn by political scientists (see McDonough et al 1998) who, using comparative survey data, discovered that whereas religiosity drove down participation where commitment to the church was associated with "quietism" (as in Spain), in Korea and Brazil, where churches helped to rally the general public against authoritarianism, the link between religiosity and political participation was strongly positive (McDonough et al 1998, 935, 939). In the aftermath of authoritarianism, Brazilians were twice as likely as Spaniards to belong to a voluntary association. The Argentine and Uruguayan Catholic bishops did not oppose authoritarianism as Brazilian cardinals and bishops did, nor did they promote grass-roots communities, or at least not the ones they could not directly control. But their counterparts in Chile did. Why, then, did commitments to the church in Chile, where the Catholic hierarchy also contested military rule, not spill over into popular participation?

Unlike in Brazil where the business community withdrew support for state authoritarianism and threw its lot in with civil society, business elites in Chile were fearful of losing a class war and until the very end of the military regime "accepted unquestioningly many state policies that were detrimental to its economic interests and acquiesced completely in the state's project of relatively autonomous domination of the political sphere" (Stepan 1985, 340). Yet however much weight the domestic economic elite exerted in facilitating a transition to democracy, arguably its impact on democratic institutions and culture would erode with time as democratic regimes enacted business-friendly policies. Thus we need to consider a third factor—the degree to which civil society was free to mobilize along new divides or was mobilized (or demobilized) along traditional lines by political parties. Though protest movements in Chile—especially beginning in 1983—were quite important in that "they allowed people to overcome fear," "revealed the military's failure to dissolve collective identities and inhibit collective action," and "reintroduced political 'space' for civil society" (Garretón 1989, 270), they did not survive and exercise the same impact on institutions and political participation in the new democracy.

This failure has been attributed to the role played by political parties. Garretón (1989, 270) contends that once the parties assumed leadership of the protests, the differences in their goals and strategies adversely affected the fate of the mobilizations. For Oxhorn (1995) party culpability went deeper: Chilean parties, which felt they bore responsibility for authoritarianism, demobilized civil society organizations that had arisen autonomously during the dictatorship. His claim is supported by Weyland's interviews with many of the principals (2014, 199–200), who revealed that during the events of 1988–1989 they saw their most urgent task as controlling the protests and general strikes that in 1983 had taken them by surprise. Unlike during the earlier mass protests, when party leaders had lost their historic "firm command" over members of affiliated associations such as trade unions, by 1988 they had "reasserted control" over mid-level politicians and associational leaders. What "reasserting control" meant was first shifting the arena of contention from the streets to the polls, a process that involved channeling the "participatory energies of centrist and leftist citizens into procedural channels" (Weyland 2014, 217–18), and second, that all necessary compromises with former regime supporters be made, even when these included accepting authoritarian institutions and institutional constraints on popular sovereignty (219–221). This interpretation is supported by Winn's account in this volume of his extraordinary conversation with Camilo Escalona, then head of the Socialist Party, who acknowledged the party was demobilizing its grassroots because it wished to avoid making promises that, if fulfilled, could jeopardize the economic model. Brazilian parties were different. In the shuffle and reshuffle of party systems after 1965, 1979, 1985, and beyond, the very instability that made those parties so woefully ineffective in Congress and as political representatives in the first decade of democracy paradoxically prepared the terrain for civil society organization to flourish. With the sole exception of the PT, no parties had any connections to social movements. Initially, the difference between these cases may have stemmed from the ways in which political actors understood the role of democratic citizens. Ultimately, however, citizens themselves pushed the limits parties set for them.

In sum, there is no clear direct relationship between the intensity of repression and the transformation of beliefs, representation, and institutions in a more democratic direction. Memory is most "productive" when its creative energies transform parties rather than are constrained by them. Democracy needs time for the seeds sown during the authoritarian past to bear fruit.

Conclusions

Memory is at work in Latin American democracies today. Self-proclaimed amnesties have been overturned by high courts, militaries have returned to their barracks now stripped of resources, prestige, and the power to govern themselves and interject themselves into politics, and impressively, new norms of citizenship and new cultures of participation have taken hold in societies once vertically organized by powerful states. Although this transformation is most evident in Brazil, democracy reaches farther across territories and down the social ladder than at any time in Latin American history. If the arguments advanced in this chapter are correct, they will have built a compelling case that the future of democracy is perhaps more promising than at any time in Latin America.

But can we confidently attribute these salutary changes to authoritarianism? After all, it could be argued, as some have, that democracy is stronger because it is externally supported, modernization has advanced, or citizens have mobilized for reasons other than memories of authoritarianism; moreover, political culture is evidently more democratic today than twenty years ago. This chapter has argued that the weight of the past has indeed shaped the politics of the present, through multiple channels. Political learning has strengthened the commitment of elite actors of the left and right, as well as that of leaders of major social institutions to democratic institutions and procedures for adjudicating conflict and distributing resources. But elite learning alone would not have necessarily created participatory institutions, reformed judiciaries, and transformed political culture. It is impossible to imagine how the dense network of civil society organizations, participatory institutions of local governance, new mechanisms of societal accountability, new political parties, escalating citizen intolerance of corruption and even clientelism and vote buying, new constitutional guarantees of rights, and new batteries of legislation to promote equality of opportunity and equal access to the law could have come into being in contemporary Brazil without the mobilization of ordinary men and women against authoritarianism. Although civil society was less visible in Chile for the first two decades of democracy, in recent years a wave of middle-school and university student protests has gripped the nation against policy moderation and compromise by the parties to such an extent that they do not appreciably differ on major policies. Even if the Chilean political class learned its lessons all too well and lost partisans along the way because of it, genuine democracy is self-correcting as well as messy. Today the second Socialist government of Michelle Bachelet promises more change.

Political scientists did not foresee just how monumental the changes I have described would be. Even the most optimistic supporters of voluntary associations did not anticipate the profound spillover effects for political institutions and political culture. The value of a volume such as this one is that it gives us the opportunity to place the political transformations of the past quarter century or more in a perspective that was obscured to contemporary observers and can be seen only with the passage of sufficient time. We now know that repression made possible a democratic political culture, stronger democratic political institutions, and the erection of new and vibrant channels of democratic participation and representation, and freedom itself. That Latin Americans remember the past is no longer a crushing weight on the brains of the living that stifles the aspirations and creativity of democratic citizens. It is a passport to a more enduring and deeper democracy than they have ever known.

Notes

1. This concept was famously used by the renowned Brazilian anthropologist Roberto da Matta (1978) to illustrate the social hierarchies embedded in a national political identity epitomized by the expression, "Do you know with whom you are speaking?"

2. Based on the published revelations of Air Force General and military *junta* member Fernando Matthei as well as his own interviews, Weyland (2014, 208–209) characterizes the human rights trials in Argentina as having made a "tremendous impression" in Santiago and having caused "consternation and alarm at the very core of Chile's authoritarian government." Reportedly in meetings of the ministerial cabinet Justice Minister Hugo Rosende even warned fellow members of the authoritarian regime that the democratic opposition would not only try military officers but hang them from the lamppost in front of Chile's presidential palace, a reference to the famous precedent of the fate suffered by President Gualberto Villarroel in Bolivia in 1946 at the hands of a mob.

3. Santiago Carillo was head of the Spanish Communist Party. This advice, offered during a strategic moment in Spain's transition to democracy, is quoted in O'Donnell and Schmitter (1986, 29).

4. Huntington (1991, 213–231) distinguished when *not* to prosecute authoritarian officials (if they retained power as a result of an authoritarian regime-led or brokered transition to democracy and hence the political costs would outweigh the moral gains), and when it was possible to prosecute top (but not middle-level or lower-ranking) officers (if the military had been displaced by the regime transition and it was "politically and morally desirable" to do so), and counseled that in either case democratizers should find a means to achieve a "full and dispassionate public accounting of how and why the crimes were committed," and above all, not to forget.

5. Salvemini was particularly eloquent: "I must acknowledge . . . that I would have been wiser had I been more moderate in my criticism of the Giolittian system. For while we Italian crusaders attacked him from the Left, accusing him of being—as he was—a corrupter of Italian democracy in the making, others assailed him from the Right because he was even too democratic for their taste. Our criticism thus did not help to direct the evolution of Italian public life toward less imperfect forms of democracy but rather toward the victory of . . . reactionary groups" (as cited in Bermeo 1992, 273).

6. According to its website, www.pastoraloperaria.org.br, the Labor Pastoral today is present in more than 80 dioceses in 16 of Brazil's 27 states; it attends to formal sector, informal sector, and unemployed workers, with the mission to "build the self-esteem of workers in their struggle for a more dignified life . . . [and] in the construction of a new society and a new culture of labor based on the fulfillment of the human person in all his dimensions; involve Christians in the commitment to the working class, reinforcing the struggle for rights and citizenship; . . . and fight for the primacy of labor over capital."

7. http://www.vanderbilt.edu/lapop/brazil/Brazil_Tech_Info_2012_W_03.12.13 .pdfhttp://www.vanderbilt.edu/lapop/brazil/Brazil_Tech_Info_2012_W_03 .12.13.pdf http://www.vanderbilt.edu/lapop/brazil/Brazil_Tech_Info_2012_W_ 03.12.13.pdf

8. In their experience attending CEB meetings, Levine and Mainwaring (1989, 219) eloquently testified to having seen countless times "once tongue-tied men and women" stepping forward to speak and share experiences, "people who were once afraid to speak out," now doing so "with confidence and vigor," and people who did not even have a rudimentary notion of their rights now standing up for them.

9. The authenticity of signatures had to be verified by a minimum of three legally constituted "associative entities."

10. In January 2006, the movement leader Hebe de Bonafini decided to end the *"Marchas de la Resistencia,"* annual marches held since 1981 because *"ya no tenemos un enemigo en la Casa Rosada."* ("We don't have an enemy in the Presidential Palace any longer"). Referring to one of the 26 meetings she had with President Kirchner during his mandate, Bonafini said *"Faltaba un pucherito en el medio para comerlo juntos, porque me sentía en mi casa."* (There was only one thing missing, a stew to eat together, because I felt at home") (Fernández-Anderson 2011, 1–2).

References

Acuña, Carlos. 1994. "Politics and Economics in the Argentina of the Nineties (Or, Why the Future Is No Longer What It Used to Be)," pp. 31–73 in William C. Smith, Carlos Acuña, and Eduardo Gamarra, eds., *Latin American Political*

Economy in the Age of Neoliberal Reform: Theoretical and Comparative Perspectives for the 1990s. Miami, FL: North-South Press.

Avritzer, Leonardo. 2009. *Participatory Institutions in Democratic Brazil.* Washington, D.C.: Woodrow Wilson Center Press and Baltimore, MD/Johns Hopkins University Press.

Bermeo, Nancy. 1992. "Democracy and the Lessons of Dictatorship." *Comparative Politics* 24, 3: 273–291.

Bermeo, Nancy. 2003. *Ordinary People in Extraordinary Times: The Citizenry and the Breakdown of Democracy.* Princeton: Princeton University Press.

Burdick, John. 2004. *Legacies of Liberation: The Progressive Catholic Church in Brazil at the Start of a New Milennium.* Hampshire, UK: Ashgate.

Cohen, Jean L. and Andrew Arato. 1992. *Civil Society and Political Theory.* Cambridge: MIT Press.

Collier, Ruth Berins and David Collier. 1991. *Shaping the Political Arena: Critical Junctures, the Labor Movement, and Regime Dynamics in Latin America.* Princeton: Princeton University Press.

Dahl, Robert A. 1971. *Polyarchy: Participation and Opposition.* New Haven: Yale University Press.

DaMatta, Roberto. 1978. *Carnavais, Malandros, e Heróis: Para uma Sociologia do Dilema Brasileiro.* Rio de Janeiro: Zahar (4th edition).

Economist. 2013. "Earth's Got Talent: The *Economist's* Country of the Year" (December 21).

Fernandez-Anderson, Cora. 2011. *The Impact of Social Movements on State Policy: Human Rights and Women's Movements in Argentina, Chile and Uruguay.* Ph.D. Dissertation, University of Notre Dame.

Fleet, Michael. 1985. *The Rise and Fall of Chilean Christian Democracy.* Princeton: Princeton University Press.

Garretón M., Manuel Antonio. 1989. "Popular Mobilization and the Military Regime in Chile: The Complexities of the Invisible Transition." Pp. 259–277 in Susan Eckstein, ed., *Power and Popular Protest: Latin American Social Movements.* Berkeley: University of California Press.

Gibson, Edward L. 2001. *Class and Conservative Parties: Argentina in Comparative Perspective.* Baltimore: Johns Hopkins University Press.

Gill, Anthony. 1998. *Rendering Unto Caesar. The Catholic Church and the State in Latin America.* Chicago: University of Chicago Press.

Gillespie, Charles G. 1991. *Negotiating Democracy: Politicians and Generals in Uruguay.* Cambridge: Cambridge University Press.

Gonzalez Ocantos, Ezequiel Alejo. 2012. "The Collapse of Impunity Regimes in Latin America: Legal Cultures, Strategic Litigation and Judicial Behavior." Ph.D. Dissertation, University of Notre Dame.

Hagopian, Frances. 1990. "'Democracy by Undemocratic Means'? Elites, Political Pacts, and Regime Transition in Brazil." *Comparative Political Studies* 23, 2: 147–170.

Hite, Katherine. 2000. *When the Romance Ended: Leaders of the Chilean Left, 1968–1998.* New York: Columbia University Press.

Holston, James P. 2008. *Insurgent Citizenship: Disjunctions of Democracy and Modernity in Brazil.* Princeton: Princeton University Press.

Huntington, Samuel P. 1991. *The Third Wave: Democratization in the Late Twentieth Century.* Norman: University of Oklahoma Press.

Karl, Terry Lynn. 1990. *Comparative Politics.* "Dilemmas of Democratization in Latin America" 23, 1(October): 1–21.

Keck, Margaret E. in Alfred Stepan, ed. 1989. Pp. 252–296 in *Democratizing Brazil: Problems of Transition and Consolidation.* New York: Oxford University Press.

Levine, Daniel H. 1993. "Popular Groups, Popular Culture, and Popular Religion." Pp. 171–225 in Daniel H. Levine, ed., *Constructing Culture and Power in Latin America.* Ann Arbor: University of Michigan Press.

Levine, Daniel H. and Scott Mainwaring. 1989. "Religion and Popular Protest in Latin America: Contrasting Experiences." Pp. 203–240 in Susan Eckstein, ed., *Power and Popular Protest: Latin American Social Movements.* Berkeley: University of California Press.

Lowenthal, Abraham F. and Sergio Bitar. Forthcoming. *Lessons Learned.* Stockholm: International IDEA.

Mainwaring, Scott. 1986. *The Catholic Church and Politics in Brazil, 1916–1985.* Stanford: Stanford University Press.

Mainwaring, Scott and Aníbal Pérez-Liñán. 2014. *Democracies and Dictatorships in Latin America: Emergency, Survival, and Fall.* Cambridge UK: Cambridge University Press.

Mainwaring, Scott and Alexander Wilde, eds. 1989. *The Progressive Church in Latin America.* Notre Dame: University of Notre Dame Press.

Martins, Luciano. 1986. "The 'Liberalization' of Authoritarian Rule in Brazil." Pp. 72–94 in Guillermo O'Donnell, Philippe C. Schmitter, and Laurence Whitehead, eds., *Transitions from Authoritarian Rule: Latin America.* Baltimore: Johns Hopkins University Press.

Marx, Karl. 1972. "The Eighteenth Brumaire of Louis Bonaparte." In Robert C. Tucker, ed., *The Marx-Engels Reader.* New York: Norton.

McDonough, Peter, Doh C. Shin, and José Álvaro Moisés, 1998. "Democratization and Participation: Comparing Spain, Brazil, and Korea." *Journal of Politics,* 60, 4: 919–953.

O'Donnell, Guillermo and Philippe C. Schmitter. 1986. *Transitions from Authoritarian Rule: Tentative Conclusions about Uncertain Democracies.* Baltimore: Johns Hopkins University Press.

Oxhorn, Philip D. 1995. *Organizing Civil Society: The Popular Sectors and the Struggle for Democracy in Chile.* University Park: Pennsylvania State University Press.

Pogrebinschi, Thany. 201. "The Squared Circle of Participatory Democracy: Scaling Up Deliberation to the National Level." *Critical Policy Studies,* 7, 3: 219–241.

Przeworski, Adam. 1989. "Democracy as a Continent Outcome of Conflicts." Pp. 59–80 in Jon Elster and Rune Slagsted, eds., *Constitutionalism and Democracy.* Cambridge UK: Cambridge University Press.

Rochon, Thomas R. and Michael J. Mitchell. 1989. "Social Bases of the Transition to Democracy in Brazil." *Comparative Politics,* 21, 3: 307–322.

Smith, Brian H. 1982. *The Church and Politics in Chile: Challenges to Modern Catholicism.* Princeton: Princeton University Press.

Stepan, Alfred. 1985. "State Power and the Strength of Civil Society in the Southern Cone of Latin America." Pp. 317–345 in Peter B. Evans, Dietrich Rueschemeyer, and Theda Skocpol, eds., *Bringing the State Back in.* Cambridge UK: Cambridge University Press.

Stepan, Alfred. 1988. *Rethinking Military Politics: Brazil and the Southern Cone.* Princeton: Princeton University Press.

Tavares de Almeida, Maria Herminia. 1987. "*Novo Sindicalismo* and Politics in Brazil." Pp. 147–178 in John D. Wirth, Edson de Oliveira Nunes, and Thomas E. Bogenschild, eds., *State and Society in Brazil: Continuity and Change.* Boulder: Westview Press.

Verba, Sidney. 1963. "Germany: The Remaking of Political Culture." Pp. 130–170 in Lucian W, Pye and Sidney Verba, eds., *Political Culture and Political Development.* Princeton: Princeton University Press.

Weffort, Francisco. 1989. "Why Democracy?" pp. 327–350 in Alfred Stepan, ed., *Democratizing Brazil: Problems of Transition and Consolidation.* New York: Oxford University Press.

Weyland, Kurt. 2104. *Making Waves: Democratic Contention in Europe and Latin America since the Revolutions of 1848.* Cambridge UK: Cambridge University Press.

10

The Memory of Politics:
Pre-Coup Democracy and
Chile's Democratic Transition

Peter Winn

Chile's peaceful transition from the harsh 17-year dictatorship of General Augusto Pinochet to a restored democracy led by Pinochet's center-left civilian opponents in the Concertación coalition has been celebrated both nationally and internationally as a model for others to follow. So has its economic "miracle," a decade of high economic growth with low inflation, low unemployment, and high foreign investment within a neo-liberal model softened by the Concertación's social welfare concerns that reduced poverty from 40 percent to 14 percent. Part of this Chilean success story, it is argued,[1] was made possible by the determination of the leaders of the Concertación to avoid the populism and other "errors" of Salvador Allende's Popular Unity coalition, which the Concertación leaders held responsible for the breakdown of Chilean democracy in 1973. Their negative memory of Chile's pre-coup democracy informed their actions, reactions, and inactions during the democratic transition from the Pinochet dictatorship to the restored democracy that the Concertación dominated from 1990 to 2010 (Winn, 1993; Garreton, 2003).

But, as Merilee Grindle and Sergio Bitar underscore elsewhere in this volume, memory and history are contested terrain, especially when what is remembered is as controversial as Chile's recent history (Grindle, 14–15). Despite 17 years of Pinochet's propaganda and leftist leaders' self-critiques of their youthful errors during the pre-coup period, not all Chileans shared these dominant negative elite assessments of the democracy of the Allende era. On the contrary, many workers, peasants, and *pobladores* (shanty-town dwellers) looked back to the Allende era with nostalgia, as a time of deepened democracy when they felt empowered politically and were protagonists of their own destiny. They also remember it as a period in which Chile's structural social and economic inequality was combated and social justice was a government priority. Most of all, they recalled the Allende years as a time of social engagement and active citizenship.

Both the actions of the workers who initiated resistance to the dictatorship during the late 1970s and convoked the social protests of 1983–1985 that began Chile's elongated transition toward democracy, and those of the shanty-town youths who were the central protagonists of that protest movement with its demand for an end to the dictatorship and the restoration of democracy, were informed in part by positive collective memories of the country's pre-coup democracy. Moreover, selectively positive memories of the Popular Unity years helped inform the recent student movement's critique of the Concertación's top-down political practice and their demand for a new, fully democratic constitution. The contested memory of pre-coup politics continues to influence the debate about Chilean democracy to this day.

It also continues to distort perceptions of Chile's violent recent past. Like Sergio Bitar, I am convinced that the political violence of the 1973 coup and the years of state terror that followed can neither be understood nor fully transcended without confronting the Allende era that led up to the coup and Chile's divided memory of that pre-coup era. For years, the most forbidden memory in Chile has not been the Pinochet era, but the Allende era that preceded it. Santiago's otherwise exemplary Museum of Memory and Human Rights, which opened in 2010, tries to avoid that political debate by beginning its permanent exhibition with the coup, leaving the visitor to guess as to its causes and the reasons for the state terror that the museum effectively details. This is a particular problem when visitors belonging to younger generations have no memories of their own of these controversial historical periods, and a central goal of the museum's pedagogy of memory is inter-generational transmission (Winn, 2013).

There are other reasons as well for focusing this essay on memories of the Allende era. I share Susan Draper's belief that "sometimes the excessive insistence on remembering atrocity cancels out the transformative potential of a notion of democracy" (Draper, in Chapter 7). It is the "transformative potential" of the deepened democracy of the pre-coup era that the coup and dictatorship set out to reverse, and it is that aspect of the period that has been lost in Chile's most recent transition toward democracy, underscoring the importance of rescuing its memory and its history from oblivion.

The transformative power of deepened democracy is a central theme of this essay. Its focus on workers and their experience of the Allende era speaks as well to Elizabeth Jelin's conference keynote argument that the political violence of the recent past should not just be viewed through the lens of human rights, but also as part of a contested battle for equity. This essay is framed within a historical memory that sees the Allende era as shaped by a struggle for social justice that the coup and state terror intended to reverse. The more limited political violence of the rightists during the Popular Unity periods sought to slow and halt the movement for social justice protagonized from below by Chile's workers, peasants and *pobladores* and aided from above by the Allende government. Its ultimate goal was to create the conditions for the military coup and dictatorship that would both reverse the advances in social equity made during the Popular Unity years and to discipline the workers, peasants, and *pobladores* so severely that they would never again have the temerity to try to carry out a social revolution that would address Chile's social injustice, economic inequality and elitist political power structure.

Within this frame, the deepened democracy of the Allende era represents an empowerment of non-elite Chileans that was key to their struggle for social justice. The memory of that empowerment and that struggle remains contested terrain today, in its deepened democracy offering Chileans an alternative model of democracy and citizenship to the current disillusioned limited participation within a constrained democracy still shaped in important ways by Pinochet's authoritarian constitution and decrees, which replaced the "model democracy" ended by his coup.

The military coup of September 11, 1973, marked a great divide in Chilean history: between democracy and dictatorship, the rule of law and state terror, socialism and neo-liberalism, egalitarianism and hierarchy, among other binaries. It is not surprising that as a result Chilean analysis of the pre-coup period has been teleological, with everything seen through the distorting lens of the coup that was to come. This is true for Chilean democracy, which before the coup was hailed as a "model democracy," but since then has been studied primarily to explain its breakdown.[2]

Pinochet propagandists promoted the view of pre-coup Chilean democracy as chaos, in order to justify his long dictatorship. But the Concertación echoed this critique, albeit in other terms, and came to power in 1990 determined to avoid the errors of the pre-coup democracy that they regarded as the cause of its breakdown. This negative memory of Chile's pre-coup democracy as "irresponsible populism" was a reason for the Concertación's continuation of the dictatorship's neo-liberal policies that they had attacked when they were in opposition, and it was largely responsible for major Concertación parties' demobilization of their own supporters and their leaders' distancing themselves from the social base that had elected them.

As Andrés Velasco, who was assistant finance minister in the first Concertación government and finance minister in the first Bachelet government, explained in a scarcely disguised critique of the Allende government and its "populist" democracy, the Concertación was "determined to break the populist cycle, in which a government is elected on promises to satisfy unmet social demands but in doing this undermines its budget, generates inflation, erodes income and is overthrown—two years of euphoria and fifteen years of penance! . . . We are not going to make the mistakes . . . of some of our predecessors" (Winn, 1993). The Concertación's negative collective memory of Popular Unity democracy, an evaluation shared by the two dominant parties of the Concertación, the Christian Democrats and the Socialists—the former opponents of the Popular Unity in the 1970s, the latter "revolutionary" socialists in the 1970s, but "renovated" socialists in the 1990s—informed its politics and policies.[3]

Yet despite Pinochet propaganda justifying his 1973 military coup and long dictatorship by attacking the democracy that he overthrew, and the Concertación's critical evaluation of the character and outcome of pre-coup democracy, not all Chileans remembered the Allende era democracy negatively. It might be a dissident collective memory, but many Chileans recalled the Popular Unity era as one of deepened democracy, when government policies prioritized social justice and made them feel empowered for the first time. In 1990, they expected the restored democracy that they had fought for to also restore some of that empowerment and some of those policies.

Foremost among these Chileans were the country's organized blue-collar workers, who had played a leading role in the resistance to the dictatorship as early as the 1970s and had convoked the social protests of the 1980s that had powerfully launched Chile's transition to democracy. Not surprisingly, Chile's workers expected to benefit from democracy's successful restoration in the 1990s under the leadership of the parties that they had supported, including Allende's Socialist Party. Chile's workers had paid a heavy price when their side lost in 1973, and they expected to be leading beneficiaries in the 1990s, now that their side had "won."[4]

Many of these workers recalled the pre-coup era as one of active citizenship and empowerment, with strong popular participation and protagonism. These memories informed their strikes and the social protests against the Pinochet dictatorship, which responded to worker appeals for monthly civil society protests, during which the protesters demanded the restoration of democracy and began the complex process that culminated in the triumph of the Concertación in the 1988 plebiscite and in the presidential and congressional elections of 1989.

It is important to underscore that the pre-coup democracy that these workers were remembering was more extensive, more profound, and more participatory than the periodic voting for political representatives that U.S. citizens understand as democracy and that has been the norm in post-1990 Chile as well. Workers participated in those periodic rites of citizenship as well during the 1964–1973 decade, when much more seemed to depend upon the outcome of this balloting, including decisions for or against reform or revolution.

But, in addition to voting in Chile's representative democracy, these workers also experienced a direct grass-roots union democracy and an economic democracy in their workplace that reshaped their lives and worldviews. This experience of active citizenship and empowerment within a multi-dimensional democracy left memories that informed their actions and those of their children under the dictatorship and shaped their expectations in 1990, when democracy returned to Chile, albeit in a more limited and constrained form. As this multi-dimensional pre-coup democracy is less well known, I will focus on it in this essay.

Perhaps most immediate for most workers was the union democracy that reached its apex in Chile during the Popular Unity period. On the one hand, the numbers of unionized workers grew to 855,000, roughly a third of the work force, the highest percentage in Chilean history before or since. On the other, the dynamics and depth of their participation intensified, as did the issues that their union democracy decided.

This emerged clearly from my reading of the minutes of the union meetings for these years of the Yarur Obrero and Empleado unions and the Ex-Yarur Sindicato Unico that merged both of these blue- and white-collar unions into one big union.[5] Interspersed with routine union business—expenditures, committees, grievances—are references to happenings of a different kind. One that leaps off the page was the vote to expel a long-time rightist company union officer, because after Allende's election as president in 1970 and the election of a leftist slate of union officers that followed, he had pulled out a pistol at a union meeting and threatened to shoot anyone who tried to take the factory away from the Yarurs. Less dramatic but equally weighty was the decision in 1971 to purchase a shuttered movie theater a few blocks away for use as a union hall. Seemingly routine to an outsider, this proposal—and the factory owner's opposition to it—reflected a history in which the blue-collar union's "free" use of company space within the Yarur mill was symbolic of the union's lack of independence and the push for it to become a "yellow" company union, while the acquisition of a union hall and office outside the enterprise was a giant step in the workers' efforts to re-establish a union independent of company control.[6]

The dynamism and saliency of union democracy at the Yarur mill emerges even more clearly from my 1970s interviews with union leaders and rank-and-file workers. They tell the story of the struggle—clandestine at first and then with Allende's election more open—to elect a leftist slate of union officers independent of company control in the most important exercise of union democracy at Yarur since the 1962 strike vote. They also recount and reveal the efforts of that now independent union to win concessions in wages, benefits, and working conditions that the Yarurs intransigently refused to negotiate, at times refusing to meet with the elected union officers or to accept their legitimacy.[7]

Together with the union minutes for April 28, 1971, these interviews tell the story of the most fateful union meeting in the history of the Yarur mill, which led to the worker takeover of the factory and—after three days of seesawing negotiations with Allende, cabinet ministers, and party leaders—culminated in the nationalization of Yarur, Inc. It was the first domestic manufacturing enterprise to be nationalized in Allende's Chile, not because it had been abandoned by its owners, but because it was a monopoly on the Popular Unity's list of enterprises to form part of the Social Property Area (APS), envisioned as the public sector of Chile's "democratic road to socialism"—and because it had a labor conflict that was threatening the production of consumer necessities, which allowed the government to take over its management.

From my reading of the union minutes and my interviews with union leaders and rank and file workers, that momentous Yarur union meeting emerges as an extraordinary exercise in direct democracy, one in which—to the surprise of the local union leaders who had "prepared the meeting" and the amazement of the national union leader sent by Allende to prevent it—the rank-and-file workers took control. Many took the floor to vent decades of resentment at company repression, exploitation and denial of union democracy. When the union president, Orlando Rojas, began to read the list of worker demands that Amador Yarur had rejected, each one was punctuated by thunderous unscripted worker applause. And when the floor was opened for discussion of what was to be done, the local union leaders and activists were surprised at the extent and depth of rank-and-file democratic participation. "Normally in meetings most *compañeros* never ask for the floor; and when they do, it is with certain prudence—trying not to attack the company," because outspoken workers risked getting fired, explained a veteran of many meetings:

But in the meeting where the strike was declared, I was amazed at the courage of many *compañeros* shouting out to demand the floor. They told the union president, Compañero Rojas, that he had to go on strike, that once and for all they had to fix the wagon of these Turkish thieves. And many *compañeros* who normally never speak valiantly, asked for the floor to say those things.[8]

If the local union leaders and activists were surprised at the spontaneous outburst that took the meeting in the direction that they wanted it to go, Ramón Fernández was amazed; he was Secretary for Conflicts for the national labor confederation (*Central Unitaria de Trabajadores de Chile*, or CUT), but also a Socialist Party member who was at the meeting as Allende's emissary with instructions not to let the workers seize the factory and demand its nationalization. Although Fernández was a veteran union leader who had attended thousands of meetings, he told me:

I have never in my life seen anything like this . . . When the union officers told them that the company didn't want to receive them and had denied all their petitions, the people stopped them and began to cry out: "Nationalization! Nationalization!" It was incredible! It was *revolution*! Two thousand workers standing and shouting: "We want nationalization!" And the women workers calling out: "No more exploitation!" They were in a state of euphoria.[9]

In the end, the workers voted overwhelmingly to go on strike and not return to work as long as the Yarurs remained; it was in effect a "strike to rule"—and a demand that the Allende government nationalize their workplace. Many workers at the Yarur factory—which was merged into Machasa in 1980—remembered that meeting even many years later as a defining event in their lives. Moreover, this union meeting was followed by similar meetings in other private sector enterprises, beginning with the textile industry and then spreading to other sectors, including enterprises too small to be incorporated into the APS according to the criteria of Allende, his cabinet, and the Popular Unity parties. In effect, it was the triumph of direct democracy from below over the representative democracy from above headed by Allende and his governing Popular Unity coalition.[10]

Nationally, the biggest advance in union democracy during the Allende years was the change in the manner of choosing the national officers of the CUT from indirect to direct elections. The CUT elections of May 1972 were the first direct elections at both the provincial and national levels. The

Communists finished first nationally, with the Socialists second and the Christian Democrats a close third, but even minor parties contested the elections, which for the first time allowed rank-and-file union members throughout Chile to vote for the national and provincial officers of the labor confederation. Earlier elections had been indirect, with the heads of CUT's constituent federation choosing the national leadership in what was a top-down undemocratic process.

Moreover, when the unions, many of them under top-down Communist Party control, failed to serve sufficiently as an agency for actualizing Allende's democratic road to socialism, "revolutionary" workers (primarily Left Socialists) invented a new bottom-up institution, the *cordón industrial*, which united the workers of an industrial belt, or a geographically defined "territory." The *cordones* enabled Chilean workers from neighboring workplaces to transcend the craft divisions of Chile's labor unions and organize together. But they also reflected the partisan divisions within the Chilean left, with the Communists refusing to participate in what they regarded as illegitimate rivals for the legal unions that they largely controlled. These *cordones industriales*, however, would play crucial roles during the final year of *la vía chilena*, defending their "territory" against attacks by rightist paramilitary groups and helping workers locked out of enterprises too small to be formally nationalized by the government to take over their workplaces and keep them functioning.[11] In diverse ways, the *cordones* would serve as a further agency of Chilean direct democracy before the coup violently suppressed them.

Political democracy was also perfected and expanded during the era before the September 1973 coup ended Chilean democracy for nearly seventeen years. Through a constitutional reform passed during the final year of the Christian Democrat government of Eduardo Frei, but implemented under the Popular Unity government of Salvador Allende, both 18- to 21-year-olds and illiterates were enfranchised, extending the vote to the last groups of disenfranchised adults. Illiterates finally got to vote in the 1973 mid-term congressional elections, signing the voter rolls with their thumbprints and recognizing the party for which they wanted to cast their ballot by their logos. Unfortunately and ironically, that election would be the last free competitive elections in Chile for fifteen years.

There was also a politicization of elections for technically non-political posts, such as that of *Rector* of the University of Chile, which during the Allende years in particular were contested as if they were national elections; this was true as well for municipal elections. As a result, when the Popular Unity won a slight majority of the vote in the municipal elections of April 1971, it was hailed as a mandate to implement their democratic road to socialism nationally. Even more striking, when the Popular Unity candidate for *Rector* of the University of Chile was defeated in March 1972 by a Christian Democrat who was also backed by the right, in an election in which students, faculty, and staff all voted, it was regarded as a Chilean rejection of Allende's socialist program and as a sign that the political momentum nationally had shifted to the right and was now moving against the Popular Unity.

Political democracy also intensified at the sub-municipal level. Chileans voted for members of their *Junta de Vecinos* in the neighborhood where they resided. These elections, which in other eras might not have been partisan politics, were politicized and hotly contested during the Frei and Allende eras, as the political parties sought to mobilize support from below and regarded every vote and local office as "trenches" in the struggle for power and as votes for or against reform or revolution. This was particularly true for residents of *campamentos* or *poblaciones callampas*, self-built squatter shanty towns that multiplied like the wild mushrooms (*callampas*) they were named for during these years, with more than two hundred land seizures during the Allende years alone, so that by 1972 one-sixth of the population of Santiago lived in *poblaciones*. Many of them were recent rural migrants who, cut loose from their conservative rural settings, were newly available for mobilization by political parties and candidates who spoke to their new situations. The Christian Democrats in the 1960s were the first to organize *pobladores* as a social category, targeting them as an unmobilized group whose incorporation into Chile's political system as Christian Democrats could alter its three thirds—one third voting left, another center, and one right—balance of power and transform Chilean Christian Democracy into a hegemonic party like their Italian counterpart. Although the Marxist left initially had problems organizing *pobladores* as anything but working class in a context in which most *pobladores* worked in the unorganized informal economy, they soon were contesting Christian Democratic control of this large group of voters. Political parties were often behind the land seizures that inaugurated squatter settlements and often intervened to prevent the expulsion of squatters by the police, in the process winning political support among the *pobladores* they had helped. Allende was a prominent example of a political leader who won the loyalty of the urban poor by being there for them in their hour of need. The Communists began to play a prominent role in the committees of the homeless (*sin techo*) that organized land seizures.[12]

Particularly striking during the Allende years was the transformation of new squatter settlements and their *pobladores* into terrains of political contest and revolutionary "consciousness-raising" by the MIR (Revolutionary Left Movement), which was founded in the 1960s by leftist students as a Guevarist guerrilla group. But after Allende's election, the MIR put its plans for "armed struggle" on hold and devoted its numerically limited but talented human resources to organizing social strata such as the *pobladores*, who had been comparatively neglected by the Communists and Socialists in their focus on class organization.[13] In the end, the MIR proved themselves better grass-roots organizers than guerrillas.

MIR *campamentos*, such as Nueva La Habana in Santiago or Campamento Lenin in Concepción, were among the best organized and most regulated of the *poblaciones*, with fledgling streets at right angles to each other and a public social center for each square block. They also practiced an intense form of both direct and representative democracy that transcended merely voting for their *Junta de Vecinos*. Every square block had a weekly meeting at which participation was obligatory and where tasks for the week were divided, from distributing food rations to cleaning the toilets in public places, and the decisions of the Directorio of the *campamento* were communicated to the residents.

In fact the Directorio was an internal local legislature, to which each square block elected its representative. At Nueva La Habana, for example, that meant the Directorio was composed of 24 square block representatives, plus seven people chosen by the entire *campamento* to be part of the executive body that governed the *campamento*, whose head was also elected. From the obligatory direct democracy of the square block to the decisions of the Directorio, MIR *campamentos* like Nueva La Habana practiced an intense form of local internal democracy that may not have been legally sanctioned by the Chilean state, but which extended and deepened democracy for their residents in ways that affected their lives and democratic participation more than the formal institutions of Chilean democracy.[14]

MIR *campamentos* also represented the extension of Chilean democracy in another direction: the normalization and intensification of street politics. Traditionally, the street in Chile had belonged to "the people," which usually meant to the left. As far back as 1919, Luis Emilio Recabarren, the "Chilean Lenin" and founder of Chile's Communist Party, had mobilized hundreds of thousands in the Santiago hunger marches protesting the postwar crisis. They included many workers who voted with their feet but did not vote in national elections. The left continued to use and control the street during the decades that followed, with memorable street politics punctuating the eras, most recently during the 1970 election campaign, but most famously in 1957, in a popular protest against rising prices.[15]

Ironically, what made the Allende years distinctive in this regard was the political use of the street by the elite and the middle class socially, and the center and right politically. Starting in December 1971 as a response to Fidel Castro's visit to Chile, elite and middle-class women of the center and right opposition to the Popular Unity marched with their maids banging empty pots, ostensibly to protest consumer shortages that were only beginning at the end of 1971, but would become serious during the year to come. The novelty of elite and middle-class women engaging in street politics increased its impact, and it became a key turning point in the political struggles of the Allende era, reviving and uniting an opposition that had seemed disoriented and demoralized by Allende's election and the Popular Unity's April 1971 municipal election victory. In retrospect, it was a democratic exercise of street politics, even though Allende partisans saw it as illegitimate, in large part because they believed that the streets "belonged" to "the people"—i.e., the left—transforming a historical description into a normative claim (Power, 2002; Baldez, 2002).

More ominous was the debut of armed neo-fascist Patria y Libertad strong-arm squads as "protection" for the women marchers. During 1972, when the center-right opposition shifted its locus of action from the halls of Congress to the streets of Santiago with demonstrations by students and other groups in search of martyrs for their cause, the left responded with armed youth groups of their own. The result was street fights that began with fists and by 1973 ended with guns, creating the images of chaos that Pinochet used over and over again to justify his dictatorship as restoring "order"—a core Chilean value that Pinochet manipulated.

Within this context in which the streets were contested terrain, the demonstrations by the left took on a new urgency. The workers of Ex-Yarur prided themselves on always being "the first in the streets" in the many crises of those years. Moreover, as they marched, taking possession of the downtown streets, they carried signs that affirmed their support for "*their* government," the "government of the workers."

The MIR, on the other hand, critical of the Allende government's "reformism" and demanding that it "arm the people," had its "revolutionary" *pobladores* march with wooden weapons chanting: "Pueblo! Fusil! MIR!" (The People, Guns, MIR). In the absence of elections, the street became a voting booth where Chileans of all views voted with their feet, signaling the intensity of their beliefs and commitments by participating in street demonstrations, thus demonstrating a deeper political commitment than mere voting.

In later years, Chilean workers, like the workers of Ex-Yarur, remembered their experience of yet another dimension of democracy that disappeared with the 1973 coup, one that was notable in Allende's Chile: *economic* democracy. This referred to worker participation in the management of their workplace, or worker co/self-management (Espinoza and Zimbalist, 1978).

It was originally a left Christian Democrat idea, part of their search for a "communitarian socialist" alternative to Communist "state socialism." Worker participation in the enterprises of the social property area was an idea brought to the Popular Unity by the MAPU (Popular Unitary Action Movement), when that small party of talented leaders split off from the Christian Democrats and joined Allende's coalition. The Socialists, with their Trotskyist strain, embraced the new structure, which included worker councilors in the top administrative body. An accord negotiated between the CUT and the Allende government provided the basic framework, but allowed each enterprise of the APS to decide for itself how to apply this framework.

At Ex-Yarur, the first enterprise of the social property area to inaugurate worker participation, local decisions made the system of self-management *more* democratic than the CUT-government accord envisioned. The new structure of self-management began on the factory floor, with an assembly in each work section that was a direct democracy, and with a production committee elected by the workers of each work section, which then chose one of its members as the section's representative on the Coordinating Committee. In the CUT-government accord, the Coordinating Committee was a non-deliberative body presided over by the local union leaders. In Ex-Yarur, however, the Coordinating Committee emerged as powerful and central to worker participation. The section delegates arrived at the weekly meetings of the Coordinating Committee with the authenticity and legitimacy of those most closely in contact with the worker experience and concerns. At the first meeting of the Coordinating Committee they elected one of the section representatives as chair, and as no one objected, this democratization of worker participation was consolidated. As a result, the chair of the Coordinating Committee became a highly visible and major leader in the self-management structure and was elected worker councilor the following year. At the same time, the Coordinating Committee meeting emerged as the most important site of worker participation, the only place where the union leaders and worker councilors—the top officials in the parallel union and participation structures—met, together with the delegates from the work sections. Increasingly, the Coordinating Committee was where worker priorities and strategy were decided, and the worker councilors were instructed to take these concerns to the Administrative Council, the socialist equivalent of the Board of Directors.

There too, the CUT-government structure as adapted at Ex-Yarur proved more democratic than the original accord. In theory, the council was composed of 5 councilors elected by the workers of the enterprise in annual secret ballots and 5 councilors named by the government, and presided over by the tie-breaking government-appointed general manager. The government councilors, however, were over-extended political leaders, labor leaders, or managers of other enterprises, who with a couple of exceptions seldom came to Ex-Yarur meetings. In practice, this meant that there was usually a worker majority at council meetings, although in the meetings that I observed decisions were made by consensus. Still, at Ex-Yarur economic democracy functioned from the factory floor to the enterprise boardroom, and both supervisors and government managers had to take account of it.

This was true as well of the top body of the worker participation structure, the General Assembly of the Workers, an exercise in direct democracy that met monthly. Refusing to be a rubber stamp, the assembly rejected an annual account by the financial manager because it was not written in a form that workers could understand and evaluate. They directed him to rewrite it in layman's language and resubmit for their approval, which he duly did. From top to bottom, then, worker self-management at Ex-Yarur not only exemplified the economic democracy of the CUT-government accord, but also its further democratization.

Worker empowerment also had material consequences, which reflected the Chilean revolution's stress on social justice. During the first two years of Allende's government the workers of Ex-Yarur received average real wage increases of 50 percent, with comparable increases in fringe benefits, although by mid-1972 those gains were being eroded by inflation. They also had new opportunities for internal promotions and special training courses to help them qualify for those positions. Worker self-management and social justice were mutually reinforcing.

Although Ex-Yarur was the first to inaugurate worker self-management, and was more successful in implementing the CUT-government accord than some other enterprises, its experience was typical of the nationalized Chilean textile industry.[16]

This became clear in mid-1972, when a meeting of worker self-management representatives from the different factories of the textile sector of the Social Property Area (APS) was held in order to evaluate their experience and to plan for the future. The assessment of this Encuentro Textil was so positive that the head of the APS, Pedro Vuskovic, the former economy minister, agreed to incorporate worker participation in the national planning process of the APS as well.

This extension of economic democracy to the highest levels of the state, unfortunately, was never carried out, a casualty of the struggle for survival of the Chilean Revolution that began in October 1972, shortly after the Encuentro Textil. But the memory of this economic democracy would help inform the resistance of Chilean workers to the dictatorship in the 1970s, their demands for democracy in the 1980s, and their expectations of a restored democracy in the 1990s.

It was Chile's organized workers, whose empowerment during Allende's democratic road to socialism and self-styled " government of the workers" was one of the salient features of the deepened democracy of that era, who took the lead in organizing and initiating resistance to the dictatorship.

Between the 1973 coup and the end of internal war declaration of the Junta in 1978 there was little that Chile's workers could do to resist the regime and its brutal repression, which first targeted resisting labor leaders and activists. The CUT and its constituent federations had been dissolved and their union leaders had been disappeared, exiled, or imprisoned. No elections were allowed, and gerontocracy had replaced democracy: the oldest union members automatically became the local union officers but were not allowed to either defend or promote labor rights, only to attend to the welfare needs of the workers, within a context of dramatically declining real wages and job security in which worker welfare was deteriorating along with the unions' powers to do anything about it.

A small opening began to emerge in 1978, when the dictatorship decided to institutionalize its neo-liberal "revolution" on the advice of political advisers like Jaime Guzmán, who were afraid that measures taken by a *régimen de fuerza* (*de facto* government) had no legitimacy and could be reversed easily by a restored democracy. A more immediate concern of Pinochet's "Chicago Boys" economic advisers was U.S. and international pressure to restore labor rights under the Carter administration, with a boycott of Chilean exports threatened by an international labor alliance that even included the anti-Communist AFL-CIO.

To avert a potentially crippling boycott for an economy increasingly dependent on exports, the Junta re-established local union elections, but tried to control their outcome by banning Allende-era union officers from running for union leadership and by calling a snap election, with only 72 hours between the announcement of the election and the polls. This was supposed to favor the slates of ostensibly "apolitical" (*gremialista*) rightist union leaders backed by the dictatorship, which these *gremialistas* had supported. But despite these duplicitous maneuvers and the banning of their established leaders, Chile's organized workers found ways to identify, nominate, and elect worker activists who shared the democratic politics of the veteran pre-coup leaders if not their years of experience. Their lack of experience would be ameliorated by the banned leaders of their dissolved national federation, who formed "consulting firms" whose services the new union leaders then bought. In this way the textile industry, a leader in union democracy before the coup, retained its leading role in the new conditions of 1978.

Nor were all the new leaders leftists. Many were centrist Christian Democrats who had moved from their support of the coup and the dictatorship's initial years to an increasingly strident opposition that brought them into alliance with Socialist and Communist labor leaders and their combative unions. One emblematic example was Manuel Bustos, who had suffered torture and interrogation at the Sumar textile mill after the coup alongside Socialist, Communist and MIR activists.

This common experience of Pinochet's repression gave Bustos credibility with the Marxist left and made him a natural bridge for Christian Democratic efforts to create alliances with the left. During the ten years that began in 1978, Bustos would play increasingly important roles; first jailed and then relegated to internal exile, he would end as the president of the new CUT when it was formed in 1988. Another centrist labor leader, the Radical Tucapél Jiménez, would become so popular and crucial to links between left and center that the dictatorship assassinated him in 1982.[17]

Between 1978 and 1982, the neo-liberal Labor Minister José Piñera (brother of the future President Sebastián Piñera) imposed a series of decrees that together added up to a new labor code, which one veteran Socialist labor leader called a "labor code written *by* a businessman *for* businessmen."[18] The new labor code made it hard to organize workers in a union, harder still to bargain collectively, and almost impossible to win a strike, which was limited to 59 days, after which the striking workers were deemed to have resigned their jobs without severance pay. In addition, the enterprise was allowed to break the strike by taking back individual workers willing to work for the old contract and to replace striking workers with strike-breakers from day one. Moreover, strike activists knew that they were likely to be fired once the strike was over, and that they risked being "disappeared" as well.[19]

Yet these labor decrees did create spaces for worker activism and union protagonism. Chile's organized workers lost little time in taking advantage of those spaces and testing their limits.

As usual it was the copper miners who took the lead in organizing active resistance to the dictatorship and its neo-liberal policies, with the textile workers close behind. Skilled workers in Chile's most strategic industry, copper miners had always enjoyed higher salaries and better benefits, as well as greater bargaining power than other Chilean workers, more especially after the nationalization of the mines in 1971. Christian Democratic and *gremialista* white collar workers at the mines had even led a strike against the Allende government in 1973 that played a role in the run-up to the coup, and which had subsequently won them the support of the Junta.

This began to change as copper workers began to push back against lower real wages, constrained labor rights, and curtailed union democracy, and as Christian Democratic activists drew closer to their Socialist and Communist peers in a common struggle against a common adversary. As early as 1977, copper workers protested their conditions with *viandazo* boycotts of the company cafeteria and wildcat strikes. They were organized from below in an echo of pre-coup democracy that rejected and marginalized the union leaders appointed by the dictatorship and the rightist *gremialista* leaders like Guillermo Medina who collaborated with Pinochet. In 1978, another copper miners' strike paralleled the formation of the Coordinadora Nacional Sindical that united Christian Democrats, Communists, and Socialists in one big labor movement for the first time since the coup of 1973.

But it was the 5,000 textile workers of Panal, one of Chile's biggest cotton mills, who in 1980 were the first to test the limits of the new labor code by going out on strike for the full 59 days that the new decree-law allowed. The 1980 Panal strike was an exercise in union democracy, which drew on memories of the democratic empowerment of workers during the Allende era to organize what was in some ways the last pre-coup-style labor action. The local union resisted efforts by leftist parties to control the strike, keeping it a non-partisan movement in which the workers, not the parties, made the decisions. The strikers drew on the surviving social solidarity and class consciousness from the Allende era, and received a flood of "solidarity" from other workers, from copper miners to informal sector workers, who identified with the Panal strikers and saw their struggle as their own, solidarity on a scale that enabled the striking workers to feed their families and pay their bills.

In other ways too the Panal strike heralded the future and marked a giant step in the labor protests against the dictatorship and its neo-liberal labor code that would initiate Chile's slow transition to democracy, a process that spanned the decade of the 1980s. The union leaders stressed the apolitical *gremialista* character of the strike and designed it so that there were no worker deaths or disappearances. They also drew on new forms of solidarity, such as the Catholic Church and the shantytowns, and new forms of protest, such as flash demonstrations on bicycles and church occupations.

The Panal strike was a test at the same time of new social movement strategies and tactics and of the limits of the spaces in the new labor code for worker activism. Historically, the Panal strike of 1980 was a key link between the worker protagonism of the Allende era's deepened democracy and the social protests and transition to democracy movements of the 1980s.

The dictatorship also saw the Panal strike as a test—both of its ability to control labor with the new labor laws and of the ability of the left to reclaim control over the Chilean industrial working class. Therefore, the regime was determined not to let the strike succeed or its leftist-led union survive.

In the end, the Panal workers sustained their strike for 59 days, the longest strike allowed under the new labor code before workers lost their jobs and severance pay. But they lost their jobs anyway when the dictatorship and the right-wing economist it had named to head Panal and supervise its integration into Machasa, a merger of three bankrupt textile enterprises, took the strike as an opportunity to close down Panal and fire *all* of its blue-collar workers (*obreros*), except for a few skilled workers who were transferred to the Yarur mill—a decision that the Panal workers were certain was political, dictated by Pinochet who considered the Panal strike a Communist conspiracy.[20]

The dismemberment of Panal was a warning to Chilean workers who might think of challenging the new labor code's unequal playing field. But the economic crisis that began in late 1981 created socio-economic conditions so bad that even workers who had been fearful of risking their jobs, lives, and liberty before were now moved to act in the face of bankruptcy and shutting down of their workplaces, including Machasa, or what remained of the textile giant after the closing of Panal.

Observers who saw hundreds of Machasa workers marching to the center of Santiago in January 1982, carrying banners demanding a return to state management of their textile mill, could be forgiven for doubting their own eyes.

The workers' use of street politics to pressure the government looked like something out of the Allende era, but it took place in 1982, under a neo-liberal Pinochet dictatorship viscerally hostile to democratic politics and worker protagonism and committed to privatization, not state management of enterprises that had already been privatized. For the Machasa workers, many of them veterans of the Yarur mill, their protest march reminded them of other eras too.

For most of them, it was suffused with memories of the Allende era, when empowered Ex-Yarur workers took over the streets of Santiago in support of the leftist "government of the workers." But for some of the older Machasa workers, including rightist union leaders, 1982 was a throwback to an even earlier memory of democratic politics, the post-World War II years, when the founder of the enterprise, "don" Juan Yarur, had his workers march downtown to pressure the government to assure his supply of imported cotton at protected prices. What both memories of politics had in common was a memory of a participatory democratic politics that inspired them to march to pressure even a dictatorship that was hostile both to their marching and to their demands. It was a memory that helped transform the Machasa workers from passive victims into protagonists of their own destiny, returning to them their historical agency.

The Machasa workers were well aware that this was 1982, not 1971 or 1953. They were not demanding worker self-management or a return to protectionism. But they *were* demanding in 1982 that the Chilean state resume management of the enterprise that it had privatized and returned to its old owners in 1974, just as the Yarur workers had demanded in 1971 that the Allende government take over the management of this same cotton mill. Moreover, the two movements of workers from the Yarur mill used similar tactics of street politics: public marches and demonstrations in combination with petitions and backroom politics to influence the decision-makers in each case. More surprising than the Yarur workers' success in persuading the Socialist Allende to accelerate his timetable and nationalize an enterprise already on his list for nationalization, was the Machasa workers' success in persuading Pinochet to violate his own neo-liberal principles, resume state management of Chile's largest cotton mill, and keep it operating with the same workers despite the bankruptcy of the enterprise. Ironically, the mill remained under state management for a longer period under Pinochet than it had under Allende. They were able to persuade Pinochet because the deepening economic crisis was threatening to undermine his political position, and adding another 5,000 workers to the already soaring unemployment statistics and with their families adding 25,000 people to the already swelling poverty rolls was not in his self-interest, especially when it involved a high-profile flagship enterprise and the fact that worker leaders asking for state management were rightists, not leftists as at Panal. The memory of politics won out over the repression of politics.

A year later, Chile's economic crisis had deepened into the most severe crisis since the Great Depression. During 1981–82, the Chilean economy actually *shrank* by 14 percent. Industries already weakened by the neo-liberal policies of Pinochet's "Chicago Boys" advisers, which had lowered Chile's tariff barriers from 100 percent to 10 percent in one year, leaving the country's manufacturing industries helpless in the face of low-cost Asian imports, now collapsed. Bankruptcies tripled. In the emblematic textile industry, a major manufacturing employer, 45 percent of the enterprises went belly up.

Textile workers were not the only ones affected by the deep economic crisis. By 1983 unemployment rose to 25 percent, and effective unemployment, including people employed in state-run dollar-a-day make-work programs, exceeded 31 percent.[21] Even the copper workers, Chile's labor aristocracy, whose leverage and wages had always been a quantum leap above the rest and whose export industry's markets were in the developed countries, were affected and moved to act.

The copper miners, inspired in part by memories of their active role in pre-coup Chile's democracy, were the first to strike against the dictatorship in 1977 and 1978. Between 1978 and 1982, leftist miners took advantage of the openings in the new labor code to reclaim control of their unions from the rightist *gremialistas* whom the dictatorship had named as union officers and who supported Pinochet.

The new leftist union leaders came from a younger generation of miners who were old enough to remember and be inspired by the Allende era, but young enough not to have been leaders in that era and thus escaped from being banned from union office by the dictatorship. Yet despite this recapture of their union and a radicalization of its demands, collective bargaining had yielded few results, while gains from strikes in 1981 and 1982 amounted to less than the workers' lost wages.

Copper miners had lost their leverage and the cost was lower real wages. Convinced by this experience that traditional forms of labor action were ineffective in the face of a neo-liberal military dictatorship, the copper miners turned to street protests as a tactic and a national alliance with opposition groups that included students and human rights groups, as a strategy.[22]

In May 1983, the copper workers issued a call for monthly protests in solidarity with their demands and in opposition to the regime's neo-liberalism and the deepening economic crisis that model had imposed on Chile.

The response from civil society was overwhelming, not entirely surprising under the circumstances. But what *was* surprising was that the biggest response and the most militant protests came not from organized workers in other sectors, but from unemployed youths in suburban shantytowns.

Many of the shantytown youth who spearheaded the protests had never held formal sector jobs and had little or no prospect of securing one in the crisis. It was a crisis in which fathers lost their jobs and ability to support their families, in which women sold their bodies to put bread on the table or pooled their poverty in *ollas comunes* (communal kitchens) that at least assured their children one nutritious meal each day. Yet the shantytown youth self-identified as "working class" and affirmed their parents' memories of a decade before under Allende's democracy, when they had jobs and when a worker's wages were enough to support a family. They had grown up in shanty towns victimized by Pinochet's repression and in families shaken by the gendered loss of jobs from Chile's neo-liberal opening of the late 1970s, with men losing their jobs and finding it difficult to find new ones, even in the informal economy.

The crisis of 1981–86, with Chile's frayed social safety net as its backdrop, was the last straw. Although it reflected the more general debt crisis of the early 1980s that engulfed almost all of Latin America, it was exacerbated in Chile by the rigid neo-liberalism of advisers like Sergio de Castro, and was blamed on Pinochet. In this context, the economic became political, and the demands for economic relief mixed with demands for the end of the dictatorship and the restoration of democracy—demands that were echoed in the middle-class drum beats on the same empty casserole pots they had used to call for Allende's ouster a decade before. Now part of the middle class joined with the poor in demanding an end to economic policies that had proved so socially costly and economically disastrous. And the Christian Democratic center united with the "democratic left" to demand a return to the democracy that they had helped destroy in the 1970s, but all now valued highly and remembered with nostalgia.

The desperation and rage of the poor was so great that it enabled them to transcend their fear of Pinochet's repression, which put 18,000 troops into the streets of Santiago where they clashed with the shantytown youth, who defied their social control behind barricades of burning tires. Implicit in the protesters' demand for democracy was a demand for an end to the repression, whose most characteristic form during the 1980s was the interrogation with torture of shantytown youth for several days following search-and-seizure operations, in specially prepared spaces within their *poblaciones*—torture that the 2003 Valech Commission on torture and political prison ignored because its comparative brevity did not fit within the commission's mandate.[23] One study of 16 of 113 Santiago *poblaciones* concluded that in those 16 alone more than 96,000 residents, most of them young, had been victims of state torture/terror.[24]

If economic desperation and hatred of the dictatorship were powerful negative incentives behind the shantytown protests, they were also inspired by positive memories of the democracy of the pre-coup era. The youthful protagonists of the protests might have only childhood memories of the Allende era, but those were often reinforced by their parents' memories of democratic empowerment during those years and by what analysts referred to as the "cultura comunista" of their families and neighbors, a leftist political culture that remained even when the political party organizations were destroyed or forced deeply underground. Moreover, these ideals, along with the new organization of the shantytown youth, were often sustained by progressive priests like Mariano Puga in La Legua and Villa Francia or André Jarlán in La Victoria. Many among these priests had participated in Christians for Socialism or some other manifestation of Liberation Theology before the coup, lent to the nascent resistance of shantytown youth the protective cover of the Catholic Church, and taught them how to organize in the new circumstances of an authoritarian Chile.[25]

Punctuated by monthly work stoppages and reinforced by middle-class *cacerolazos,* the monthly shantytown protests assumed a rhythm and power that grew to threaten Pinochet's support within the military and the stability of his dictatorship. Protesters began to chant "y va a caer"—"he's going to fall"—with the wish becoming father to the thought. Pinochet, however, did not fall in 1983–85. He proved to be a shrewd political manipulator when mere force was no longer enough: he maneuvered by firing his neo-liberal economic czar Sergio de Castro and appointing a traditional rightist civilian politician, Sergio Onfre Jarpa, as super minister to negotiate with the opposition; and rehabilitating the Christian Democrats to give him safe interlocutors with whom to negotiate to gain time, but then making sure that those negotiations went nowhere and petered out when the crisis died down.

In the end, neither the monthly worker strikes nor the shantytown protests were able to oust the Pinochet dictatorship, but together they began the elongated transition to democracy in Chile that would culminate in the plebiscite victory of the Concertación for the NO in 1988 that ensured the end of the dictatorship, the electoral victory of the Concertación in the presidential and congressional elections of 1989, and the inauguration of Patricio Aylwin in 1990 as the first elected civilian president since the

coup of 1973. Among their many impacts, the strikes and protests persuaded the conservative Reagan administration that Pinochet could be the
next Somoza, who had to be removed from power before his overthrow left
Communists in control, as they believed had happened in Nicaragua. As a
result, the second Reagan administration actively promoted a controlled,
pacted transition to democracy in Chile that made it a major supporter
of the 1988 plebiscite and of the Concertación for the NO coalition that
opposed Pinochet in the plebiscite, even providing a parallel computer
network whose quick vote count would make it difficult for the dictator
to fraudulently steal the plebiscite of October 5, 1988, and would make it
clear if he did try.[26]

I was an international observer for that plebiscite as part of a LASA team
of Chile experts that probably was the most knowledgeable international
observer group for the 1988 plebiscite. The areas that I observed were the
rural zone of Melipilla, which I had first known in 1972 as a conflict-ridden
zone of the agrarian reform under Allende, and Talagante, a suburban area
with a complex social and political profile. The balloting took place on a
hot day, its relentless sun more like summer than spring. The lines were
long and voters had to wait hours in the hot sun to cast their ballots, yet no
one complained—or went home without casting a ballot. On the contrary,
elderly peasants with leathery faces waited patiently to vote for the first
time in 15 years, while the many young faces in a country with a majority
born since the coup waited excitedly for the opportunity to vote for the
first time. One very pregnant woman went into labor, but insisted on being
helped to the voting booth before being transported to the hospital. An
elderly nun became faint but insisted on voting.

Below this diversity and behind this determination was a common
appreciation of democracy, which they had been denied for fifteen years.
For many there were strong memories of democratic politics from before
the coup. Pinochet tried to spin those memories of pre-coup politics by
projecting images of chaos and conflict from 1973 in his 1988 TV spots,
but a solid majority of Chileans rejected him—and his manufactured
memory of pre-coup politics—on October 5th. That evening I watched
the vote count of paper ballots in Melipilla and Talagante, as activists
surrounded each table to make sure there was no fraud in the count and
cheered the triumph of the "No" in district after district, at both the men's
and women's tables.[27]

Later that night, when he realized that he was losing, Pinochet stopped
the continuous election coverage on national television and contemplated
another coup. But it was too late. The phoned-in quick count by the "No"

campaign showed its decisive victory, which first Sergio Jarpa, Pinochet's ex-super minister, and then General Fernando Matthei, the head of the Air Force, confirmed on national television. Pinochet had lost! A brutal dictatorship that had seized power with bullets had been ousted by ballots. Democracy had triumphed over doubts and fears.

The following days of celebration almost justified the Concertación's vapid slogan : "La alegría ya viene." Smiling people went around flashing victory signs to perfect strangers, while youths did line dances down the central Alameda boulevard chanting "Y ya cayó"—he has already fallen—with new certainty that this time they were right.

The big organized "fiesta popular" was held a couple of days after the plebiscite in the Parque O'Higgins, the "people's park," but also the site of the annual Independence Day military parade. It was an optimistically sunny day, and as an oral historian with journalist credentials, I went around asking people what their expectations were of the restoration of democracy during the years to come. The responses were varied, but many brought out vivid memories of the pre-coup democracy and the popular empowerment and social welfare that had accompanied it. While the Concertación leadership was acutely conscious of the failures of that pre-coup democracy, which Pinochet's propaganda campaign had underscored and reinforced, significant sectors of the Concertacion's social base regarded that pre-coup democracy as an idealized memory and expected it to be revived, along with social and economic policies designed to benefit the majority of Chileans, people like themselves, not the big capitalists or land-owners. Several phrased it in terms of political victory: now that that their side had won, and the civilian right and the military had lost, they expected that they would be the beneficiaries, in terms both of social and economic policies and political process.

What was equally striking was that private sector entrepreneurs and managers also anticipated changes from a Concertación government that would reverse many of the authoritarian, neo-liberal, and inegalitar-ian measures of the Pinochet dictatorship. Their side had lost, and they expected their opponents to follow up their electoral victory with policy shifts, including an increase in democratic empowerment of their work-ers and unions. Workers and union leaders too expected that the Pinochet labor laws would be reversed—or at least heavily revised to create a level playing field. They also believed that the power of unions and of workers within workplaces would be greatly increased.

Chilean workers may not have anticipated a return to Allende-era economic democracy, but their expectations were inflected with their pre-coup experience of democracy and empowerment. What they did look forward to was a democracy in which their political participation was encouraged and not just at election time. Instead, what they experienced was the opposite: the political leaders with whom they had worked and voted for distanced themselves from the people who had put them in office and *de*mobilized them. Christian Democratic and Socialist union leaders had counted on government officials from their party to use their new power to reverse the anti-labor laws of the Pinochet era, protect Chilean industrial jobs, and support union leaders from their party. Instead, politicians imposed party discipline on the union leaders from their party and pressed them to keep the lid on worker demands and mobilization, arguing that it could threaten the transition. Moreover, not only were the grass-roots party organizations in working-class *poblaciones* demobilized; so were the social movements that many analysts had seen in the 1980s as the successors and preferable alternatives to the political parties.[28]

The most striking example of these changes was the Socialist Party, which had been more "revolutionary" than the Communists during the 1970s, but in the 1990s was a big tent party, in effect the Popular Unity coalition without the Radicals (who survived as a small social democratic party within the Concertación) and the Communists, also excluded from the Concertación (although the Socialist Party after 1990 contained many *ex*-Communists). It was also the party whose leaders had undergone the biggest conversion experience in exile, which transformed the young "revolutionary" Socialists of the Popular Unity years into the "renovated" neo-liberal Socialists of the Concertación era (Hite, 2000).

I was aware of this, but still unprepared for my conversation with Camilo Escalona, then head both of the Socialist Party and its most leftist faction. It took place in Villa Grimaldi, once the national intelligence agency's most notorious clandestine center of detention, torture and extermination, where, in 1997, Escalona had come to inaugurate a monument to the Socialists who had disappeared there, including top central committee leaders. I had been invited by a fellow historian and veteran Socialist who was himself unhappy with the direction his party had taken. He arranged for a conversation with Escalona, after his eulogy of the Socialist comrades who, he claimed, had died there in defense of democracy.

I framed my question carefully to be a naive query, professing ignorance of politics but with some knowledge of Chile's 20th-century history, including the history of his party. In the past the Socialists had always been a party that mobilized its grass roots and had strong local organizations in working-class areas. Escalona agreed. But that was no longer true, I said. On the contrary, the Socialist Party seemed to be *de*mobilizing its grass-roots bases, and its local organizations were withering away. Escalona agreed that was true; the Socialists no longer mobilized. "But why?" I asked. "If we mobilize the people," he explained, "then we will have to make promises, and if we are elected we will have to fulfill those promises."

"Yes," I responded. "That is democracy." "But, if we do that, we run the risk of falling into populism," he warned, "and that could jeopardize the economic model."

It was all too clear. Escalona's prime loyalty was to the neo-liberal economic model that the Socialists had first criticized, then accepted reluctantly as strategy, but by 1997 had embraced as converts to its success, the Chilean economic miracle, with a decade of rapid growth with low inflation and unemployment and declining poverty. To control those in the Socialist Party who might challenge this turn to the right, Escalona reinforced party discipline and reduced the autonomy of the local party organizations.

Yet 1997 was also the year that saw the publication of Tomás Moulian's *Chile Actual*, a leftist critique of the Concertación's pacted transition and limited democracy that was a surprise bestseller because it hit a nerve and articulated what many Chileans were thinking and feeling at the time (Moulian, 1997). As it happened, 1997 was the last year too of the Chilean economic miracle. The following year the Asian crisis revealed how vulnerable the neo-liberal model was to imported shocks and international crises beyond Chile's control. The following year was the year of Pinochet's arrest in London and of the stock-taking on all sides that it detonated.

Within the Concertación, there was a shift to the left that would elect two successive Socialist presidents in the 21st century, Ricardo Lagos and Michelle Bachelet. Within the Socialist Party, a group of *autoflagelantes* emerged within the leadership to begin a leftist self-critique that would lead several to leave the party. Bachelet herself ran in 2005 as an anti-party candidate who promised to replace the distanced government of political elites with a "citizens' government," implicitly harkening back to the democracy of the Allende era. Once in office, however, she seemed unable to fulfill that electoral promise, perhaps because of the opposition of party leaders whom she had depended on to win the runoff election for president in 2006.

At the same time, to the left of the Concertación, Communists, Anarchists and Autonomists began to contest Concertación control over student organizations, reflecting a generational discontent with the transition and the limited democracy that the Concertación had negotiated and practiced. At first, their alienation manifested itself in a refusal to register that left over 2 million Chileans, most of them young, not participating in the democracy that their parents had fought for, a boycott of the political system that worried the leaders of all the political parties. This youthful discontent would first break through the veil of media silence in the 2006 "Penguin" secondary school movement, which the Concertación was able to co-opt. But it would really come of age and change the national discourse in the 2011 university-led student protest movement that was at once a critique of the Concertación's top-down, distanced elitist representative democracy, and a demonstration of the dynamic, bottom-up direct democracy that both looked back to the grass-roots democracy of the Allende era and forward to a future under a new, fully democratic constitution that was the ultimate student demand.

When I asked student leaders, all of whom were born since the Pinochet dictatorship, what collective memory of the Allende era inspired them, they underscored the importance of a democratic politics that mobilizes "the people" and the realization that one cannot make the changes Chile needs without empowering the people. They also stressed the lesson that it is the social movements that should define the agenda and create this popular protagonism.

The student movement's own strategy of mass direct democracy protests was itself an Allende-era legacy—filtered through the memory of their grandparents or parents and their own study of history and often reflecting the historical memory of teachers and authors.[29]

In 2013, Michelle Bachelet was once again elected president of Chile, this time in a landslide victory that increased her power and autonomy from the party leaders of the Concertación. What remains to be seen is whether Bachelet is willing and able to create a "citizens' government" in her second term in office, a government that implicitly looks back to the deep democracy of the Allende era, rather than to the limited democracy of the Concertación that was shaped by negative memories of that era. Success or lack of it may depend on the willingness of the younger generation to tolerate Pinochet's much-reformed, but still authoritarian constitution, which has framed the Concertación era.

Whatever the politics of memory in today's Chile and in its democratic transition, it is driven by the politics of the past, democratic and dictatorial, distant and recent, as well as by current concerns. Allende and his era continue to shadow his successors and their politics to inform the positions taken on all sides.

In Chile, the politics of memory reflects the memory of politics.

Notes

1. For my analysis of the political violence of the Allende era and critique of opposition allegations that the Allende government was responsible for the creation of a "climate of violence," see Winn, "The Furies of the Andes," in *A Century of Revolution,* Grandin and Joseph.
2. See, for example, Valenzuela, *The Breakdown.*
3. For an illuminating account of this Socialist transformation, see Hite, *When the Romance Ended.*
4. Many workers, however, internalized the negative dominant memory of the pre-coup era, or were persuaded by Pinochet's repression to keep silent about it. Moreover, even those who retained a positive evaluation of the pre-coup democracy often qualified that judgment with criticisms of "excesses" or lamented the "immaturity" of Chile's "working class" when it was in a position to excercise power. Still, as the Allende posters that sprouted defiantly in Chile's shantytowns underscored, the historical memory of that era remained contested terrain, with many defending the positive dissident memory of pre-coup democracy. (For an account of this battle for historical memory under the Pinochet dictatorship and the Concertación, see Stern, *The Battle for Hearts and Minds* and *Reckoning with Pinochet*); and Stern and Winn, "El tortuoso camino chileno" in *No hay mañana sin ayer,* Winn, ed., pp. 261–410).
5. The distinction between *obrero* and *empleado* corresponds roughly to the differentiation between blue- and white-collar workers. It was instituted in the labor reform of the mid-1920s as a way of dividing the Chilean working class and weakening their unions, which were then recognized as legal by the state for the first time. Over time, the superior status of the *empleado* led supervisors, technicians and skilled blue-collar workers to seek to be defined as *empleados,* eroding the correspondence between *empleado* status and white-collar work. For an illuminating, historical account and expert analysis of this distinction see Morris, *Elites.*
6. Drawn from my reading of Sindicato Industrial SA Yarur, Manufacturas Chilenas de Algodón, *Minutes,* 1970–71. But meanings can change with the context. Ironically, with the nationalization of SA Yarur in 1971 by the Allende government, the union leaders moved their offices back into the factory, with their takeover of prime space inside it now seen as a sign of their increased power within the nationalized textile mill.
7. For a fuller account of this story, see Winn, *Weavers.*
8. Silvio Castillo, quoted in Winn, *Weavers,* p. 174. The factory owners, the Yarurs, were children of Palestinian Arabs who had fled Turkish persecution in the years before World War I. But because they had arrived in Chile with Turkish passports, they were still known as *turcos* generations later.
9. Ramón Fernández, Secretary for Conflicts, Central Unica de Trabajadores (CUT).

10. For fuller excerpts from my interviews on this story, see *The Chile Reader,* Hutchison, Milanich, Klubock and Winn, eds., pp. 393–399.

11. For a more detailed account of the cordones industriales through oral histories, cf. Gaudichaud, *Poder popular.*

12. For the history of squatter settlements in Santiago, see Garcés, *Tomando su sitio.*

13. For reflections on the MIR and the speeches of their leader Miguel Enríquez, see *Miguel Enríquez,* Naranjo, Ahumada, Garcés and Pinto, eds.

14. For an account of the MIR and Nueva La Habana, see Cofre S., *Campamento Nueva.*

15. Although the MIR imprint on the *campamentos* it organized was strong and the organization internally practiced a Leninist democratic centralism that was far from democratic in our sense of the term, not all the *pobladores* who lived in MIR–led campamentos were Miristas. This political heterogeneity gave the local leaders a relative autonomy from the national leadership that grew with time, making them more representative of the *pobladores* they governed. (Marian Schlotterbeck)

16. In private sector firms, worker participation was limited to Vigilance Committees, whose role was to make sure the owners were not sabotaging production.

17. In 2001, in an unprecedented act for Chile, the retired army Major Carlos Herrera, on national television, confessed to the murder of Tucapél Jiménez two decades before and asked the assassinated labor leader's son, a congressional deputy, for forgiveness. Identifying himself as the accused in the ongoing trial, Herrera went on to explain: "Pero por una cuestión de conciencia, sentía que me faltaba realizar una acción de cuyo preponderante tratar de explicar lo inexplicable y pedir perdón."

    Herrera said that he was ordered to kill Jiménez because the latter was "*un traidor.*"

    He revealed that "*por largo tiempo me sentí orgulloso de que había prestado semejante servicio a la Patria,*" but that "*con el paso del tiempo y los trece años de prisión que tengo en el cuerpo, comprendí que aquello fue un desgraciado, torpe e irracional homicidio que no tiene ninguna justificación.*"

    ["Mayor (r) Carlos Herrera pide perdón por asesinato de Tucapél Jiménez." [http://www.emol.com/noticias/todas/2001/04/26/53287. Accessed 3/21/2014]

18. Arturo Martínez, then Vice-President, CUT, Santiago. Conversation of July 4, 1991.

19. For a summary of the laws that made up the new labor code, see my chapter, "The Pinochet Era," in Winn, *Victims,* pp. 32–35.

20. This account of the Panal strike draws on my research and interviews for a larger as yet unpublished project, "Military Cloth: The Chilean Textile Industry in the Pinochet Era."

21. For an incisive analysis of the Chilean economic crisis, see Meller, *Un siglo.*

22. For an account of the copper workers, their organizations and actions during this period, see Klubock, "Class, Community and Neoliberalism," in Winn, *Victims*, pp. 222–235.

23. The restricted mandate of the Valech Commission was underscored by a commissioner who sympathized with the *poblador* complaint. (Elizabeth Lira, Commissioner, National Commission on Political Prison and Torture, Santiago, July 22, 2009).

24. Colectivo de Memoria Histórica José Domingo Cañas, *Tortura en poblaciones*. Their study made clear that the total number of *pobladores* tortured would be far higher if they had been able to study all the *poblaciones* in Greater Santiago.

25. In a prize-winning Ph.D. dissertation, Alison Bruey traced the evolution of resistance movements in La Legua and Villa Francia, from the coup of 1973 to the protests of 1983, showing how progressive priests and leftist political culture reinforced each other to enable resistance to survive despite the harsh repression of the post-coup era and then provide the organizational base and experience on which the social protests of the 1980s would be built. (See Bruey, "Organizing Community.")

26. In part, that rejection reflected the more appealing "No" publicity campaign, with its rainbow banner, humorous ads and upbeat TV spots with famous actors. But for the most part, it reflected a grass-roots door-to-door effort by the NO campaign to educate voters and persuade them that their vote would count and their ballot would be secret. When the final demonstration of the NO campaign attracted miles of marchers under a diversity of banners, I knew that the NO would win a majority of the votes, but was still uncertain that Pinochet would accept defeat in the plebiscite the following Sunday.

27. Chile's gendered voting system is "separate but equal." Men and women vote in different polling booths and their vote counts are separate, so the gender breakdown of the vote is known immediately. Historically, there has been a "gender gap" in Chilean politics that is the reverse of the United States, with Chilean women voting more conservatively on average than Chilean men. This was true as well in 1988, so when Pinochet lost the female vote, it was clear that he had been rejected by Chilean society.

28. For social movements in the 1980s, see for example Oxhorn, *Organizing Civil Society*.

29. Winn, *La revolución chilena*, pp. 145–150.

References

Baldez, Lisa. 2002. *Why Women Protest: Women's Movements in Chile*. New York: Cambridge University Press.

Bruey, Alison J., 2007. "Organizing Community: Defying Dictatorship in Working-Class Santiago de Chile, 1973–1983." PhD dissertation, Yale University.

Cofre Boris. 2007. *Campamento Nueva la Habana: El MIR y el movimiento de pobladores, 1970–1973*. Concepción: Ediciones Escaparate.

Colectivo de Memoria Histórica José Domingo Cañas. 2005. *Tortura en poblaciones del Gran Santiago (1973–1990)*. Santiago: Self-published.

Espinoza, Juan Guillermo and Andrew Zimbalist. 1978. *Economic Democracy: Workers' Participation in Chilean Industry, 1970–1973*. New York: Academic Press.

Figueroa, Francisco. 2013. *Llegamos para quedarnos: Crónicas de la revuelta estudiantil* . Santiago: LOM.

Garcés, Mario. 2002. *Tomando su sitio: el movimiento de pobladores de Santiago*. Santiago: LOM.

Garreton, Manuel Antonio. 2003. *Incomplete Democracy: Political Democratization in Chile and Latin America*. Chapel Hill, NC: University of North Carolina Press.

Gaudichaud, Franck. 2004. *Poder popular y cordones industriales*. Santiago: LOM.

Grandin, Greg and Gilbert M. Joseph, eds. 2010. *A Century of Revolution: Insurgent and Counterinsurgent Violence During Latin America's Long Cold War*. Durham, NC: Duke University Press.

Hite, Katherine. 2000. *When the Romance Ended: Leaders of the Chilean Left, 1968– 1998*. New York: Columbia University Press.

Hutchison, Elizabeth, Nara Milanich, Thomas M. Klubock and Peter Winn. eds. 2013. *The Chile Reader: History, Politics, Culture*. Durham, NC: Duke University Press.

Meller, Patricio. 1996. *Un siglo de economía política chilena (1890–1990)*. Santiago: Ed. Andrés Bello, 1996.

Milos, Pedro. 2007. *2de abril de 1957*. Santiago: LOM.

Morris, James O. 1966. *Elites, Intellectuals and Consensus*. Ithaca, NY: Cornell University Press.

Moulian, Tomás. 1997. *Chile actual: Anatomía de un mito*. Santiago: LOM.

Naranjo, Pedro, Mauricio Ahumada, Mario Garcés and Julio Pinto, eds. 2004. *Miguel Enríquez y el proyecto revolucionario en Chile*. Santiago: LOM.

Oxhorn, Philip. 1995. *Organizing Civil Society: The Popular Sectors and the Struggle for Democracy in Chile*. College Park, PA: Penn State University Press,

Power, Margaret. 2002. *Right-wing Women in Chile : Feminine Power and the Struggle against Allende, 1964–1973*. College Park, PA: Penn State University Press.

Sindicato Industrial SA Yarur, Manufacturas Chilenas de Algodón, *Minutes*, 1970–71.

Stern, Steve J. 2006. *The Battle for Hearts and Minds: Memory Struggles in Pinochet's Chile, 1973–1988*. Durham, NC: Duke University Press.

2010. *Reckoning with Pinochet: The Memory Question in Democratic Chile, 1989– 2006*. Durham, NC: Duke University Press.

Steve Stern and Peter Winn. 2013. "El tortuoso camino chileno a la memorialización (1990–2011), in *No hay mañana sin ayer,*, ed. Winn, pp. 261–410.

Valenzuela, Arturo. 1971. *The Breakdown of Democratic Regimes: Chile*. Baltimore: Johns Hopkins University Press.

Winn, Peter. 1993. *Americas: The Changing Face of Latin America and the Caribbean*. New York: Pantheon.

Winn, Peter. 2013. *La revolución chilena.* Santiago: LOM.

Winn, Peter, ed. 2013. *No hay mañana sin ayer: Batallas por la memoria histórica en el Cono Sur.* Lima: Instituto de Estudios Peruanos.

Winn, Peter, ed. 2004. *Victims of the Chilean Miracle: Workers and Neoliberalism in the Pinochet Era, 1973–2002.* Durham, NC: Duke University Press.

Winn, Peter. 1986. *Weavers of Revolution: The Yarur Workers and Chile's Road to Socialism.* New York: Oxford University Press.

11

A Place for the Dead in the City of the Living: The Central Cemetery of Bogotá

Paolo Vignolo

This text has been translated from Spanish by Andy Klatt. All translations, unless otherwise indicated, are his own. Some parts have been published in Spanish and French in Vignolo (2013a and 2013b).

Memory policies and practices are at the very heart of today's Colombian public debates. Despite widespread skepticism, many analysts believe that the reelection of President Juan Manuel Santos in May 2014 will clear the path to a peace agreement between the government and the FARC (Revolutionary Armed Forces of Colombia) guerrillas, ending a violent conflict that began in 1964. Starting the count in 1984 alone, the conflict has left more than 6 million victims (Semana, Feb. 9, 2014). The possibility of a more democratic future for Colombia will depend, in good part, on how society confronts its violent past as it moves towards social justice and the reduction of impunity.

In this chapter I focus on the importance of participatory democratic processes and active citizenship for memory building in public spaces. The inspiration for this discussion stems from an interdisciplinary project I am involved in to develop in the area of the Central Cemetery of Bogotá.[1] Our central hypothesis is that Bogotá's city of the dead is becoming the capital's main site to "perform" national memory, and a place where different historical perspectives struggle to make themselves visible. The chapter is divided into four parts.

In the first part of the chapter, "Performing the Past," I outline the general considerations on the emergence, over the last decade, of two different devices of memory in Colombia: cultural patrimony and historical memory. Each device has its own narrative, grammar, and public-space performance. In "The Central Cemetery as an Open-air Museum" and "The Cults of Popular Saints" I focus on the metamorphosis of the cemetery over the last 40 years. In these sections, I pay special attention to the surprising practices, rituals and commemorations that take place on the burial grounds. In "The Avenue of Memory," I address the competing strategies and tactics of various stakeholders who are engaged with the urban transformations in the larger metropolitan area surrounding the cemetery. In "The April 9 March," I describe how recent political rallies use these places for the performance of memory. Finally, in "The Future of the City of the Dead," I sketch out the perspectives and proposals arising from our project.

Performing the Past

As June Erlick argues in her letter from the editor in the "Democracy and Memory" issue of *ReVista*, Colombia is a laboratory for memory studies and practices. In my opinion, this situation is unique for three reasons, each of which raises crucial questions. First, unlike the Nazi Holocaust, the democratic transitions in the Southern Cone, and post-apartheid South Africa, the dispute over memory in Colombia takes place in the middle of an armed conflict with no negotiated end in sight. Any eventual demobilization by the FARC would not in itself be sufficient to bring about peace in the country, since armed criminal gangs, drug traffickers, and the National Liberation Army (ELN) guerrillas are currently operating. If the aim of government policies is to generate a democratic culture of memory, to move forward and bring national reconciliation, they must confront the country's generalized impunity and its social inequality, both of which are among the highest in the world and reflect deeply ingrained social oppressions. At the same time, we must answer the question posed by Elizabeth Jelin: can we address political violence through the lens of social justice, and not only through the lens of human rights?

A second factor that makes Colombia *sui generis* is that the state is not the only one that systematically violated human rights. In fact, sometimes the state was not the biggest perpetrator. For this reason, the process of transitional justice cannot be limited to a reparative act by the state to compensate for its own criminal acts. Historical memory cannot be accurate when criminal organizations and illegal armed groups dominate a conflict. What kind of public history can we develop in a social context ruled by mafias?

A third point has to do with memory-building as a bottom-up, participatory process. For decades, victims' associations, trade unions, social movements, and "memory communities" have struggled against forgetting and impunity. These organizations had faced violent repression for their actions.

Only in the last three to four years have these movements been supported by public entities. We celebrate this sudden change. It is undeniable that decentralized, grass-roots decision-making must be supported by public institutions. This support ensures that the distributions of powers are more equitable. Still, this new process brings new dangers, as argued by Peter Winn´s chapter on Chile. Is there a way to avoid the co-optation of movements that are focused on resistance and social transformation? Can we avoid paving the way for mechanisms that maintain the *status quo*? How do we address the risk of memory networks becoming mere bureaucratic tools that herald new post-conflict rhetoric?

These questions are still unanswered in Colombia and elsewhere. The challenge we face in our project at the Central Cemetery is discerning how to collectively build and perform a shared memory in such a complex scenario.

Two very different narratives dominate Colombia's past. One describes a country full of happy, hard-working people who live at peace in a paradise of natural beauty and great natural wealth, defying the vile misdeeds of a handful of criminals. This is the vision promoted by the advertising slogan and national branding campaign, "Colombia is Passion." An alternative narrative emphasizes the pervasive violence, insecurity, and corruption that have marked generations of Colombians: an entirely different passion that recalls Jesus' suffering on the Vía Dolorosa (Vignolo 2009; Garcia 2013). These alternating visions reflect the two devices that refer to the public use of history in Colombia today. The first is cultural patrimony. Affirmation of this has come from international sources such as new UNESCO directives on intangible cultural heritage, as well as national ones, particularly the effects of the multicultural and pluriethnic Constitution of 1991, but also stimulated by the rise of populist neo-nationalism, taking different forms on the right and the left (Moncusi Ferré 2005; Castro-Gómez 2009; Chaves, Montenegro, Zambrano 2010 y 2014; Vignolo 2011).

The second device is associated with the concept of historical memory that is promoted from the bottom up by victims' associations, activist groups, and social movements. This second device has recently been assimilated by the state for top-down policy promotion.

The goal for those who prioritize cultural patrimony is to produce what I would call "least common multipliers." They focus exclusively on fragments of the past that are perceived as worthy of remembering by a large majority of the population. In cultural patrimony, there is little room for diverging narratives or disputed interpretations. Any reference to conflict arising from class, race, or gender is suppressed or relegated to a distant place. When traumatic events such as slavery, massacres, or political violence are declared to be part of the shared patrimony, the values that underlie such a declaration are assumed to be universal.

In contrast, the mnemonic technique engaged by historical memory stresses the "greatest common divisers" of social life: un-ameliorated offenses, unresolved conflicts, and dreams deferred (Antequera Guzmán 2011, Ortega 2011). This approach leads to an emphasis on making conflicts visible but hinders an appreciation of life-affirming projects and the texture of daily life (De Certeau 1975). As Kristin Ross puts it,

> We automatically associate memory of the recent past with memory of atrocity (trauma). This makes the idea of people working together to take charge of their collective lives sound unfamiliar. It also makes us wonder how to "figure" a memory that brings pleasure, power, excitement, happiness, disappointment—instead of trauma (quoted by Draper in this volume).

Cultural patrimony evokes the everlasting glory of the idealized nation and relegates the exotic "other" to the realm of folklore. Historical memory tends to memorialize victims and reify the past. Each operation highlights the rescue of certain legacies to be bequeathed to future generations, at the same time running the risk—if no form of dialogue and accommodation between the two is found—of undermining the potential for the active citizenship and cultural agency required to produce a collective, durable reinterpretation of the past (see Grindle, Jelin, Hagopian, Winn, and Lerner Febres, in this volume).

Given the importance of Bogotá's Central Cemetery as a place of memory in the heart of the capital, the patrimonial legacy and conflictive history of Colombia coexist within its walls.

The Central Cemetery as an Open-air Museum

In order to better understand the city of the living, it is worth looking at events in the neighboring city of the dead. Bogotá's Central Cemetery was declared to be a National Monument in 1984, and it may be one of the most extraordinary sites dedicated to memory in Colombia. Concentrated in this small space located in the heart of the capital city are diverse practices and representations motivated by contradictory narratives regarding national history from Independence to the present (Escovar Wilson-White 2002 and 2003).

Men and women representing all political stripes, social origins, and generations lie next to one another in the cemetery (Tovar Zambrano 1997).

Over the years, different population groups have developed funerary practices, ancestor cults, and different ways to evoke memory, making the cemetery a privileged space to communicate with the beyond, but privileged also for the exercise of active citizenship and to reassert ethnic, political, and cultural meanings (Martín-Barbero 1981, Calvo Isaza 1998, Vignolo 2013). As an example of "written history" in the living fabric of the metropolis, the Central Cemetery exemplifies the metaphor with which De Certeau described the role of historiography: "at the same time [that] it functions as an inverted image, it is susceptible to omission and dissembling; it relates the past in ways that are the equivalent of cemeteries in cities; it exorcises and admits to the presence of death amidst the living" (1994: 103).

The Central Cemetery was established during the struggle for the nation's independence and has been one of the most vibrant places in the social life of the capital, particularly in the 1930s, 1940s, and 1950s. In those decades, funeral ceremonies were well-attended public events where entire families from working-class neighborhoods came to hear funeral orations and sermons while the ladies and gentlemen of high society promenaded in their most elegant finery amidst a thriving market for objects both sacred and profane. Life in the city of the dead faithfully reproduced the implacable hierarchies of the city of the living. Clergy and laity, artisans and workers, elite families, widely divergent social classes, and partisans of implacably antagonistic political parties intermingled amidst the hustle and bustle of a shared space.

By the mid-twentieth century, however, the growth of Bogotá had so accelerated that the Central Cemetery could no longer meet the needs of what was rapidly becoming a modern metropolis, and a need arose for a new approach to the ever more frequent funerals. Rural migrants filled densely populated settlements to the south of the traditional city center and did not bury their dead in the Central Cemetery. Instead, new cemeteries were established on the city's periphery (Arturo 1994, Torres Tovar 2009). At the same time, the city's urban plan expanded to the north and elite population sectors migrated to gated housing developments where elegant shopping malls reflected their ideal for modern living. The *post-mortem* representations of their new lifestyle were known as "memorial gardens," Catholic adaptations of Protestant cemetery design (Calvo Isaza 1998: 65). Early in the 1980s, Jesús Martín Barbero (1981: 13) compared the old and new styles of spaces:

> Like a *plaza de mercado*[2] the Central Cemetery spreads to the surrounding area outside its walls [with activities such as] the sale of

gravestones, flowers, candles, and religious objects, but also lottery tickets, horoscopes, grilled meat, books, and talismans such as coral, monkeys' paws, blackbirds' beaks, etc. . . . And as in a *plaza de mercado*, there is disorder inside the cemetery where a multiplicity of objects is thrown together haphazardly [including] grave markers of all sizes from simple wooden crosses driven into the ground to elaborate monuments of stone, bronze, or marble . . . In contrast to the expressive heterogeneity of the traditional cemetery, the new memorial gardens offer . . . uniform and symmetrical areas divided into marked-off sections, each with a similar-looking statue and an abstract name like Garden of Peace or Garden of Eternity. Each of these sections has the same exact number of identical gravesites measuring 1.8 by 3 meters. The gravesites are also equidistant, arranged symmetrically with identical headstones and bronze vases for flower arrangements.

The logic of spatial segregation based on economic strata[3] and guaranteed by the variable annual fees owed to funeral agencies, replaced the jarring physical and corporal promiscuity of the hierarchical society of old. As the Central Cemetery, the old city of the dead, falls increasingly into disuse as a burial place, it is becoming a place of memory, or rather of competing memories where official history confronts and contends with what Susan Draper (in this volume) calls counter-memories, alternative visions of the past held by subaltern groups. Two phenomena coexist: the cemetery is ever more museumified while it is increasingly used in the cult worship of "popular saints." Since the 1960s, the Central Cemetery has become a sort of open-air museum, where national history is exhibited in the form of tombs, mausoleums, and shrines to emblematic public figures. By means of this process, which Tovar Zambrano (1997: 158–159) defines as the "symbolic mummification" of great statesmen, the cemetery is a place for worship of established power, but also for representations of the political struggles that have caused Colombia so much pain in the last half-century.

The 20th century's most distinguished heads of state lie along the main road through the city of the dead, pompously enough called the Way of the Immortals. They include Liberals and Conservatives and some who held office during the period of the Violence.[4] Others include General Rojas Pinilla and Admiral Rubén Piedrahita, the leader and another member of the military junta that governed the country from 1953 to 1957, and a long line of historical figures made up almost exclusively of white men from powerful families. The line of notables starts with the simple tomb of

López Michelsen just behind the Pietà at the entrance and leads to that of the traditionalist Catholic politician Laureano Gómez, tellingly located in front of the cemetery's church (Correa 2014).

To many politicians and popular leaders, the idea of being buried in the Central Cemetery meant that they and their ideas would have a place in the national memory. This was especially important to leftist parties, which, despite being excluded from political representation during the 1958–1974 National Front, were nonetheless permitted to memorialize the lives of their leaders. Thanks to public subsidies and financing by political parties and mutual aid societies, it was possible for unionists, Communist leaders, and even former guerrillas to be ushered triumphantly into monumental posterity beside distinguished generals, presidents, and captains of business and industry. Their admission to the *necropolis* was compensation for having been denied access to the *polis*, to political life.

A wave of political violence in the late 1980s and early 1990s played a particularly important role in placing new tombs in the monumental sector of the cemetery. Here lie three of the presidential candidates assassinated by an alliance between drug traffickers and paramilitaries with the complicity of some officials of the Colombian state: Liberal Luis Carlos Galán, whose road to the presidency was thought to be unstoppable, was killed in 1989 by assassins in the pay of Pablo Escobar; Candidate Carlos Pizarro Leongómez, the last commander of the M-19 guerrillas, was shot down in 1990 when he entered electoral politics after 20 years as a guerrilla fighter; and Jaime Pardo Leal was gunned down in 1987 along with more than 3,000 other members of the *Unión Patriótica* (Patriotic Union) political party killed in the 1980s and 1990s.

The massive political funeral that followed each of these killings reaffirmed the importance of the Central Cemetery as a reference point in the country's cartography of memory (Correa, 2014). This was the place where multitudes gathered to denounce the assassinations and commemorate the lives of political leaders whose violent deaths stained Colombian society with their blood. From those tumultuous days on, antagonistic visions have competed for inclusion in the hegemonic rendering of national history. Each of these visions is inscribed in the form of patriotic phrases on imported marble and eulogized with flowers, song, and revolutionary graffiti.

The Cults of Popular Saints

The transformation of the cemetery into a museum space has doubtless represented an important change since it has allowed for the performance there of what Cohen (1994: 1–23) calls "the production of history" that has expanded conventional history and the historiographic tradition. In a more subtle but perhaps more powerful way, daily practices in the Central Cemetery have also been changing, "moving beyond the realm of spectacle to include memories that are more communal and collective, if less epic moments" as Susan Draper puts it. Massive waves of migration from rural areas to Bogotá beginning in the 1950s had led to exponential growth in the city's population and created the conditions for the reappropriation of the cemetery by *campesinos* new to the capital. These new *bogotanos* found in the cemetery an ideal space in which to reestablish relations with the other world that their new urban life seemed to deny them. Calvo Isaza, picking up on some seminal reflections by José Luis Romero (1976) writes,

> Through non-institutionalised cults, magic and superstition, these settlers sought to integrate themselves into the city on acceptable terms, in accordance with the social and economic expectations that had sustained them thus far, but armed with formulas inherited from peasant life . . . The cemetery offered a place laden with meaning that allowed them direct contact with a supernatural world and [a way] to manipulate an often openly hostile social reality. (1998: 78, 82)

The cemetery is seen as a porous place where it's easier to establish all kinds of communication, traffic, and intercourse between the dead and the living. It has become a place of pilgrimage for the cults of so-called "popular saints," people buried there who for some reason are considered intermediaries with the world beyond death.

Leo Kopp (1858–1927) is one example. He was a businessman of German origin who promoted the industrialization of the city in the early twentieth century. "He founded the Bavaria brewery and the Fenicia glassworks, among the most important of that era. He is remembered for how well he cared for his workers, always responding to their petitions, and at the present time his tomb has become an important pilgrimage site in the cemetery. Miraculous powers are attributed to it" (Escovar Wilson-White 2003: 114). Kopp's paternalistic attitude at the dawn of Colombian industrialization (Archila Neira 1991: 128) transformed him into a sort of patron saint for the unemployed. His statue mimics the posture of Rodin's thinker, and every week devotees wait their turn in long lines to whisper supplications into his ear.

Political figures are also objects of public devotion. The most prominent among them is the above-mentioned Carlos Pizarro Leongómez, the last of the M-19 commanders, who died young and handsome and was known popularly as *Comandante Papito*, "Commander Hottie." The slogan of his brief presidential campaign had been "All together we will change Colombian history—that's a promise." He had pledged to demonstrate his commitment to peaceful change and participate in democratic politics, but he was killed by a paid assassin within a month of declaring his candidacy, apparently at the orders of paramilitaries with the complicity of Colombian security agencies (Correa 2014). His tomb is engraved with an image of the sword of Bolívar, a reference to the theft of this historic object by M-19 in their first public action on January 17, 1974 (Vignolo and Murillo 2012: 593).

Now, though, Carlos Pizarro is remembered not only as a charismatic former guerrilla leader, but as a saint with supernatural powers. His tomb is adorned with messages expressing thanks for favors granted. He is visited by two distinct memory communities: former M-19 militants and a growing number of devotees with no connection to his political commitment, who come to ask for his intercession in the other world. Strikingly, the religious connection is increasingly overshadowing his political heritage.

Then there is the cult of the Afro-Colombian José Raquel Mercado, a musician and laborer at the port of Cartagena who became the president of the CTC national labor federation (*Confederación de Trabajadores de Colombia*). The M-19 guerrillas kidnapped him in early 1976 and accused him of being a traitor to the people, selling out strikers and collaborating with the government and with the United States. The guerrillas urged people to "vote" with graffiti on whether or not he should be executed, and they eventually sentenced him to death. When the unionist's body was found, people were so indignant that the Bogotá mayor donated a lot for his burial. Ironically, the tomb of M-19 commander Carlos Pizarro was later placed just a few steps away (Correa 2014). Mercado's tomb has become a magnet to the denizens of some black communities in Bogotá, not in recognition of his leadership in the labor movement, but because of the African physiognomy of the bust on his mausoleum. Today he is one of the most venerated saints in the cemetery.

Every Monday the cemetery comes alive with performances and symbols of a popular religiosity, modified from the official Catholic liturgy. It is an extraordinary example of the subversion and reassignment of cultural meaning drawn from official history via spontaneous practices that elude the controls of dogma. Miniature images of the Madonna of Carmen, the baby Jesus, or the Sacred Heart (Vignolo 2009: 85–128), which figure in the iconography recognized by the Catholic Church, are venerated in rituals involving flowers and candles characteristic of indigenous Andean traditions.

In addition, "images and graffiti inscribed on the gravestones and mausoleums evoke curses and blessings, black and white magic, the evil eye, witchcraft, and exorcism. Potions, wax effigies, feathers, and bones figure in the cult repertoire together with elements of Catholic liturgy such as bibles, white capes, crucifixes, goblets, and missals" (Peláez 1994: 147–160). Other elements include mariachi performances, the reading of love letters and poems, and the singeing of coins.

The practice of "adopting" anonymous deceased persons by those seeking intercessors in the afterlife is common here, as it is in many parts of the country (Nieto 2012). We might trace an analogy between these collective patchworks of performing practices and Chilean *arpilleras* poetically described by Marjorie Agosín, in the sense that that they generate a bond of empathy between an anonymous dead person and the one who becomes the guardian of the grave, implicitly making "a call for justice and accountability, an aesthetic rendering of memory that serves as political testimony" (Agosín, in this volume).

In De Certeau's (1999) terms, these practices lead to tactics in the invention of everyday life. The protagonists are persons who little by little become leading points of reference in the cemetery. One example would be the *escaleristas,* or "ladder workers," who live by renting ladders to people wishing to pay their respects to a dead person whose remains are stored in cubicles at the higher levels of the external vaults. Others are the so-called "people's priests" who, while not authorized to perform sacraments, will for a few pesos officiate outdoor masses in honor of the deceased.

Depending on circumstances, the church hierarchy has alternated between repression and tolerance of these practices. In certain periods they are considered to be examples of idolatry that must be exterminated, just as weeds threaten to suffocate the closed garden of the ellipse, a metaphor in the Catholic tradition for both the garden of Eden and the "closed womb" of the Virgin Mary. At other times, however, they are seen in a positive light as seeds among the ignorant from which the true faith may grow. The best-known popular saint may be María Salomé. She is often represented as a prostitute, but as often occurs in mythological systems her story has many versions. In the words of Gloria Inés Peláez (1994: 155):

> Each of Salomé's followers can relate a fragment of her story, but these many fragments have elements in common which taken together can be understood as a single story . . . She was a prostitute who also sold candles in the cemetery and took in laundry. She lived in the neighborhoods of Egipto and La Perseverancia. She was very poor but

exceptionally charitable. She had an unhappy marriage and her son made her life miserable. Her husband beat her and her mother killed her. She died of uremia; she was burned to death; she was dragged until dead; she was mutilated. These are the most common elements that are repeated and while they don't coincide with each other, what they have in common is that her life was one of misery and violence that caused her terrible suffering. While the specific circumstances vary, Salomé is always a victim.

But there is more. It happens that the tomb next to that of María Salomé is the burial place of Julio Garavito, an important figure in the history of Colombian science (Escovar Wilson-White 2003: 124). In 1970 the International Astronomical Union named a crater on the moon in his honor. It's on the dark side of the moon, but still, it's on the moon! Most of us in Colombia don't know anything about Garavito's scientific works, though. What we do know is that his face appears on the 20,000-peso note.

It is for this reason that devotees of Maria Salomé have extended all sorts of rituals to the neighboring tomb. They stroke the truncated column of Garavito's tomb with 20,000 peso notes; they smoke marijuana with him; and they adorn his monument with candles and flowers, with all sorts of objects. However, some of Garavito's descendents have protested angrily. They are insulted that their illustrious forebearer lies in eternal repose beside a woman of such ill repute, and that he is continually accosted by the disreputable people who dedicate themselves to her cult. Pilgrimages to the tomb of Salomé increased to such an extent by 1980 that the cemetery administration decided to relocate her body. The popular saint was exhumed and transferred to a new resting place in the south of the city, where the pilgrimages and cult activities have continued.

Even so, Salomé's fame is such that some devotees continue to flock to her now-empty tomb in the Central Cemetery, particularly some in the LGBT community as well as sex workers from the nearby neighborhood of Santa Fe. Despite the dramatic differences between María Salomé and Julio Garavito in life, in death they have become the joint objects of cults. It isn't easy to prevent devotees seeking contact with the next world from worshiping a man like Garavito, who has his name written on the moon– and on the 20,000-peso bill.

The Avenue of Memory

If the city of the dead can give us useful insights on the city of the living, the reverse is also true. Changes in the metropolis have a big impact within the necropolis. The old cemetery—embedded between an industrial area and some rundown neighborhoods—is currently at the material and symbolic center of a major reorganization of land use in the Colombian capital. Since the beginning of the 1990s Bogotá has embarked on an ambitious plan for comprehensive urban transformation. The plan includes a new public transportation system of dedicated bus lanes and elevated platforms called the Transmilenio, the revitalization of the historical center, the construction of public buildings—above all libraries, schools, and public archive—and the expansion of the international airport.

The Avenida El Dorado, which connects downtown Bogotá with the airport and runs alongside the cemetery, is taking shape as the great boulevard of the 21st century metropolis, with the construction of gated communities and huge shopping malls catering to the middle and upper classes, and modern buildings housing major foreign and domestic corporations. Moreover, the Avenida El Dorado is increasing playing the role of the "Avenue of Memory," a geographical reference point in the new millennium from which to recount the country's past.

Over the last 15 years, every city administration has carried out significant construction projects in the area, albeit with ambiguous outcomes. At the end of the 1990s the administration of Enrique Peñalosa sought to transform an old and abandoned section of the Central Cemetery into a park, rather pompously named Renaissance Park, referring to its history and playing on the artistic pretensions of the place. This operation was a complete failure, its planners having been inattentive to the *genius loci* of the place. Despite all their efforts the park is not experiencing a rebirth. On the contrary, it continues to be a funereal location that is most often deserted.

The following administration of Antanas Mockus took up the question of what to do with the above-ground vaults, enormous crumbling structures with rows of niches at several levels which until a few years ago served as resting places for the dead of humble families. The dilemma was whether to pull them down or invent another function for them (Rodriguez 2009). Mockus decided to transform them into a symbol of his efforts to lower the homicide rate in the city. Through a minimal intervention, Mockus has these shadowy monuments to death made into an artistic installation (Mockus 2004). Once the scene had been set, he used the site to stage symbolic acts of civic resistance. For example, he summoned citizens to the cemetery for an act of solidarity with the victims of a bloody February 2002 FARC attack on the Nogal social club, and for the international day against the death penalty in December of the same year (Mockus 2005:

38). This was a rare example of civil society initiatives being systematically promoted top-down by city authorities (Sommer 2005: 2).

The administration of Gustavo Petro recently held a public competition to paint graffiti and murals along a large portion of the Avenida El Dorado. Walls alongside the cemetery are now adorned with images and words that explicitly refer to the struggle for memory in the country. Also on the Avenida El Dorado, the country's tallest building—the Colpatria Tower—is illuminated at night with images inspired by a neo-nationalism whose fundamental element is pride in the country's cultural and biological diversity. It has become necessary for any political or economic actor who wants to be visible in Colombia somehow to make its existence known along the Avenida.

Of course these changes have created conflicts related to the political uses of public history. The neighbors of Independence Park have been struggling for years to block Transmilenio construction on the Avenida El Dorado for which dozens of centuries-old trees have been sacrificed and which threatens other elements of cultural and environmental patrimony. Somewhat farther from the historic city center, a planned expansion of the government's National Administrative Center threatens to encroach on the campus of the National University. The Administrative Center would be the largest urban renovation project in Latin America since the construction of Brasilia (*El Tiempo*, 24-08-2013).

Along the avenue, two memorials stand out as places of memory, each representing an opposing vision of the country's history. The first is the Monument to the Heroes Fallen in Combat, built by newly elected president Alvaro Uribe in 2003 and located across the street from the Ministry of Defense. From its beginnings, the grounds of this monument have been used as a staging area for military parades and other commemorative events organized by the armed forces. An inscription on the monument reads: "Colombia extends its thanks to our valiant heroes of all times who died defending the soil of the Fatherland, Freedom, and the Law. Their names are known unto God."

Over the course of his eight years as president (2002–2010), Uribe insisted that the main problem in Colombia was that groups of criminals, outlaws, and terrorists held the great majority of good people hostage, hindering the country's social progress and economic development, and that only the courage and dedication of the armed forces could bring about the revival of the fatherland. A publicity campaign was launched, proclaiming that "Yes, there are heroes in Colombia," referring to the police and the military, but also implicitly to Uribe, the strongman who would pacify the country at whatever cost by implementing the hard-line anti-insurgent policy known as Democratic Security.

Paradoxically, those who supported this aggressive approach also denied the existence of the armed conflict, since to have acknowledged its reality would have required them to recognize that the insurgents had a role to play in the country. The doctrine of Democratic Security reconfigured large parts of Colombian public affairs. It was proclaimed as a hegemonic project to reorient national culture, and the communication media were saturated with this message, defining political friends and enemies and rewriting national history from its own ideological standpoint (Vignolo and Murillo 2012: 604).

The second memorial is the Center for Memory, Peace, and Reconciliation, built on the grounds of the city's Central Cemetery close to where many victims of political violence are buried. The Center is a monolith that resembles a large gravestone, penetrating into the entrails of the city's past, into the earth, and into the root of the Colombian conflict. It suggests that the victims of that conflict are provided a door through which they may reemerge symbolically. A public space has been constructed under this monument including an auditorium, an exhibition center, and offices and meeting rooms for grass-roots organizations (López Obregón 2009).

The Center was established on the initiative of civil society organizations with the support of the city government, to demand the right to memory as an exercise in active citizenship. Some of the authors of this volume and conference participants, namely Elisabeth Jelin, Sergio Bitar and Salomón Lerner Febres, have been among the inspirers of the principles of the Center, where memory is assumed as a social exercise

> . . . which should not be understood as a simple evocation of events that have occurred nor as a mere intellectual experience. We speak more of a communion of experiences tinged with affect, and which aims to bridge the gap between the past and present for the reassignation of a new, higher meaning to events that, as mere facts, have been closed off by the passage of time. (Lerner Febres, Chapter 5 in this volume)

The Center was to open in 2010 for the celebration of the Bicentennial of Independence, but in 2009 excavators working on the site unexpectedly uncovered the city's historic Paupers' Cemetery. The city government then had to decide whether to proceed with construction or call a halt in order to identify the anonymous human remains that had been found, which in fact no one was demanding.

By that time, Colombians had discovered that in recent years ten to thirty thousand people had been buried in thousands of mass graves around the country. The dead were victims of selective killings, massacres, and extrajudicial executions carried out by paramilitaries, guerrillas, and the armed forces (Navas 2009: 163). The terror at the horrific discoveries coexisted, however, with the all too common indifference, and in this climate it was decided that unearthing the largest mass grave in the capital city's oldest cemetery could not be treated as a routine administrative problem. To Camilo González Posso, director of the Center since its establishment, it is important that this place be recognized as a space of memory and reflection: "It must not be forgotten that for over a century many people were buried there. We are not seeking to invoke the tragedy, but to dignify the memory of those who are no longer with us" (in Rodríguez 2009).

Construction of the Center was delayed while thousands of remains dating from 1827 to 1970 were carefully processed. This was one of the most extensive forensic examinations of modern urban history ever undertaken in Latin America. According to the project's coordinator of archaeology Karen Quintero, the research helps us to reconstruct daily life by scrutinizing the remains of the city's most humble inhabitants (*El Tiempo*, 7 July 2011). Due to this effort, the memorial site was until recently but a large hole in the ground where engineers and laborers toiled alongside forensic anthropologists working to restore dignity to the anonymous dead of Bogota just as their colleagues were doing with the remains of victims of the conflict hastily buried in rural fields all around the country. The mass grave underlying the Center of Memory was an apt but terrible reminder that only emphasized the urgent need to come to terms with the past and exorcize the demons of war. The Center finally opened its doors to the public in late 2012 and is now positioning itself as the most active space in town on issues related to historical memory.

The April 9 March

Perhaps the most convincing evidence of the enormous symbolic importance of the Avenida El Dorado—and above all of the Central Cemetery—was the march of April 9, 2013, when tens of thousands of citizens filled the streets of Bogotá in a massive demonstration "for peace, democracy, and the defense of the public good." Many of them had traveled from the farthest reaches of rural Colombia to march with poor, working, and middle-class city dwellers in support of the negotiations being held between the government and the FARC guerrillas.

Among the people fed up with the militarization of daily life and brought together by a coalition of the government, labor unions, and parts of the left were those from the invisible and marginalized face of the country: settlers from far-flung rural areas, Indians defending their traditional form of property; representatives of black communities on the Pacific coast with their own collective property rights; and *campesinos* from every part of the country.

The institutional performance of April 9 was meticulously choreographed to maximize its symbolic value. President Santos began the day by delivering a deeply patriotic speech to an audience of generals and other military and police personnel at the Monument to the Heroes Fallen in Combat. Then he walked up the Avenida El Dorado to the Center for Memory, Peace, and Reconciliation with a group of top government officials to pay his respects to civilian victims. There they were met by Bogota's new Mayor Gustavo Petro, Vice-President Angelino Garzón, a group of foreign diplomats, and top city officials.

The event brought together a president who had been minister of defense during some of the most violent years of the conflict, a vice president who was a former union leader and former vice president of the leftist political party the Patriotic Union, and a mayor who was a former member of the M-19 guerrilla movement. Together they planted a tree of peace in the cemetery in honor of anonymous victims of political violence. This remarkable event received the backing of the international community, the blessings of the high command of the ELN guerrilla group and the approval of the FARC negotiating team in Havana. The only significant expression of opposition came from former president Alvaro Uribe, who lashed out at the April 9 mobilization as a "march with terrorists" (*Caracol*: April, 8, 2013).

The date chosen by the organizers also marked the first-ever official commemoration of the April 9, 1948, assassination of Jorge Eliécer Gaitán, a traumatic event that led to a spontaneous insurrection called the *Bogotazo* and a civil war known as *La Violencia,* the Violence, leaving gaping social wounds that remain unhealed to this day. Until a few months before the march it had seemed that the Colombian state had nothing to say with respect to the day that had fundamentally changed the country's destiny. For decades there were no public commemorations or military parades, not even symbolic acts. A systematic policy of forgetting sought to erase any memory of the *Bogotazo* and the Violence from the public sphere and the public consciousness. In the face of this silence it was left to grass-roots organizations to keep the collective memory alive.[5]

This situation took an unexpected turn when Juan Manuel Santos became president. In order to promote large-scale mining, agricultural exports, and infrastructural development, the new governing coalition led by Santos decided to seek a peace agreement with the FARC. After all, the ravages of an ongoing war would hinder or preclude capitalist investment in many rural areas of the country that had been battered over the previous 20 years with the forced displacement of more than 4 million people through death threats, selective killings, and massacres; the illegal seizure of more than 12 million acres of land by drug traffickers and paramilitaries; kidnappings for political advantage or for profit; the indiscriminate use of anti-personnel mines by the guerrillas; and a chaotic land titling regime. All of these obstacles to development had been either caused or exacerbated by the armed conflict.

One element that distinguishes the current negotiations from innumerable frustrated peace processes in the past is that this time the government went to the table having passed the 2011 Law on Victims and Land Restitution. Indeed, this law—a top priority of the Santos government—was designed as an important tool to bring about an overall reorganization of rural territory and determine the fate of the beleaguered rural population. Thus far the policies devoted to returning land to its original owners are still viewed as ineffective and dangerous for rural leaders: "Nobody looks for land in order to be buried there," as one *campesino* put it (Ronderos 2014: 30). Still, the Law on Victims and Land Restitution has framed a new official narrative on the horrors that have swept Colombia, through normative definitions of the armed conflict itself, its duration, its actors and its victims (Antequera Guzmán 2011).

As minister of defense under Uribe, Santos had denied the existence of an armed conflict, despite glaring evidence to the contrary. As president he was forced to alter this position, given the need to implement transitional justice. Remarkably, Colombia transitioned from a supposed non-conflict to a post-conflict scenario without ever coming to terms with the conflict itself. In addition to economic reparation, the need for visible acts of symbolic reparation led to the proclamation of April 9 as National Victims Day, to mention just one example of the revised narrative.

But the government was not alone in revisiting the traumas of the past with an eye to its current political interests. The opposition also hoped to gain political space by pointing to unresolved crimes that had been committed against it. Some sectors of the left under the leadership of Liberal Party activist Piedad Córdoba came together in a new organization called the Marcha Patriótica. The name of the new organization clearly evokes the experience of the Unión Patriótica, the electoral party that emerged decades earlier from a previous set of peace negotiations with the FARC and other guerrilla groups and was then brutally persecuted. It is a clear allusion to the specter of a peace process that ended in an extermination campaign whose perpetrators enjoy impunity to this day. Peace with the guerrillas will be possible only if the state can provide guaranties that this macabre history will not be repeated.

On April 9, 2013, the Marcha Patriótica put all its impressive political and electoral potential on display in the streets of the capital. Long-deceased victims of unpunished atrocities were vicariously endowed with legal standing and embodied by the demonstrators, raising their voices to demand an end to hostilities. This event represented a new vision of the country's national memory and promises to be remembered as a turning point when relations among allies and adversaries entered uncharted territory, opening possibilities theretofore considered unimaginable.

On the day of its 65th anniversary of the murder of Gaitán, a neglected but pivotal tragedy became a reference point for the memory of its immolated victims in a conflict whose existence was officially denied just a few months before. The phantasmagorical presence of an unacknowledged past now plays a role in influencing the course of present-day struggles.

The most noteworthy aspect of the April 9 march with respect to both institutional and popular participation was the unexpected convergence of antithetical ways of remembering the past, interpreting the present, and imagining the future. By participating in the April 9 mass march up the Avenida El Dorado that ended on the grounds of the Central Cemetery, President Santos hoped to conciliate antagonistic anniversaries, spaces, and narratives along with these two uses of memory. It is to be hoped that his gesture will prove to be something more than a short-term maneuver to further his prospects for reelection, helping instead to bring into being a deeply yearned for ceasefire with the FARC. Making reference to the Colombian case, Salomón Lerner Febres warns,

> Today, the most notorious case might be that of Colombia, where peace negotiations to put an end to an almost half-century of violence have the moral charge of responding not only to the interests of political figures and armed actors, as they would have before, but now also, and most importantly, to the victims' rights to truth, justice, reparations, and guarantees that such atrocities will never happen again (Lernes Febres, in this volume).

The Future of the City of the Dead

The starting point for our intervention in urban affairs has been to ask ourselves what might be the future for the city of the dead, given the radical transformations taking place in the city of the living that surrounds it. As we have seen, the old cemetery happens to be located in the most strategic area of the capital, in terms of both property values and cultural significance. While major changes are on their way, it is not yet clear what they will be. Many options are at stake in a subtle dispute to take control of the area.

Will the role of this urban space as an open-air museum be strengthened, or will it revert to a memorial site? Are popular pilgrimages or political demonstrations going to become massive gatherings, as has happened in the past? Is it at risk of becoming a no man's land due to a lack of internal governance? Or will it be transformed into a theme park, as the initiative of some private companies might suggest? Above all, what is the vision for the future of the cemetery of those who spend long hours there for work, emotional, or spiritual reasons?

A team of researchers, artists, activists, and public officials who for different reasons had already been working in the area have come together to seek answers to what at first seemed like a few simple academic questions. The entire collective process has been oriented around three important principles: participation, poetic representation, and political representation.

Participation, or How to Involve Local Cultural Agents

On the one hand, the cemetery displays monuments considered to be part of the cultural heritage that do not seem to make sense to a non-specialized observer. On the other hand, powerful cultural practices are reshaping the space of the dead in innovative and rather subversive forms, even if they are still marginalized and outside of public recognition. As Mario Rufer (2012: 31–32) states, these practices:

[. . . reproduce] hegemonic re-accommodations by the state, which uses the past and defines "new" memories, but also tries to impose limits on what may or may not be included in "the new." At the same time, these re-accommodations become interwoven with the interpretations and demands of subaltern sectors as they "read" these attempts at establishing hegemony. In this performative reading they make them say "something else" or offer the historical continuities of inequality, exclusion, or the limits of citizenship in the nation as a contrast.

In this sense the cemetery, as both an open-air museum and a place of ritual, is a paradigmatic example of the distinction Ian Assmann (2011) draws between communicative memory and cultural memory. Astrid Erll (2012: 37–38) summarizes the question thus:

> *Communicative memory* stems from daily interactions and its content is made up of the historical experience of contemporaries. For this reason it never refers to anything beyond a limited temporal horizon, always in motion, of about 80–100 years. The contents of *communicative memory* change and they are never assigned a fixed meaning. For the purposes of *communicative memory*, all individuals are considered equally competent to remember and interpret the shared past. . . . *Cultural memory*, on the other hand, is a present memory associated with fixed objectifications. It is highly artificial and is represented in ceremonies, above all in the temporal and cultural dimensions of celebrations. *Cultural memory* has a fixed inventory of contents and established meanings, and specialists such as priests, shamans, or archivists are trained to carry out its continuation and interpretation. . . . There is a floating gap, a lacuna moving between that which is remembered by *communicative memory* and that which is remembered by *cultural memory*.

In our work concerning the cemetery we wish to fill this floating gap by means of participatory processes involving people who have an emotional or work relationship with the place: relatives and friends of the deceased, groups of victims, workers, and scholars. These are the cultural agents who activate the transformative potential of living memories present in the area. The goal is to legitimize communicative memory as expressed in popular cults, subaltern devotional practices, and unofficial tributes and commemorations, and at the same time democratize—that is, spread knowledge of, among those who congregate there—the cultural memory represented at the cemetery by its monuments and documents. Since the beginning there has been an emphasis on participation. For example, since mid-2013 the theater collective Vividero has been working on a theater production called An Act of Grace with a group of transgender sex workers, a social group that is very active in cult activities around the tombs of María Salomé and Julio Garavito.

At almost the same time, we at the National University have proposed a participatory action research project (Fals Borda 1986 and 1998; Kemmis and McTaggart 2000) with people involved in work relevant to historical memory and to the cultural patrimony of the Central Cemetery. These included guards, flower and candle sellers, tombstone and monument workers, "popular priests," and "ladder workers," but also relatives and devotees of Carlos Pizarro, Leo Kopp, and Raquel Mercado, among others. The staff of the Center of Memory, Peace, and Reconciliation, for their part, mobilized people who were already holding commemorative and ritual activities in the cemetery to take part in the project as cultural agents. This latter group included political activists, indigenous communities, and victims' associations.

Poetic Representation, or How to Propitiate an "Alchemy of Narratives"

In the Central Cemetery, military mausoleums sit side by side with tombs of guerrilla leaders; presidential cenotaphs may be found next to the burial sites of anonymous bodies; spaces may be shared by mass graves and monuments to leading historical figures; and patriotic memorials coexist with contemporary artistic installations. There is probably no other public space in Colombia with such a dense concentration of divergent narratives. A chaotic and hazardous sedimentation allows thousands of individual histories to challenge the official history of the nation.

We asked ourselves, therefore, how to collect, organize, and give life to a polyphony of voices, often silenced, that would reflect "the heterogeneity of multi-faceted discourses that constitute our micro and macro histories" (IDPC, 2013). Francisco Ortega calls this an "alchemy of narrative":

> Listening to testimony requires imagination. If the language of science remains impervious before the scene of social devastation, those who speak scientifically will have to borrow, steal, concoct words, insinuate and modulate in order to break the silence . . . After all, it is such an exercise of imagination that makes empathy possible, the attribute that knowledge lacks in order to arrive at true comprehension . . . Today, once again, arts, literature and social sciences are called forth to play an important role in the recovery of languages and memories of pain, true laboratories to construct the conviviality of the future, one in which death is no longer the structuring center of social life. We cannot renounce such an urgent task.

The research group's collective decision was to create a *mise-en-scène* with these voices called "Songs for the Living and the Dead," which was performed for the first time last November and presented during Holy Week at the Fourteenth Ibero-American Theater Festival of Bogotá. The people who spend their days in the cemetery led the visitors on a nocturnal tour and a rediscovery of its unknown corners, unrecognized areas, and unexplored territories where fragments of its affective archives generate a montage of common experiences. The premise of this exercise is that in order to work with a social fabric torn asunder by decades of abandonment and micro-conflicts, it is important to call upon living experiences as felt by individuals. On the basis of this corporal memory it is possible to conjugate the orality of popular cults with the grammar of funerary art, urban legends with national history, and the fervor of devotees with the concepts of experts.

Secondly, we wish to bring together, symbolically and materially, the fragmented and disjointed elements of the cemetery. We created montage that presents a journey through the memory of Bogota and Colombia from Independence to our own times; it begins at the monumental entrance to the cemetery, crosses the ellipse, passes in front of mausoleums dedicated to unionists and members of the armed forces, crosses the street where flower and tombstone vendors ply their trade, and includes the abandoned potter's field and the vaults with multiple individual niches, before arriving at the new Center of Memory, Peace, and Reconciliation.

Finally we bring out the act of naming as the minimal act of remembering. The name of a person is the last vestige of the past that historians grasp in our Sisyphean struggle against forgetting, disappearance, and anonymity. This is reflected in the monument inscriptions of the cemetery. A display of lights designed by the Escuela-Taller highlights the names of well-known deceased persons, in contrast with the unidentified bodies whose remains are stored in old multi-niched vaults where Beatriz Gonzales has installed her work Anonymous Auras. The incremental process of losing the names of the deceased, the steady loss of the minimal trace of recognition, and the constant struggle to rescue the identity of those whose identity has been disappeared is the guiding thread that runs through our experience before arriving at the Memorial, in homage to the victims of the violence that has characterized the country's history.

We are aware of the dangers: to perform memory in the middle of an ongoing conflict may be something akin to acting as sorcerers' apprentices seeking alchemical formulas. There is the risk of biased readings of national history that ignore crucial people and episodes, or of creating a version of history that conforms to the needs of the conjuncture. And there is also the danger of adopting a post-conflict discourse that as Castillejo Cuellar (2012: 386) points out, tends to depoliticize, fossilize, and naturalize otherwise divergent interpretations in the context of a form of transitional justice "with its own gospel of truth, reconciliation, and pardon as precursors of a future moral community." But in Colombia we have no option. We cannot wait for the end of a never-ending war to develop serious participatory work on memory.

Political Representation, or the Past as a Common Good

When we first started working in the Central Cemetery we were quickly struck by the ungovernability of the site. The city of the dead is technically the responsibility of several public and private institutions, but in fact it is a no man's land without effective governance. Over the years, the fragmentation of institutional responsibilities and the lack of communication among the different entities responsible for maintaining the site has generally led to its neglect. There is no electrical service in large areas; the provision of water is inadequate; trees that have not yet been felled are in terrible condition; access roads are dangerous; security is so poor that many tombs have been robbed or profaned; and a system of gates, padlocks, and checkpoints make it feel more like a penitentiary than a final resting place for the dead.

Nevertheless, if we had begun our intervention by trying to convince multiple entities to engage in a dialogue on institutional governance and seek to define needed changes and improvements, the initiative probably would have degenerated into a series of exhausting and inconclusive meetings. The simple act of calling the parties together to discuss an artistic proposal, however, awakened their enthusiasm and inspired them to make commitments that can now be translated into practical policies for urban transformation. The work that was undertaken in those months led to the mutual confidence and recognition between people and institutions that enabled us to consolidate our cooperative relations and form a viable collaborative network that would be difficult to ignore, and any future proposal regarding the Central Cemetery will have to take the current participatory process into consideration.

A first step has been the collective production of a "cartography of memory" of the area of the Central Cemetery. This was accomplished by collecting life stories of individuals and collective memories of groups that are active in the area. The goal is more ambitious in the medium to long term, though. We would like the area's new land-use plan to incorporate the proposals for cultural policythat have emerged from grass-root practices to become socially grounded and negotiated among different local cultural agents.

As a group we are interested in the "axis of memory" along the length of the Avenida Eldorado, in which the area of the Central Cemetery would be the primary staging area for citizen initiatives related to possible interpretations of the past. The only way to accommodate the horrors of the past is to frame them with a subjective reflexivity in relation to matters of the present, providing a means to promote active citizenship in the future.

For this path to go beyond an official history proffered by the state or a collection of fragmented and unconnected personal stories, it must entail more than an opposition between public and private memory, instead allowing the past to be seen as a common good. The debate over "the commons" underlines the relational character of memory based on the dynamics of exchange and circulation, a logic of sharing outside market dynamics or the ubiquity of the state (Chomsky 2002; Mattei, 2011). This approach also suggests confronting each situation empirically on the basis of its local and historical characteristics rather than attempting to apply highly formalized or universalist models (Ostrom, 1990).

Finally, it is clear that referring to the past as a common good necessarily implies the existence of memory communities (Erll 2012). In Lerner Febres's words: "*Ese pasado es común, y por tanto, la memoria, para tener relevancia colectiva, ha de ser fruto de un diálogo intersubjetivo, de una suerte de pacto de nuestros afectos*" (in this volume). To avoid a naïve approach or a fall into a deceptive essentialism, however, it is important to underline that these communities are complex collectivities with their own mechanisms of inclusion and exclusion, internal hierarchies, and forms of discrimination. Esposito (2003) reminds us that behind any *communitas* there is always a system of immunities. Cohen (1985) also indicates that in addition to being geographical and social entities, communities are symbolic constructs.

Given the extraordinary social energy that has been displayed in massive citizen mobilizations against forgetting, it is possible to imagine the construction of common memories that allow for the agency of subjects previously relegated to the margins of national life, in the process reducing the armed actors' room for maneuver. This would also require the repressive apparatus of the state to accede to the rule of law, allowing for the viability of a participatory government based on a shared past. In this sense the struggle for memory establishes the conditions for a negotiated peace and a consensual future. In the words of Michel De Certeau: "'To mark a past' is to make a place for the dead, but also to redistribute the space of possibilities, to determine what *must be done*, and—as a consequence—to use the narrativity that buries the dead as a way of establishing a place for the living."

This is an enormous challenge, but the ongoing transformations in the Central Cemetery and the events of April 9, 2013 allow us to discern on the horizon its taking shape as a distinct possibility.

Notes

1. The on-going project is being developed by a group of researchers at the National University of Colombia along with the Center of Memory, Peace and Reconciliation, the Interdisciplinary Network of Live Arts, the *Escuela-Taller* and the Cultural Institute of the City of Bogotá.
2. *Plaza de mercado* is a closed urban market space where agricultural and other producers sell their goods to city dwellers.
3. In Colombia all urban housing units are officially categorized into six strata representing the presumed economic condition of inhabitants. Prices paid for public services such as water, electricity, and gas correspond to the stratum assigned to each place of residence.
4. *La Violencia,* 1948–1957.
5. On the 60th anniversary of the *Bogotazo* in 2008, for example, grass-roots organizations undertook a multiplicity of independent initiatives that included street theater, the painting of murals, musical performances and flash-mobs.

References

Antequera Guzmán, José. 2011. *La memoria histórica como relato emblemático.* Bogotá: Agència Catalana de Cooperació al Desenvelupament, Alcaldía Mayor de Bogotá. Web: January 15, 2014 http://es.scribd.com/doc/103059651/La-memoria-historica-como-relato-emblematico#page=11

Archila Neira, Mauricio. 1991. *Cultura e identidad obrera: Colombia 1910–1945.* Bogotá: CINEP.

Arturo Julián (editor). 1994. *Pobladores urbanos: Ciudades y espacios.* Bogotá: Instituto Colombiano de Antropología e Historia.

Assmann, Jan. *2011. Cultural Memory and Early Civilization: Writing, Remembrance, and Political Imagination.* Cambridge UK: *Cambridge University Press.*

Calvo Isaza, Oscar. 1998. *El cementerio central: Bogotá, la vida urbana y la muerte.* En colaboración con Marta Saade y Fabio Jiménez. Bogotá: Observatorio de Cultura urbana.

Castillejo Cuéllar, Alejandro. 2012. "Reparando el futuro. La verdad, el archivo y las articulaciones del Pasado en Colombia y Sudáfrica." In: *Seminario internacional. Desafíos para la reparación integral a las víctimas del conflicto armado interno en Colombia. Memorias.* Bogotá: Alcaldía Mayor.

Castro Gómez, Santiago. 2009. "Las políticas culturales como un patrimonio de la nación." En *Compendio de políticas culturales*, Ministerio de Cultura de la República de Colombia. Web: January 15, 2013. http://www.mincultura.gov.co/?idcategoria=1825

Castro Gómez, Santiago. 2011. Historia de la gubernamentalidad. Bogotá: Siglo del Hombre.

Certeau, Michel de. 1975. *L'Ecriture de l'Histoire.* Paris: Editions Gallimard.

Certeau, Michel de. 2010. *La invención de lo cotidiano.* México: Universidad Iberoamericana.

Chaves, Margarita; Montenegro, Mauricio; Zambrano, Marta. 2010. Mercado, consumo y patrimonialización cultural. In: *Revista Colombiana de Antropología*. N. 46, vol. 1, January-June, pp. 7–26. Bogotá, Instituto Colombiano de Antropología e Historia. Web: January 15, 2014. http://www.redalyc.org/articulo.oa?id=105015237001

Chaves, Margarita; Montenegro, Mauricio; Zambrano, Marta (editors) 2014. El valor del patrimonio. Bogotá, Instituto Colombiano de Antropología e Historia.

Chomsky, Noam. 2002. *The Common Good*: Interviews with David Barsamian, Berkeley, CA: *Odonian Press.*

Cohen, Anthony P. 1985. *The Symbolic Construction of Community*. London: Tavistock.

Cohen, David William. 1994. The combing of history. Chicago: University of Chicago Press.

Correa, Fabián. 2014. Textos de la cartografía. *Cartografía del cementerio central*. Centro de memoria, Paz y Reconciliación, Escuela-Taller, Universidad Nacional de Colombia.

Erlick, June. 2013. "The past is present." In: *Memory: in search of history and democracy. ReVista. Harvard Review of Latin America.* Fall, vol. XIII n. 1, p. 1.

Erll, Astrid. 2012. *Memoria colectiva y culturas del recuerdo. Estudio introductorio.* Bogotá: Universidad de los Andes, ediciones Uniandes.

Escovar Wilson-White, Alberto. 2003. *Guía del Cementerio Central de Bogotá.* Bogotá: Alcaldía Mayor de Bogotá, Corporación la Candelaria.

Escovar Wilson-White, Alberto. 2002. *El cementerio central de Bogotá y los primeros cementerios católicos.* Edición en la Biblioteca Virtual del Banco de la República. Web: January 15, 2014 http://www.banrepcultural.org/book/export/html/86408

Esposito, Roberto. 2003. *Communitas. Origen y destino de la comunidad.* Madrid: Amorrortu.

Fals Borda, Orlando. 1986. *La investigación-acción participativa: Política y epistemología*, en Álvaro Camacho G. (ed.), *La Colombia de hoy*, Bogotá, Cerec,. pp. 21–38.

Fals Borda, Orlando. 1998. *El territorio como construcción social*, Revista Foro.

García-Moreno, Diego. 2010. *Beatriz González. ¿Por qué llora, si ya reí?* Documental, Colombia, 80 m.

Kemmis, S. and McTaggart, R. 2000."Participatory action research," in N.K. Denzin and Y.S. Lincoln (editores) *Handbook of Qualitative Research* (2a ed.). Sage, CA, pp. 567–605.

Londoño Calle, Viviana. 2011. "El mensaje de los muertos." En: *El Espectador,* 07 de Julio de 2011. Web January 15, 2014 www.elespectador.com

López Obregón, Clara. 2009. *Presentación del diseño arquitectónico del centro de memoria y del centro virtual.* January 15, 2014 http://www.centromemoria.gov.co/documentos-relacionados/188-discursos-pronunciamientos

Martín-Barbero, Jesús. 1981. "Prácticas de comunicación en la cultura popular. Mercados, plazas, cementerios y espacios de ocio." En: *Comunicación alternativa y cambio social*. M. Simpson compilador. México: UNAM. Web: March 11, 2013 http://es.scribd.com/doc/6334231/Practicas-de-comunicacion-en-la-cultur a-popular-mercados-plazas-cementerios-y-espacios-de-ocio (Consultado el 11 de marzo de 2013).

Mockus Antanas. 2014. *Cultura ciudadana. Programa contra la violencia en Santa Fe de Bogotá, Colombia.* New York: División de Desarrollo Social, Banco Interamericano de Desarrollo, 2002. Web: January 15, 2014 http://es.scribd.com/ doc/63048/Colombia-Cultura-Ciudadana-Experiencia-Bogota

Mockus, Antanas. 2004. "Ampliación de los modos de hacer política." En: *La démocratie en Amérique latine: un renouvellement du personnel politique?* Colloque CERI. December 2–3. Web: January 15, 2014 http://www.ceri-sciences-po.org/ archive/mai05/artam.pdf

Mockus, Antanas. 2005. "Resistencia civil en Bogotá 2002–2003." En: *Acción política no-violenta, una opción para Colombia.* Freddy Cante and Luisa Ortiz editores. Bogotá: Universidad del Rosario.

Moncusi Ferré, Albert. 2005. "La activación patrimonial y la identidad." En: *La memoria construida: Patrimonio cultural y modernidad.* Albert Rodrigo, María Hernàndez, Gil M. Martí, Albert Moncusí Ferré, Beatriz Santamarina Campos. Valencia: Tirant-lo-Blanch.

Mattei, Ugo. 2011. *Beni comuni: un manifesto*. Laterza: Roma-Bari.

Navas, María Elena. 2009. "En busca de fosas comunes en Colombia." BBC 26 de Mayo de 2009. En: *Ciudadanías en escena: performance y derechos culturales en Colombia.* Paolo Vignolo editor. Bogotá: Universidad Nacional de Colombia, 162–163.

Nieto, Patricia. 2012. *Los escogidos*. Medellín: Sílaba.

Ortega Martínez, Francisco A. (editor). 2011. *Trauma, cultura e historia: reflexiones interdisciplinarias para el nuevo milenio.* Facultad de Ciencias Humanas, Centro de Estudios Sociales CES, Universidad Nacional de Colombia, Bogotá.

Ortega, Francisco. 2013. "The Alchemy of Narrative." In: *Memory: in search of history and democracy. Re-Vista. Harvard Review of Latin America.* Fall, vol. XIII n. 1, pp. 30–35.

Ostrom Elinor. 1990. *Governing the Commons. The Evolution of Institutions for Collective Action*, Cambridge, Cambridge University Press.

Peláez, Gloria Inés. 1994. "Magia, religión y mito en el Cementerio Central de Santafé de Bogotá." En: *Pobladores urbanos: en busca de identidad.* Julián Arturo compilador. Bogotá: Tercer Mundo Editores, ICAN-Colcultura.Vol. 2, pp. 147–160.

Rodríguez, Dominique. 2009. "La artista Beatriz González interviene los columbarios del Cementerio Central." En: *Revista Cambio*, May 10. Web: January 15, 2014 http://esferapublica.org/nfblog/?p=8326 http://www.cambio.com.co/ culturacambio/827/ARTICULO-WEBNOTA_INTERIOR_CAMBIO-5147907. html

Romero, José Luis. 1976. *Latinoamérica: las ciudades y las ideas*. Buenos Aires: Siglo XXI editores.

Ronderos, María Teresa. 2014. "¿Tierra para enterrar campesinos?" In: *El Espectador*, January 31, 2014, 30.

Rufer, Mario. 2012. *La nación en escenas. Memoria pública y usos del pasado en contextos poscoloniales*. México: Colegio de México.

Silva, Alicia Eugenia. 2009. *Bogotá, de la construcción al deterioro (1995–2007)*. Bogotá: Cámara de Comercio, Universidad del Rosario. January 15, 2014. http://books.google.com.co/books?id=zjD1hkHtqrcC&pg=PA6&lpg=PA6&dq =silva+politicas+bogotana+2009&source=bl&ots=XXzCLQoNhT&sig =5ixYH63UxdrSgO1k8UKDrn9rrpc&hl=en&sa=X&ei=pxUgUYOCK4ig8Q-S7wIG4CA&ved=0CGIQ6AEwBw#v=onepage&q=silva%20politicas%20 bogotana%202009&f=false

Sommer, Doris. 2005. *Cultural Agency in the Americas*. Durham: Duke University Press.

Torres Tovar, Carlos Alberto. 2009. *Ciudad informal colombiana. Barrios construidos por la gente*. Bogotá: Universidad Nacional de Colombia.

Tovar Zambrano, Bernardo. 1997. "Porque los muertos mandan. El imaginario patriótico de la historia colombiana." En: *Pensar el Pasado*. Carlos Miguel Ortiz Sarmiento y Bernardo Tovar Zambrano editores. Bogotá: Universidad Nacional de Colombia - Archivo General de la Nación.

Vignolo, Paolo. (editor). 2009. *Ciudadanías en escena: performance y derechos culturales en Colombia*. Paolo Vignolo editor. Bogotá: Universidad Nacional de Colombia.

Vignolo, Paolo. 2011. "Paradojas de la patrimonialización" En AA.VV. La cultura: identidad, economía y políticas públicas. Bogotá: Politécnico Grancolombiano, Corporación Escenarios, Departamento Nacional de Planeación, 144–155. February 15, 2014 http://www.poligran.edu.co/comunica/paipa_2010_html/ index.html

Vignolo, Paolo y Murillo Ramírez, Oscar. 2012. Un arma de doble filo: la espada de Bolívar y el resurgir de los nacionalismos en Colombia Y Venezuela. In: Bernardo Tovar Zambrano (editor) *Independencia: historia diversa*. 50 años del Departamento de Historia. Bogotá: Universidad Nacional de Colombia.

Vignolo, Paolo. 2013. Prospects of Peace. Sharing Historical Memory in Colombia. In: *Memory: in search of history and democracy. Re-Vista. Harvard Review of Latin America*. Fall, vol. XIII n. 1, pp. 20–23.

Vignolo, Paolo. 2013. Qui gouverne la ville des morts? Politiques de la mémoire et développement urbain à Bogotá. In: *De la ville à la métropole. Les défis de la gouvernance*. (Christian Lefèvre, Nathalie Roseau, Tommaso Vitale editores). Science Po - L´OEeil d´or, Paris, pp. 305–322 (¿Quién gobierna la ciudad de los muertos? Políticas de la memoria y desarrollo urbano en Bogotá. En: *Memoria y Sociedad*. Vol.17 / No. 35, *Políticas de la memoria y usos públicos de la historia*. July-December, 125–142. January 15, 2014 http://memoriaysociedad.javeriana. edu.co/articulos.php?id=46

12

Summing Up: Many Voices, Many Histories, Many Memories

Erin Goodman

Over two days in November 2013, the David Rockefeller Center for Latin American Studies at Harvard University convened 29 scholars to consider the role of memory and its impact on democracy in Latin America. Seven distinct panels focused on the psychological, journalistic, artistic, interpretive, and catalytic aspects of memory as it influences justice and democratic transitions. Provocative questions came to the fore: How are memories formed and are they malleable? How does memory interact with democracy? What factors color the universal experience of memory? Who writes or rewrites the narrative of a country? How do we commemorate the past while considering shifting interpretations of the same events over time? Which forces distort memory from excavated records and archives? How do they impact the formation of truth and the quest for justice? The conference provided the opportunity for academics and practitioners from different countries, different generations, and different disciplines to come together.

Civil society and government share equal responsibilitiy in addressing these questions, as each actor—individually and collectively—has a role to play. In excavating the evidence of the past, archivists and journalists uncover physical records helping us to understand the lines of command in the carrying out of atrocities. By identifying evidence of horrible acts that previously relied on subjective memory alone, the analysis of these records can inform a historical truth. In designing and building public spaces, artistic events, and monuments to commemorate the past, architects and curators bring to physical fruition a collection of memories that acknowledge the past and, perhaps, can serve as a warning against repeating it. International entities, advocates, lawyers, politicians, the media and even funding agencies can provide the necessary catalysts to bring about justice and to begin to acknowledge the past through tangible or judicial recognition.

Individually and together the contributors to this volume and the additional conference presenters offer insights on the interaction of memory and democracy. In this review I aim to provide a summary of the conference presentations that are not among the chapters in this volume.

"What Type of Memory for What Kind of Democracy? Challenges in the Link Between Past and Future"

Keynote speaker Elizabeth Jelin, Argentine sociologist and Senior Researcher at the National Council of Scientific Research in Argentina, set the stage by encouraging participants to question a number of perceptions of democracy and memory. Challenging the concept of collective memory, which implies a totalitarian, undemocratic society, Jelin described what she calls the "uncertain relationship" between memory and democracy. She asked us to consider the relationship between temporality and memory and urged caution when linking the past to the future: which past are we considering for this present?

"We are all committed to human rights," declared Jelin. "We believe there is something about human dignity and the human condition that is a threshold for humanity, a humanity for which we are all responsible." However, ideas about human rights and crimes of horror have evolved over time. Since events unfolded in Latin America and elsewhere on different scales, in different ways, it is impossible to identify a comparative unit of analysis. Jelin emphasized that transitional justice cannot be a one-size-fits-all package that travels from one place to another. Highlighting the limits of collective memory, Jelin provided a thought-provoking framework from which to view the subsequent presentations.

Committing to Democratic Values and Institutions in Latin America

The first panel of the conference explored the roots of commitment to democratic politics in Latin America. The panel included presentations by Katherine Hite and Juan Mendez, as well as Peter Winn (Chapter 10 of this volume).

Katherine Hite, Professor of Political Science at Vassar College and author of *The Politics of Memory in Chile* (2013), asserted that political scientists historically steered clear of memory when studying processes of democratization, perhaps because it was easier to study institutions than subjective memory. Like Jelin, Hite emphasized the importance of political timing: as we reach back to mark a moment in time, our sensitivity to the periodization of political processes is heightened; memories are about timing and the construction of myth, symbolism, association, and contestation in media and public opinion.

Hite reminded us to consider the appropriation and manipulation of memory toward political ends. Collective memory can be channeled to destructive political ends. People of different generations, classes, or political views may interpret the same event differently. When reacting to different narratives of the past, we must consider the correlations to power at times of transition. Radically different interpretations of the same events can make a national reconciliation difficult or even impossible. Despite attempts by the dominant political actors to mobilize memory in one direction, opposing narratives often coexist. Inclusionary national projects allow wide forms of expression leading to a more representative political society.

Juan Mendez, United Nations Special Rapporteur on Torture, discussed the importance of international law in the domestic politics of nations in his talk, "Evolving Standards in International Law Regarding Mass Atrocities and their Contribution to Memory and Democracy." International actors and organizations often serve as catalysts for truth seeking and reconciliation on a national level. If we consider that the role of international law is to impose a minimum standard for justice, allowing states to decide how to prosecute, Mendez opened by challenging the term "standards": is it possible for "evolving standards" to have acquired an equivocal meaning? As standards evolve, will there be different standards in the future?

Historically, there has been an obligation on the part of the state to confront the past. Since the Nuremberg trials following World War II, an obligation to intervene has become ingrained in the field of human rights. Most international law relates to the obligation to punish, but only under the conditions of due process and fairness of trial. Standards have existed at least since 1945, beginning with the concept of crimes against humanity. In international human rights law, crimes against humanity elicit an obligation to prosecute and to punish, and they call up a duty to ensure the right of the victim to redress. Rights cannot be suspended during an emergency or *ex post facto* by a decision not to investigate.

Mendez highlighted four significant components in the transitional justice paradigm: truth, reparations, justice, and institutional reform. The state must attempt to fulfill each of these components although it cannot oblige people to remember or to forget. Our understanding of what societies owe to victims has been clarified by decisions made by international human rights tribunals in the context of transitions. The standards by which these decisions were made are not new and were applied equally to societies in transition as well as established democracies. While international law does not mandate memory, it can create conditions conducive to memory. Though neither international law nor the state can require it of citizens, Mendez considers remembering to be a civic duty. Commemorating public spaces, naming streets, monuments, schools and other public places can also serve this role.

Journalism and the Role of New Media in the Construction of Memory

Panelists Stephen Kinzer, Maria Teresa Ronderos, June Erlick, and Michèle Montas (Chapters 3 and 4 of this volume, the last two) considered the role of journalists in contributing to the construction of memory through investigation and reporting. The role of the press in determining which topics are openly discussed and given importance, nationally and internationally, was a consistent theme throughout the panel.

Stephen Kinzer, Journalist-in-Residence at the Watson Institute for International Studies at Brown University and co-author with Stephen Schlessinger of *Bitter Fruit: The Story of the American Coup in Guatemala*, discussed the international influences and dimensions of political events in Guatemala in a talk titled "Guatemala Looks Back: The Arbenz Centennial and the Rios Montt Trial." Kinzer expressed hope about the emergence of new forms of media and the changing perspectives of younger generations regarding the role of the press. He considers these the main factors galvanizing Guatemala to look back at the positive and negative aspects of its past.

Kinzer highlighted four recent pivotal media moments in Guatemala. The first was the September 2013 commemoration of Jacobo Arbenz's 100th birthday. The commemoration of the former president's short tenure (1951–1954), during which he implemented several social reform policies including a land reform policy that was unfavorable with elites, indicates a turnaround in the way people regard the former president's controversial legacy. The second was the opening of the innovative online news forum Plaza Pública around the trial of Efraín Rios Montt. Plaza Pública is privately funded and its reporters do not observe previous codes of silence. Thanks to this type of open media innovation, citizens are better informed about events in Guatemala. The third was the striking discovery of the Police Archive, unearthing eighty million documents, 15 million of which have now been digitized and processed by teams of document-forensics experts and archivists. "They paint a very cold but intimate self-portrait of the terror state," said Kinzer. The final powerful tipping point, Kinzer indicated, was the reaction to the re-emergence of indigenous movements in Guatemala in the forms of protests and strikes. Though the state views them as subversive, the violent police response to the incidents has been met with dissent on social media, revolutionizing the way the populace responds.

Despite the plethora and immediacy of news coverage today, Kinzer cautioned that the bombardment of daily news coverage detracts from the reflective process of considering what happened in the past and the bigger questions of what might happen in the future. "Times have changed," he concluded. "One of the greatest sins of journalism is to accept the agenda of power, the dominant narrative. Why should what is being mentioned by the elite be what is journalistically 'important'?"

Maria Teresa Ronderos is a Colombian journalist and former Visiting Scholar at the David Rockefeller Center for Latin American Studies. She previously directed the online news site VerdadAbierta (www.verdadabierta.com), which she discussed is her presentation, "How a Better Memory of Colombia's Conflict is Contributing to Enhance its Democracy." Verdad-Abierta encourages debate about Colombia's past and present through the provision and dissemination of information from different perspectives.

Although Colombia is one of the Latin America's most stable democracies and successful economies, it has experienced hundreds of thousands of political assassinations in the past few decades, including 1,200 mostly young political leaders and 1,400 social leaders. Following the signing by the Colombian government of peace accords in 2005, a wealth of new testimony became available. When VerdadAbierta was first created, it collected testimony from former paramilitaries; today it also collects testimony from the FARC (Fuerzas Armadas Revolucionarias de Colombia).

According to Ronderos, the role of the press in today's recovery of memory is to expose the involvement of certain actors and to denounce complicity. "My journalism has changed," said Ronderos. "I still verify my sources and check my facts, but I have this hope of connecting with citizens in a different way . . . I want people to be encouraged to reclaim, to be inspired to resist, and to show that unethical political institutions that partner with criminals have increased the spread of violence." Verdad-Abierta's mission speaks directly to Kinzer's concern that the past and the future not be lost on the present.

New media is delving into the past in a strong and independent way: "This form of journalism is restructuring and rebuilding stories from thirty years ago, not just from today . . . When arrests are made, there are people everywhere doing investigative work and putting pieces together." This, according to Ronderos, is very new. She mentioned collaborations across several Latin American news outlets, thus telling across borders the stories that journalists were not allowed to tell in their own countries.

Just as international law and human rights organizations play an important role in domestic criminal justice, pressure from international media and collaborations across borders have helped broaden the dialogue. Ronderos and Kinzer asserted that the role of the media today is to encourage public discussion about what kind of country is being constructed, and at the expense of which citizens; this in addition to telling and sharing stories in revolutionary new ways.

Paper Mountains

The preservation of written and oral records and what is learned from forensic data was addressed by panelists John Dinges and Kirsten Weld, and by Ava Berinstein (Chapter 8 of this volume). Both Dinges and Weld focused on the role of archives and archivists in documenting the past and in the reconstruction of democratic societies.

John Dinges, Godfrey Lowell Cabot Professor of Journalism at Columbia Journalism School, emphasized the importance of journalistic credibility and veracity in the construction of democracy in his presentation, "The Document Troves Leading to the Detention of General Pinochet and Operation Condor." Documents themselves are not always factually accurate, but they seldom lie, said Dinges. Secret documents reveal what their drafters were communicating to other, often clandestine, actors at the time. And unlike individual memory, documents do not change over time. This imposes on academics and journalists the obligation to scrutinize the documents to determine historical accuracy. At the same time, Dinges maintained that we must also interview the protagonists—not just the victims—and try to understand their motives and determine what happened.

Factual investigation is what earns credibility, whereas speculation, opinion, and political correct analysis may be attractive, but end up damaging credibility, especially in the long run. Dinges asked, "Does it matter if documents are authentic, and how do we know they are so? . . . Does it matter in Argentina whether there were 10,000 or 30,000 people killed?" He answered this question with an emphatic "yes." This is the difference in the number of deaths carefully documented by the truth commission versus the number that human rights activists claim were killed.

Dinges pointed to large document collections that are now available, collections that couldn't have been handled without the digital tools of the past fifteen years. "We must interrogate the data," says Dinges, "to ask and try to get answers from this data." Collections cited included the Vicaria Testimonies in Chile, the FBI Extradition Packet on Manuel Contreras, the files of Arancibia Clavel, the Chilean and Argentine documents declassified by the Clinton administration after Pinochet's London detention, and the Archives of Terror in Paraguay.

Dinges pointed to the incredible wealth of data and knowledge that could be accessible in the future thanks to a new software that would search these documents in a heuristic way for patterns of content beyond the numerical. This would help historians deal with lines of responsibility and the massive nature of these document collections. "So many people search these documents looking for the smoking gun, which is not easily found," said Dinges. Instead, one must show the chain of custody and the chain of transmission of information in an attempt to pinpoint account-ability. Following all of the chains is currently only possible through reading over every document, a daunting task without the help of digital tools.

Kirsten Weld, Assistant Professor of History at Harvard University, gave a presentation titled "The Promise and Peril of Terror Archives in the Americas." Though archival preservation is not often singled out as essential to democracy, several recent initiatives have altered this dynamic, Weld asserted, highlighting the important 2005 discovery of the archives of Guatemala's notorious National Police. The idea of *habeas data* has been paralleled with a movement for the "right to truth," enshrined by the Organization of American States and the United Nations, wherein governmental violence against documents is considered to be a form of violence against citizens. In a landmark case in the Inter-American Court about the 1970s forced disappearance of guerrillas in Brazil, an "obligation to investigate" was marked judicially. This was the beginning of the archival cascade, similar to the "justice cascade." Weld cautioned against a new phenomenon: the tendency to "juridify the past" as new evidence is uncovered by archiving for the purpose of criminal justice, individualizing blame and victimhood, and sidestepping structural and economic analyses of repression.

Like Dinges, Weld pointed to the discovery of several collections of documents and efforts for truth-seeking: the Archives of Terror in Paraguay (1992), the Stroessner Commission (2005), the archives of the defunct national police in Guatemala, in Brazil the creation under Lula of the website Memórias Reveladas (2009, http://www.memoriasreveladas.gov.br), and the declassification of records from the regime in Argentina. However, the process of opening archives is more complex than it seems at first, she noted, pointing as an example to the discovery of police archives in a corner of a station in Guatemala. Weld contended that the Guatemalan government had stonewalled the country's Historical Clarification Commission regarding access to documents, alleging that there were no archives or that they had been burned. When the archives "reappeared," families were armed with evidentiary testimonies and documents. Now these "archives of terror" are in the hands of the state, provoking backlash from conservative sectors, including acts against archival staff and documents.

The aim of generating evidence in order to prosecute wartime criminals has grown into a project of international scale. Before the 2005 Guatemalan discovery, no convictions had been made. Now there have been some trials because of the access to state documents, but the reliance of projects on foreign funding presents its own challenges. Archives with an obvious human rights dimension are prioritized over other important and underfunded issues, such as records of land titles.

The problem is not a lack of knowledge, said Weld: we know what we are trying to bring to light, and we have a rich resource base; yet more knowledge does not in itself lead to changes in the balance of power and in the building of real democracy. The potential promise of archives to modify political subjectivities and hold political leaders accountable is huge; however, reifying victimhood and reducing history into instrumentalized memory are real perils. The Guatemalan case shows how local actors have navigated the promise and peril of terror archives in order to bring about real political change on the ground.

We can conclude that the primary duties of the investigative journalist are to ensure authenticity and to make the written record a basis of historical record and therefore a form of truth, and accessible to the public, in order to put these collections to use to find answers and to bring about justice.

Monumental Commemorations of Memory

Two panels were comprised of scholars and artists interpreting memory. The first panel explored the art and literary production that exhumes and explains memories of collective experiences. Panelists Marjorie Agosín, Susana Draper, and Marguerite Feitlowitz have all contributed to this volume (Prologue, Chapter 7, and Chapter 6 of this book, respectively). The second of these panels considered the role of museums and public spaces in preserving and interpreting memory of collective experiences. The panel included presentations by Julian Bonder and Gustavo Buntinx, as well as Paolo Vignolo (Chapter 11 of this volume).

Julian Bonder, Professor of Architecture at Roger Williams University and partner at Wodiczko+Bonder Architecture, Art, Design, discussed several award-winning international commemorative projects that his firm has completed. Bonder's intention in designing monuments and transforming space has been to attempt to share untold stories and voices without presuming to speak for them. New uses of architecture have created a theater for actions affirming life and the past. As monuments and memorials have been inserted into built environment on an unprecedented scale, there are more and more reminders of war, genocide, and crimes against humanity. Monuments are archives in the ground; they serve people who are in search of memory and of names. "They leave traces on the skin of the earth," said Bonder.

Ethics, Bonder maintained, are the ideas of action. The act of remembering references a person or event in the past, bringing it into action. Memory is a marker of contemporary culture, influencing the design and interpretation of architecture and public art. The space between the stories told and remembered, in the context of designing spaces and buildings, forces us to ask, how can we contribute to allow ethical descriptions of "space of appearance"? Marked by exile and temporality, ethical transformation means establishing conversations in space and time. Bonder concluded by reminding us that despite significant risks, it is possible both to put aesthetics at the service of ethics and to bear collective responsibility.

Gustavo Buntinx is director of the Micromuseo "Al Fondo Hay Sitio" in Peru. "The 'micro-museum' is a response to the Peruvian museum void," said Buntinx. This is due to a lack of documentation of "harrowing experiences of uncivil war and dictatorship in memorial." His presentation was entitled "'His Body is an Island Turned into Rubble': Archaeologies of Memory Amongst the Ruins of the Prison Island of El Frontón." El Frontón is an offshore prison in Peru where over 100 people were killed in the jail massacre of 1996. Today nature and birds have reclaimed the island. He calls the memorialization of this space a "political archaeology," an "awakening" that might evolve into a "waking up." Through photographs, Buntinx showed that there are perforations in the ruined architecture of the jail, the "poetic fiber of exposure to the water." The act of unearthing or reclaiming a burial place, a place where people have been killed, breathes life into their memory and acknowledges their place in history. Vignolo's example of the National Cementery in Bogotá and Buntinx's El Frontón both serve as cases to which we can apply Bonder's principle of "ethics of space."

Memory and the Role of Religion

The panel "Triggering and Healing Memory" provided a discussion of the effects of trauma on current and later generations and the role of spirituality in understanding and coming to terms with injustice and violence in public ways. The panel included presentations by Kimberly Theidon and Alexander Wilde, as well as Salomón Lerner Febres (Chapter 5 of this volume).

Kimberly Theidon, then John L. Loeb Associate Professor of the Social Sciences in the Department of Anthropology at Harvard University, is currently the Henry J. Leir Chair in International Humanitarian Studies at the Fletcher School, Tufts University. For over a decade, Theidon has worked with demobilization and reintegration programs in Colombia. Her presentation entitled "Pasts Imperfect: Working with Former Combatants in Colombia," focused on former combatants' conversion to evangelical Christianity and reintegration into civil society.

There are multiple transitions implied in reintegration, and in balancing demands for peace with those of justice and social repair. Theidon called the transition from combatant to civilian a "psychosocial black box process." She has found that as former combatants and guerrillas begin new lives, they often find themselves at the doors of evangelical churches. Perhaps the attraction lies in the familiarity of seeking a dogma and a philosophy to live by. Theidon posited that part of the draw to the church is that religious practice focuses on rupture, wherein converts leave their old identities behind. This fits with the rhetoric of transitional justice: meta-constructs of "a before and an after." Theidon recalled a question she had posed to a member of the FARC: "Why join the demobilization?" He responded: "What we are searching for is forgetting. We don't forget what we have learned . . . [but] you need to leave the war behind, find a way to evacuate it from the mind."

"Justice repertoires," as Theidon called them, draw upon the idea of shedding a past life linked to "justice-as-revenge." Throughout the region, many pastors share the dark pasts of their new converts. One ex-paramilitary subject told Theidon: "I can only be forgiven by God, I cannot be forgiven by most people." There is a notable absence of the state as an actor in adjudication: some former combatants speak of their faith in divine justice and claim that certain accounts can only be settled before God. Thus, in situations where some citizens find the actions of the state either insufficient or unrelatable, religion has filled the void in their search for justice and forgiveness.

Alexander Wilde is Research Fellow for the Center for Latin American and Latino Studies at American University. In his presentation titled "Historical Memory, Transitional Justice, and the Chilean Catholic Church," Wilde noted that remarkably little has been written on the role of the church in democratic transitions. He focused his presentation on the central questions of memory construction and how the church contributed to that construction.

As an institution, the Catholic Church in Chile is proud of its defense of human rights during the dictatorship. Since the country's transition to democracy in 1990, it has focused on doctrinal orthodoxy and personal piety, stepping back from the prominent role it had played in the public sphere during the dictatorship, except in questions related to traditional teaching on divorce and abortion, says Wilde. Nonetheless, the institutional church and individual Catholics contributed to the country's memory through state policies regarding human rights violations during the dictatorship.

The church has played an active role in creating historical memory during Chile's transition and by influencing public policy in several concrete ways. It has legitimated major policy initiatives, firmly supporting the two official truth commissions and providing detailed records of events and impeccable archives that informed their reports. Wilde contends that when the Rettig Commission issued its report in 1991, the church's support contrasted sharply with the hostility of other large national institutions—notably the armed forces, the Supreme Court, professional *gremios*, and the political right—all of which rejected its findings. The work of the Valech Commission, which began its work in 2003, continued in a new phase that ended only in August 2011. It established with "moral certainty" that nearly 40,000 individuals were tortured as part of an official policy implemented through the 17 years of dictatorship, at 1,100 sites in every province of the national territory.

Wilde concluded his presentation by emphasizing the distinctive character of the Catholic Church's role in contributing to historical memory and transitional justice in Chile. The church views both victimizers and victims through a different prism than the law-based practices usual in transition justice. A belief in forgiveness, mercy, and reparation has led them to a different perspective on punishment of victimizers. They also perceive, according to Wilde, a blurring of lines between victim, victimizer, and bystander as a reality in Chile and some other Latin American countries. Another important role of the Chilean Catholic Church during the dictatorship was to help alleviate widespread suffering in ways that engendered human agency in constructing a better society. Wilde suggests that if we want to understand and contribute to processes of moral healing in societies that have undergone severe trauma, we should pay more attention to the dimension of religion.

The Comparative Case of Post-Franco Spain

The final capstone panel, "Memory and the Future of Democracy," explored perspectives on the future of democracy in Latin America. This panel included a presentation by Marysa Navarro using the comparative case of Spain, as well as presentations by Frances Hagopian (Chapter 9 of this volume) and Elizabeth Jelin.

Marysa Navarro is Charles and Elfriede Collis Professor of History Emerita at Dartmouth College and Resident Scholar at the David Rockefeller Center for Latin American Studies. In her presentation, "The Politics of History and Memory in Spain," Navarro discussed the Spanish transition, viewed until recently as a resounding success. Though marred by violence, it had nevertheless avoided the possibility of a major bloody confrontation and permitted the peaceful transformation of Spain into a constitutional monarchy. It had achieved the reconciliation of most Spaniards by drawing a "*cortina del olvido*" over the horror of the Spanish civil war (1936–1939) and the long years of Generalissimo Francisco Franco's dictatorship (1936–1975). Four hundred thousand people had died in the Spanish civil war, with 300,000 or more exiled and another 40,000 jailed. Although the impact of the Civil War was painfully alive for thousands of Spaniards, there was no public discussion of it during the transition. In many cases in Spain, memory has never been confronted—there has been only one historical narrative. Navarro argued that now is the time for Spain to address its past.

By the time the civil war ended in 1939, Franco's power was unquestioned—he was generalissimo of the armed forces, "caudillo by the grace of God," Prime Minister, and Head of State. He appointed all ministers and was the ultimate source of legitimate authority. However, since 1947, he declared Spain to be a monarchy, with a vacant throne. In 1969, he gave a new title to Prince Juan Carlos de Borbón: Prince of Spain.

Upon Franco's death in November 1975, it had seemed impossible to most observers as well as to most Spaniards that the end of the dictatorship would not bring about chaos or another civil war. Before he died, he named King Juan Carlos I as his successor and gave instructions for the transition with the now-famous maxim, "*el paquete está atado,*" later emulated by Pinochet in Chile. Though he was dead, his power remained in the structure he left and in the hands of the armed forces, and therefore enabled Spaniards to maintain a "*paz de olvido*" (peaceful forgetting/non-remembering). One important component of success was the promulgation of an amnesty law that pardoned the crimes committed from the moment Franco led the war against the Republic until the end of his regime.

Franco's death did, however, bring about extended periods of social agitation, though largely peaceful. By 1977 political parties were allowed. By 1978 Spain had a new Parliament and a new constitution for the first time since 1931. Amnesty laws were passed. Freedom of speech and most trappings of democracy returned, and political prisoners were freed. However, though there was a construction bubble in the 1990s, the current state of affairs in Spain leaves much to be desired, argued Navarro, particularly regarding the economic crisis and youth unemployment.

Navarro proposed that Spain has failed to address the role of the monarchy and the role of fascism in society today. There are now increasing numbers of denunciations of missing relatives, and a human rights organization "boom" in order to reclaim loved ones. Navarro expressed her hope that human rights redress and democratic construction come sooner in Latin America than they have in Spain.

Conclusion

Just as individuals remember events differently, there are different ways of commemorating history and honoring deceased loved ones through monuments and other public spaces, varied ways of addressing and prosecuting human rights violations, and unique ways of collecting and disseminating information about the past. Similarly, there are different ways of thinking about a collective future. The exercise of considering what kind of future for what kind of country brings us back to Jelin's urging for us to consider temporality, Bonder's questions of how future generations might interpret monuments and objects of the past, Hite's caution that collective memory can be misdirected, and Mendez's reminder that international legal standards can be subjective and culturally variable. Over the course of the two-day conference, and as evidenced in the chapters in this volume, we learned that there are infinite perspectives on what and how the wrongs of the past must be righted and remembered.

Appendix

Conference Program: Democracy and Memory in Latin America

Friday, November 1 & Saturday, November 2, 2013

CGIS S-010 Tsai Auditorium, 1730 Cambridge St., Cambridge, MA

Friday, November 1, 2013

1:30 PM	Conference Registration
2:00 PM	Keynote Address ***What type of memory for what kind of democracy? Challenges in the link between past and future*** ELIZABETH JELIN, Senior Researcher at the National Council of Scientific Research in Argentina
2:45–4:15 PM	**Panel I Committing to Democratic Values and Institutions in Latin America** This panel, composed of political scientists, sociologists, and historians, will explore the roots of commitment to democratic politics in Latin America. MARYSA NAVARRO (CHAIR), Professor Emerita, Department of History, Dartmouth College; DRCLAS Resident Scholar *How Memory Can Help Democratization and Reconciliation (My Personal Experiences in Chile)* SERGIO BITAR, Senior Fellow, Inter-American Dialogue *The Politics of Memory* KATHERINE HITE, Professor of Political Science, Vassar College *Evolving Standards in International Law Regarding Mass Atrocities and Their Contribution to Memory and Democracy* JUAN MENDEZ, U.N. Special Rapporteur on Torture *The Memory of Politics* PETER WINN, Professor of History, Tufts University

4:15–5:30 PM   **Panel II Constructing Memory**
Featuring the role of journalists and others in contributing
to the construction of memory through investigation and
reporting on events and personal stories of those whose
lives have been affected by repression and resistance.

JUNE CAROLYN ERLICK (CHAIR), Publications Director,
DRCLAS

*Guatemala Looks Back: The Arbenz Centennial and the Rios
Montt Trial*
STEPHEN KINZER, Visiting Fellow at the Watson Institute
for International Studies, Brown University

*How a Better Memory of Colombia's Conflict is Contributing
to Enhance its Democracy*
MARIA TERESA RONDEROS, Director, Verdad Abierta.com

*The Jean Claude Duvalier Trial: Unearthing Haiti's
Buried Memories*
MICHÈLE MONTAS

Saturday, November 2, 2013

8:45–10:00 AM   **Panel III Recording Memory**
Featuring historians and archivists discussing the preservation of written records of the past, and archeologists
and human rights specialists discussing what is learned
from forensic data.

WILLIAM FASH (CHAIR), Charles P. Bowditch Professor
of Central American and Mexican Archaeology and
Ethnology, Harvard University

*The Preservation of Mayan Oral Literature Through
Recorded Memories*
AVA BERINSTEIN, Linguistics Advisor, Cultural Survival

*The Document Troves Leading to the Detention of General
Pinochet and Operation Condor*
JOHN DINGES, Godfrey Lowell Cabot Professor of
Journalism, Columbia Journalism School

The Promise and Peril of Terror Archives in the Americas
KIRSTEN WELD, Assistant Professor of History,
Harvard University

10:00–11:15 AM Panel IV Interpreting Memory I
Featuring art historians and literary scholars discussing art and literary production that exhumes and explains memories of collective experiences.

DIANA SORENSEN (CHAIR), Dean of the Arts and Humanities; James F. Rothenberg Professor of Romance Languages and Literatures; Professor of Comparative Literature, Harvard University

At Night the Memories
MARJORIE AGOSÍN, Luella LaMer Slaner Professor in Latin American Studies, Wellesley College

Acts of Opening, Acts of Freedom: Mexico 1968 Other/wise
SUSANA DRAPER, Associate Professor of Comparative Literature, Princeton University

"Operation Memory": Contemporary Novelists Wrestle with History
MARGUERITE FEITLOWITZ, Professor, Literature Department, Bennington College

11:30 AM–12:45 PM Panel V Interpreting Memory II
Featuring architects and curators to explore the role of museums and public spaces in preserving and interpreting memory of collective experiences.

DORIS SOMMER (CHAIR), Ira Jewell Williams Professor of Romance Languages and Literatures, Director of Graduate Studies in Spanish, Harvard University

Memory-Works: Works on Memory
JULIAN BONDER, Partner, Wodiczko+Bonder Architecture, Art, Design; Professor of Architecture, Roger Williams University

"Su cuerpo es una isla en escombros": Arqueologías de la memoria entre las ruinas de la isla prisión del Frontón
"His Body is an Island Turned into Rubble": Archaeologies of Memory Amongst the Ruins of the Prison Island of El Frontón
GUSTAVO BUNTINX, Conductor, Micromuseo "Al Fondo Hay Sitio"

A Place for the Dead. The Central Cemetery of Bogotá as a Realm of Historical Memory for Post-Conflict Colombia
PAOLO VIGNOLO, Associate Professor at the Center of Social Studies, Universidad Nacional de Colombia

2:00–3:15 PM   **Panel VI Triggering and Healing Memory**
Featuring scientists and psychologists discussing the
effects of trauma on current and later generations;
scholars of religion discussing role of spirituality in
understanding and coming to terms with injustice and
violence in public ways.

DAVID CARRASCO (CHAIR), Neil L. Rudenstine
Professor of the Study of Latin America, Department of
Anthropology in the Faculty of Arts and Sciences/Harvard
Divinity School

*La búsqueda de la verdad y sus contribuciones a la
consolidación democrática*
SALOMÓN LERNER FEBRES, Former President of the
Truth and Reconciliation Commission of Peru; Executive
President of the Center for Democracy and Human
Rights, Pontifical Catholic University of Peru

*Pasts Imperfect: Working with Former Combatants
in Colombia*
KIMBERLY THEIDON, John L. Loeb Associate Professor
of the Social Sciences, Department of Anthropology,
Harvard University

*Historical Memory, Transitional Justice and the Chilean
Catholic Church*
ALEXANDER WILDE, Research Fellow, Center for Latin
American and Latino Studies, American University

3:15–4:30 PM   **Panel VII Memory and the Future of Democracy**
Capstone panel featuring scholars from a variety of fields
exploring the relevance of their disciplines to the future of
democracy in Latin America.

MERILEE GRINDLE (CHAIR), Director, DRCLAS, Edward
S. Mason Professor of International Development,
Harvard Kennedy School

*The Weight of the Past, the Politics of the Present, and the
Future of Democracy in Brazil, the Southern Cone, and Beyond*
FRANCES HAGOPIAN, Jorge Paulo Lemann Visiting
Associate Professor for Brazil Studies, Department of
Government, Harvard University

ELIZABETH JELIN, Senior Researcher at the National
Council of Scientific Research in Argentina

The Politics of Memory and History in Spain
MARYSA NAVARRO, Professor Emerita, Department of
History, Dartmouth College; DRCLAS Resident Scholar